THE
SECOND CRUSADE
AND THE
CISTERCIANS

Also by Michael Gervers

THE HOSPITALLER CARTULARY IN THE BRITISH LIBRARY (Cotton MS Nero E VI). A Study of the Manuscript and its Composition, with a Critical Edition of Two Fragments of Earlier Cartularies for Essex

THE CARTULARY OF THE KNIGHTS OF ST. JOHN OF JERUSALEM IN ENGLAND, SECUNDA CAMERA: ESSEX

CONVERSION AND CONTINUITY: Indigenous Christian Communities in Islamic Lands, Eighth to Eighteenth Centuries (co-edited with Ramzi J. Bikhazi)

THE CARTULARY OF THE KNIGHTS OF ST. JOHN OF JERUSALEM IN ENGLAND, PRIMA CAMERA: ESSEX

THE
SECOND CRUSADE
AND THE
CISTERCIANS

Edited by
MICHAEL GERVERS

St. Martin's Press
New York

D
162.2
.S43
1992

For Marc

All rights reserved. For information, write:
Scholarly and Reference Division
St. Martin's Press, Inc., 175 Fifth Avenue,
New York, N.Y. 10010

First published in the United Staes of America in 1992

Printed in the United States of America

ISBN 0-312-05607-9

Library of Congress Cataloging-in-Publication Data

The Second Crusade and the Cistercians / edited by Michael Gervers.
    p. cm.
  Includes bibliographical references and index.
  ISBN 0-312-05607-9
  1. Crusades—Second, 1147-1149. 2. Cistercians. 3. Bernard, of
Clairnaux, Saint, 1090 or 91-1153. I. Gervers, Michael, 1942- .
D162.2.S43 1992
909.07—dc20   91-26968
                                                        CIP

CONTENTS

PART I: BACKGROUND AND IDEOLOGY

LIST OF FIGURES

LIST OF MAPS

ABBREVIATIONS

attr.	attributed
Beds.	Bedfordshire
bk(s).	book(s)
BN	Bibliothèque Nationale
BSAJ	British School of Archaeology in Jerusalem
C.	*Causa*
c.	*capitulum*, circa
cf.	compare
ch(s).	chapter(s)
col(s).	column(s)
comp.	compiled by
cm.	centimeter(s)
d.	pence
ed(s).	edited by, edition, editor(s)
e.g.	for example
Eng.	English
epist.	*epistola*, letter
esp.	especially
et al.	and others
Ez.	Ezekial
fasc.	fascicule
ff.	and page(s) following
fig(s).	figure(s)
f$^{o(s)}$	folio(s)
Fr./fr.	French
Herts.	Hertfordshire
Hosp.	Hospitaller(s)
ibid.	same as above
km.	kilometer(s)
Lat./lat.	Latin
Leics.	Leicestershire

m.	meter(s)
ms.	manuscript
n.	note
n.s.	new series
no(s).	number(s)
Notts.	Nottinghamshire
p.	page
para(s).	paragraph(s)
pl(s).	plate(s)
pp.	pages
pr.	*praefatio*
Ps.	Psalm
pt(s).	part(s)
publ.	published
q.	*questio*
ref.	reference
reg.	register/*registrum*
rev.	revised
rpt.	reprinted
RS	Rolls Series
s.	shilling(s)
ser.	series
St.	Saint
s.v.	*sub verbo* (under the word)
tr(s).	translated by, translator(s)
v.	*verbo*
vol(s).	volume(s)
Wm.	William
Yorks.	Yorkshire

EDITOR'S PREFACE

The present volume was conceived by members of the Society for the Study of the Crusades and the Latin East, and represents the collaborative effort of twenty scholars from six nations on three continents. The Society recognized that although many crusades to the Holy Land failed to meet their objectives, none has received so little attention in modern crusade historiography as the Second. The various chapters appearing here were solicited in order to redress that lacuna, and to show how important the Second Crusade was in shaping what was clearly the most significant, long-term political and religious institutional movement of medieval Europe in the post-millenium period. Equally important is the close link established in every chapter between that movement and the Cistercians. The wide range of subjects touched upon by the contributors to this study is a harbinger of the new directions presently being explored by historians, art historians, archaeologists and musicologists alike.

The preparation of this volume for publication was as much a collaborative undertaking as was its writing. The editor is particularly indebted to David Harvie for his assistance in all aspects of the project, particularly the compilation of the Bibliography, the standardization of the notes, and matters concerning computer software. A splendid job of text editing was performed by Sarah Brierley*, Gillian Long* and Martha Smith*. Martha, together with Carol Stoppel*, developed the maps, while Carol prepared the Index. The maps were drawn in the cartography office of the University of Toronto by Jane Davie under the direction of Professor Geoffrey Matthews. Much help was generously provided by the staff of the Robarts Library of the University of Toronto and of the Pontifical Institute of Mediaeval Studies, particularly by Mary English, the Rev. Donald F. Finlay, Nancy McElwee, Mary McTavish and Caroline Suma. The layout of the Bibliography was established by Pawel D. Thommée using WORDPERFECT macros. Fig. 5 was produced in SAS by Rodolfo Fiallos* and Thong Nguyen*. Dr. Ramzi J. Bikhazi offered valuable advice and editorial assistance at the commencement of the project. Financial support was kindly made available by the University of Toronto and, for those persons marked with an asterisk, by the Canadian Job Strategy Programme, a division of Canada Employment and Immigration. Secretarial support was offered by Barbara Gover through the good graces of Professor John Warden, Chair of Humanities, Scarborough Campus, University of Toronto.

All citations in the notes have been abbreviated, with full references corresponding to those abbreviations appearing in the Bibliography. Containing as it does over seven hundred entries, the Bibliography is itself a unique source of reference for the study of the Second Crusade.

Toronto, May 7, 1991

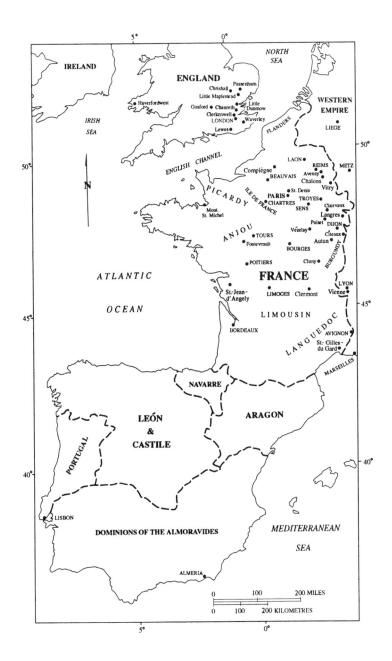

Map 1. Western Europe at the time of the Second Crusade

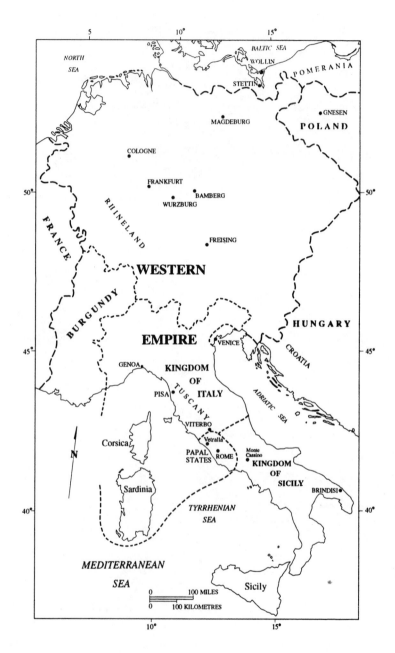

Map 2. Central Europe and the Italian Peninsula at the time of the Second Crusade

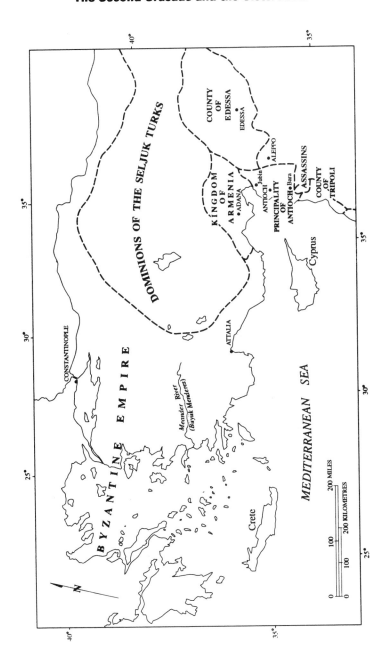

Map 3. The North Eastern Mediterranean at the time of the Second Crusade

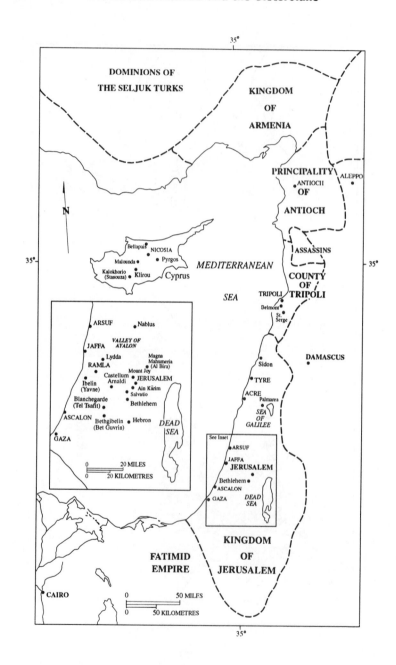

Map 4. The Latin East at the time of the Second Crusade

Introduction

Giles Constable

Bernard of Clairvaux and the Second Crusade, whether or not we like them, were of central importance in the history of the twelfth century. The connection between the spiritual leader of the Cistercians and the warlike campaigns against the enemies of Christendom remains a question of endless fascination. In spite of all that has been written on the subject, the essays in this volume show there is still much work to be done, and that many broad questions as well as points of detail need to be examined. I shall not try in this introduction to summarize their individual contributions, since each article speaks for itself. I shall attempt, rather, to place them within a larger setting of religious and crusading history, and to draw attention to some of the questions they raise about Bernard and the crusades.

One of the central problems for historians lies in the term "Second Crusade", which implies a degree of continuity and institutionalization which became apparent after the fact. For contemporaries, there was nothing inevitable about the crusades. The First Crusade was an event rather than an institution, and was preceded and followed by more or less similar, though smaller, expeditions, to the East and elsewhere. At the same time, missionary work, especially in eastern Europe, continued and developed as a peaceful alternative, or parallel, to warlike activity. It was in the course of the twelfth century, and as a result of developments in the church and secular society as well as outside Christendom, that the crusades took on their distinctive character as an aspect of Christian expansion and aggression.

The part played by Bernard of Clairvaux in this development was more that of a catalyst than an initiator, and there is no reason to believe that events would have taken a substantially different course, or that the crusades would have had a different character, if he had not been drawn into preaching the Second Crusade. His spiritual enthusiasm and charismatic personality brought a special coherence and fervor, however, which raised the expectations for the success of the Crusade, and thus contributed to the disappointment at its failure. Bernard drew together many threads in contemporary culture and spirituality, as several of these essays show, and wove them into a concept of crusade, which involved the monastic and military orders as well as the crusading expeditions. The crusaders and Templars were parallel to monks in their spiritual orientation and acceptance, each in their own way, of the special opportunity for salvation offered to them by God. The theme of distant love found in crusader songs reflected at the same time the unfulfilled yearnings of the soul for its destiny in God, the homesickness of the pilgrim and traveller, and the desire of the lover separated from the object of his love. The fact that Bernard neither initiated or created these themes is beside the point. He used them to shape a vision of crusading and the crusader which inspired not only his contemporaries but also future generations of crusaders.

The extent to which these ideas influenced the practical course of events is another problem for historians, and is raised in several articles in this volume. Although the Second Crusade generated widespread support, it was not a spontaneous movement, and the questions of who took the initiative in summoning the crusaders to arms, and of who responded to the call, and why, have long puzzled scholars. The two accounts of the origin of the crusade found in the works of Otto of Freising and Odo of Deuil are not entirely compatible, and the differences between them furnish some clues to determining whether the king of France or the pope took the initiative. It seems clear that Bernard of Clairvaux became involved after Louis VII and Eugenius III, but that he soon took the lead. The question of who participated in the Crusade is also more complicated than appears on the surface, and is intimately connected with the internal histories both of the royal house of France, and especially the relation between Louis VII and Eleanor of Aquitaine, and of noble families whose members had traditionally participated in the crusading movement. They went as armed pilgrims determined to visit Jerusalem and the Holy Land, but they were also trained soldiers who brought with them the traditions of warfare and strategy learned in the West.

In spite of its impressive sponsorship and widespread appeal, the Second Crusade lives in history less for its achievement than for its failure, which impressed itself on the collective psyche of Latin Christendom in the middle of the twelfth century, and of which the memory was preserved in later annals and chronicles. The reaction to the failure involved not only the unsuccessful effort to organize another crusade, but also a serious blow to the prestige of the organizers of the crusade, and, to a lesser extent, of the crusading movement. Bernard bore, or at least assumed, the brunt of the criticism, but some of the blame fell on the Cistercians generally, and, at least later, on the Templars, who came to share the responsibility for the military defeat. This may be reflected in the pattern of declining donations to the Cistercians and Templars, at least in England, and in the increase of donations to the Hospitallers, who were less involved in military activities, and whose reputation came through relatively unscathed. It would be a mistake to overemphasize the effects of the failure, however. Literature and art, in addition to later events, show that the crusading spirit was only temporarily dampened, and that the ideals preached by Bernard survived the setback of the specific expedition he inspired. Many of the most glorious (or notorious, depending on the point of view) moments of the history of the crusades still lay in the future.

Meanwhile, the Latin Kingdom of Jerusalem had its own destiny, which was only peripherally determined by the waves of crusaders from the West. It took shape after the First Crusade, during the first half of the twelfth century, and developed its traditions in terms of its own military, economic, and social needs. In many respects the Second Crusade seems to have had less effect in the East than in the West. The art and architecture in the Holy Land were comparatively untouched by the influx of crusaders, and the Cistercians founded their first houses in the Latin Kingdom in the 1150s and 1160s, precisely when their prestige was ebbing in the West. It may be that the willingness of the order to establish houses in the East, which Bernard had opposed, was precisely on account of a slackening of the tight control that marked the order during its early years. These kinds of developments are not recorded in annals or chronicles, and some of the most interesting articles in this volume are those using sources which help historians to penetrate below the level of written sources, and to see the silent continuities as well as the dramatic changes which mark the surface of history.

PART I

BACKGROUND AND IDEOLOGY

1

The Second Crusade and the Redefinition of *Ecclesia, Christianitas* and Papal Coercive Power

Yael Katzir

Scholars studying the crusades have underemphasized the far-reaching changes that took place in the papacy as a result of the crusading movement in the years 1095-1147. It has often been suggested that the First Crusade represented a papal triumph.[1] However, historians have neglected to analyze the changes that occurred in the concepts of *Ecclesia* and *Christianitas* because of that crusade. Theretofore, principles of the Gregorian Reform movement had been applied to the clergy and to the monarchs. But with the First Crusade, these principles were extended further, in a conscious and coherent fashion, to the laity at large, and more specifically to members of the knighthood. Historians have also failed to examine the differences, as well as the links and developments, between the First and Second Crusades. The Second Crusade was institutionalized and juristically defined to a much greater extent than was the First, due to the far-reaching changes that took place within the Church as a juridical institution during the first half of the twelfth century. There was also a development in the concept of the coercive power of the papacy.[2] Evidence for such changes in papal power can be found in the writings of both Gratian and Bernard of Clairvaux.

The First Crusade affected the Gregorian Reform movement in several ways. To begin with, it transformed the Gregorian concept of *Ecclesia*. Church historians, such as Jean Rupp, Gerhart Ladner, and Jan Van

Laarhoven,[3] have provided new insight into the evolution of the idea of *Ecclesia* during the eleventh century. It is well known that ninth-century Carolingian theologians developed a complex theory of *Ecclesia* that saw the pope and the emperor as the supreme officials of two parallel hierarchies, one clerical and one lay, both within the framework of the *Ecclesia*. This Carolingian ecclesiology was widely accepted well into the mid-eleventh century. At this time, however, the Gregorian reformers began to attack this concept, and eventually came to assume that *Ecclesia* comprised only the clergy, and that the laity were no more than passive communicants within it. With the First Crusade, though, a new structure emerged in the Latin West: a purely clerical *Ecclesia* surrounded by, and forming part of, a larger Christian society that some contemporaries called *Christianitas*. The laity were deprived of a leading role within this newly defined and more narrowly conceived *Ecclesia*. This did not mean that they were relegated to the role of passive observers. Rather, by participating actively in the First Crusade, the laity were able to play a vital role within *Christianitas*.

Traditionally, the Gregorian Reform movement[4] has been viewed as having had three major objectives: the liberation of the Church from secular domination and even, to some extent, from all secular contacts; the reform of the clergy; and the establishment of the Roman Church as the "Mother of all Churches"—the embodiment of the Universal Church, the Church of which all others are members, the absolute, paramount authority. When these reform objectives were discussed in relationship to the *Ecclesia*, it was understood that the concept referred primarily to the clergy. Correspondingly, the Gregorian program concerned itself with the laity only negatively, that is, by excluding its members from interference with the clergy. The First Crusade introduces two new elements to the Reform program. Both were manifest in the Clermont address, which applied the idea of reform to the laity in a way that had previously been confined to the clergy. Rather than focussing on the liberation of the Church from secular domination, the address focussed on the liberation of Christendom from its external enemies (the Saracens) and on the defense of the Eastern Christians.[5] It also called, not for the reform of the clergy, but for the reform of the laity, or more specifically, the lay nobility.

Previous religious wars—against the Saracens and other infidels—had been local or regional in character. In contrast, the Clermont address was universal in its appeal, for it dealt with the liberation of Jerusalem, "the place connected with Christ in whom we all share."[6] Jerusalem was, needless to say, the only place—apart from Rome—that had a universal redemptive meaning in the economy of Christian salvation. It also lay beyond the boundaries and immediate interests of the "powers" in Europe.

The call for the reform of the lay nobility can be traced back to the Peace and Truce of God in the mid-eleventh century. During the First Crusade, however, the Church sought to transform the unruly knighthood of Western Europe into a new Christian militia.[7] This new militia was no *militia sancti Petri*, fighting for the papacy in Italy, Spain or Asia Minor. Rather, the militia created in 1095 acquired a universal character: that of the *militia Christi*. Under the direct leadership of Christ, the new militia would serve and defend the Church and Christendom, and the new Christian knight would imitate Christ. In the words of the *Gesta Francorum*: "If any man would come after me let him deny himself and take up the cross and follow me."[8]

The First Crusade thus rendered explicit what had been implicit since the pontificate of Gregory VII, or even that of Leo IX: it forged an unbreakable link between the idea of a crusade and the idea of reform. Of course, the success of Urban II's ecclesiastical statesmanship in 1095 exceeded all expectations, including those of Urban himself. But his success was not accidental, nor perhaps should it have been so surprising. It grew out of the general atmosphere of reform, an atmosphere charged with eschatological and apocalyptic expectations.[9] The striking fact is the degree to which Urban gave a new dimension of universality to papal authority and to papal strivings for reform. The laity were now partners in the reform movement, and had their own particular task within it. And although this reform movement was centered in France, it was felt throughout Europe.

The universality of the pope's address at Clermont, represented by the transformation of the *militia sancti Petri* to that of the *militia Christi*,[10] may be linked to a development in the second quarter of the twelfth century. At that time, the papal title, Vicar of St. Peter (*Vicarius Petri*) was superseded by the title, Vicar of Christ (*Vicarius Christi*).[11] This new title was intimately associated with the papal claim to the "Fullness of Power" (*Plenitudo Potestatis*). Moreover, the new title implied both a different kind of jurisdictional power and a true universality of power.[12] In this sense, the transition from the *militia Petri* to the *militia Christi* of the First Crusade constituted the first phase of a slightly later development—the transformation of the pope into the "Ordinary Judge of All", the *Iudex Ordinarius Omnium*.

Several important developments between 1095 and 1147 help explain the differences between the First and Second Crusades: the crusading experience in Europe and Outremer[13]; the Concordat of Worms (which, by ending the investiture struggle, removed the last barrier to papal-monarchical cooperation in the crusades); the publication of Gratian's *Decretum* around 1140; and the impact of St. Bernard of Clairvaux.

Perhaps the most distinct characteristic of the Second Crusade was the development of the Church's coercive power. Of course, ecclesiastics had long argued—it was commonplace in the eleventh century—that the Church had the right and duty to order secular princes to repress heresy. This use of the Church's coercive power was frequently symbolized by the sword that the Church entrusted to a secular prince. In fact, the eleventh century was fully familiar with the idea that the symbolic "two swords" of Luke 22:38 represented the twin powers of the Church: that of spiritual coercion (excommunication) and that of material coercion (the commissioning of secular princes to use armed force against heretics and other enemies of the Church and Christendom).[14]

Neither in the Clermont address nor elsewhere, however, was the First Crusade justified by reference to the Church's coercive power. One could argue that the contemporaries of the First Crusade had in mind something like the Church's coercive power as the ultimate justification for the crusade, and that they were limited by the lack of an adequately developed jurisdictional language and terminology. But the only evidence for this would be the late—and thus unreliable—account of the Clermont address as rendered by William of Tyre between 1169 and 1184. In William's account, Urban II quotes Psalm 44:5, "Gird thy sword upon thy thigh, O most mighty."[15] This same quotation is also incorporated into the "Rite for the Dubbing of the Knight."[16] It could be argued, therefore, that the layman was exposed to the idea that the sword represented the Church's coercive power. But this reflects the thinking of the mid-twelfth century and after, rather than the thinking of 1095. In the period just before and just after the First Crusade, no one associated the crusade with the Church's right and duty to delegate the "sword" of coercive power to the lay prince.[17] Rather, the First Crusade was perceived by all as being a "just war."[18]

Between the late 1120s and the early 1140s, the idea of the Church's coercive power was transformed and decisively linked with the idea of a crusade. This development is evident in the writings of both Gratian and Bernard of Clairvaux. In his massive *Decretum*, Gratian devoted *Causa* 23 to defining and discussing the meaning of "just war" and all of its variants. A crusade, that is, a war against nonbelievers and enemies of the Church, automatically became an occasion for the legitimate exercise of coercive power.[19] In Question 8 of *Causa* 23, Gratian focussed on the use of coercive power against heretics; he also examined the problem arising from the feudal obligation of military service to the prelates.[20] Gratian did not limit himself to examples of wars against heretics; rather, he included within this larger category texts that concerned wars against the Saracens. Hence, all canonists after 1140 had to consider the crusade as a jurisdictionally defined war: one in which the Church, or more accurately, the papacy, delegated the material sword of coercive power to the lay prince as the bearer of arms against the Saracens, or other enemies of the Church.

It is perhaps paradoxical that Bernard of Clairvaux contributed at least as much as Gratian to the jurisdictional definition of the crusade as the preeminent expression of the Church's material coercive power.[21] For, of course, Bernard was not a canonist, was not educated in canon law, and did not often demonstrate what we might call a juristical style of thought.[22] In his own way, and within the framework of monastic life and language, Bernard was propelled by the major experience of his life: conversion. In its modified application to the surrounding society, conversion is more easily understood, as well as accepted, when labeled "reform".

Prior to Gratian, and long before the Second Crusade, Bernard identified the crusade with the Church's coercive power. In his treatise *In Praise of the New Knighthood*, which was written as propaganda for the newly established Order of the Templars around 1136, he wrote: "Let both swords [the two swords of the Church's coercive power] held by the faithful be drawn against the necks of the enemies [of the Christian people]."[23] He also wrote, "When a man of both types [a monk-knight of the kind exemplified in the Templars] powerfully girds his sword and nobly distinguishes himself by his cuirass, who would not consider this . . . worthy of admiration?"[24]

The idea of the Church's coercive power caused considerable confusion in twelfth-century thought.[25] Twelfth-century interpretations of the idea contributed much to new hierocratic theories about the papacy's jurisdiction over the emperor and over lay monarchs in general. These theories raised important questions. For example, if the Church delegates the material sword to the lay monarch, does monarchy itself become simply a part of the *Ecclesia* and thereby lose its autonomy? Or, to pose the question differently, does the Church's coercive power swallow up kingship? No one in the first half of the twelfth century had a clearer grasp of these issues than Bernard of Clairvaux. Indeed, Bernard gave a more satisfactory answer to these questions than any canonist before Hugacio at the end of the twelfth century. In the mid-1140s, Bernard wrote to Conrad III, the king of Germany and Italy. Conrad III was also the emperor-elect of the Romans, and thus held a special responsibility for the defense of the Roman Church. Bernard urged Conrad to take up arms against the commune of Rome, which had rebelled against the pope. In this context, his rhetoric formulated a crucial distinction:

Is not Rome at once both the Apostolic See and the capital of the Empire? To say nothing of the Church, is it to the King's honor to rule a dismembered Empire. . . ? Wherefore I say to you, gird your sword upon your thigh, most powerful one [Note the quotation from Psalm 44:5]. And let Caesar restore to himself what is Caesar's, and to God what is God's. It is clearly the concern of the Caesar both to protect his own crown and to defend the Church. The one benefits the king, the other the defender of the Church.[26]

Here Bernard distinguished sharply between two offices: the kingship, which was autonomous, and the *Defensor Ecclesiae*, which would use the material sword at the Church's command and on the Church's behalf.[27]

Bernard's ideas had an influence on Pope Eugenius III, who had been one of his Cistercian disciples. Bernard's influence is obvious in the famous bull *Quantum praedecessores nostrum*, in which the pope summons Louis VII of France to take part in the Second Crusade. Thus, for the first time, the call for the crusade was directly addressed to a European monarch. The bull calls upon the king and his lords "to gird themselves manfully and so to defend the Church and all of Christendom."[28] Echoing Psalm 44:5, it calls upon the king to exercise the Church's material sword in the crusade. With that sword, the king must defend the Church not only in his own kingdom, but wherever he is needed in Christendom. It is important to note the contrast between this summons and Urban II's address at Clermont. In 1095, Urban created a new militia of the nobility. In 1145, Eugenius III officially institutionalized the crusade in two ways: first, he identified the crusade explicitly as the Church's material sword; secondly, he appointed the lay monarchs as the natural heads of the crusading army. In these ways, a new institutional structure was created which allowed for the exercise of the Church's coercive power. This new framework, combined with the granting of spiritual and temporal privileges to those who exercised the Church's coercive power, made the papacy much more powerful.

It is possible that Bernard himself viewed the Second Crusade as a new reform movement. The First Crusade extended the Gregorian reform principles from the clergy to the lay nobility, from *Ecclesia* to the more broadly conceived *Christianitas*, through the creation of a new militia, the *militia Christi*. However, the Second Crusade caused even more extensive reform to occur. This crusade extended the reform to the highest level of feudal society—to the kings—by asking them to take up the sword in defense of the Church and all Christendom. Moreover, by giving greater weight to the penitential character of the crusade, the Second Crusade extended the reform to all those who, in Bernard's words, "are blessed to be alive in this year of Jubilee",[29] and who undertook the obligation to imitate Christ.

The Second Crusade thus represented another important stage in the development of papal power. It detached from the crusading idea the concrete goal of liberating the city of Jerusalem, which, although in danger, was after all again in Christian hands. The Second Crusade placed greater emphasis on the reward of a heavenly Jerusalem, a reward that was promised by the holders of the keys of St. Peter to all those exercising the Church's material coercive power—that is, to all those who would take up the Cross.

NOTES

1. Munro, "Popes"; Munro, "Speech"; Richard, "Papauté"; Baldwin, "Papacy"; Duncalf; Fliche; Krey, "Urban's Crusade"; La Monte, "Papauté"; Holtzmann; Gilchrist, "Canon Law". Riley-Smith, *Crusades* does not deal with the crusades from our specific point of view. The same is true of: Murphy; and especially: Gilchrist, "Erdmann".

2. The concept "papal coercive power" refers to the two swords of Peter. Although the theory of the two swords of Peter should be distinguished from the theory of the two swords (separating secular from religious power), the two theories intersect at one point. Here, the focus is on a series of well-defined cases, where the failure of the spiritual sword to enforce discipline led the papacy to make use of its right to coercive power. In these cases, the pope delegated the material sword to the nobility or the monarch, who could rightfully represent him.

3. Rupp; Ladner; Laarhoven. The linguistic differentiation between *Ecclesia* and *Christianitas* evolved slowly. The two terms continued to have more than one meaning and occasionally were used interchangeably.

4. Fliche & Martin, vol. 8 (1944, rpt. 1950).

5. Tellenbach. The principle of "liberation" is emphasized also in the words of Pope Urban II at Clermont, when he tried to impose the ideas of the Gregorian reform on the clergy, as rendered by Fulcher of Chartres: "Ecclesiam cum suis ordinibus omnimode liberam ab omni saeculari potestate sustentate . . .". So far the regular demand and then: "Necesse est enim, quatinus confratribus vestris in Orientali plaga conversantibus, auxilio vestro jam saepe acclamato indigis, accelerato itinere succurratis" (Fulcher, *Historia* 1, pp. 322-23).

6. The call to reform the fighting nobility is repeated in some versions of the pope's address: "Quid dicimus, fratres? Audite et intelligite: Vos accincti cingulo militiae, magno superbitis supercilio; fratres vestros laniatis, atque inter vos dissecamini. Non est haec Militia-Christi, . . . vos pupillorum oppressores, vos viduarum praedones, vos homicidae, vos sacrilegi . . . vos pro effundendo sanguine Christiano expectatis latrocinantium stipendia . .

.. Certe via ista pessima est .... Porro si vultis animabus vestris consuli, aut istiusmodi militiae cingulum quantocius deponite aut Christi milites audacer procedite, et ad defendendam Orientalem Ecclesiam velocius concurrite" (Baldric of Bourgueil, p. 14). Writing in Europe after the crusade, Baldric of Bourgueil is reflecting on the way in which the papal address was construed among the clergy.

7. "Si quis vult post me venire, abneget semetipsum, et tollat crucem suam, et sequatur me" (*Gesta Francorum*, p. 1).

8. Chenu.

9. "Si inter ecclesias toto orbe diffusas ... *privilegia majora* traduntur ... illi potissimum ecclesiae deberemus ex qua gratiam redemptionis et totius originem christianitatis acceptimus ... semen nostrum Christus est in quo salus et omnium gentium benedicto est" (Guibert of Nogent, *Gesta*, p. 137).

10. Erdmann, *Entstehung*, pp. 185-211.

11. Maccaronne, p. 85.

12. Benson, "Plenitudo".

13. Constable, "Second Crusade". This important paper on the Second Crusade approaches the subject from a different angle.

14. Stickler, "Gladius"; Stickler, "Anselmo da Lucca"; Arquillière.

15. "Vos igitur, delectissimi, armamini zelo Del *accingimini unusquisque gladio suo super femur suum potentissime*" (Wm. of Tyre, *Historia*, p. 41). This psalm is also quoted in Baudric of Bourgueil's version, though there its use was strictly limited to the idea of the reform of the knighthood: "Accingere, o homo unusquisque, gladio tuo super femur tuum, potentissime. Jam nunc igitur auctoritate loquamur prophetica . . . . Accingimini, inquam, et estote filii potentes" (Baldric of Bourgueil, p. 15).

16. Ackerman.

17. A good example of the lack of juridical language would be in the Clermont version as rendered by Guibert of Nogent, *Gesta* (p. 139): "Si ergo piorum praeliorum exercitio studentis." In the first quarter of the twelfth century, the terms "bellum iustum" and "coercive power" were not yet common, although the beginnings of legal language were emerging.

18. Villey; Pissard; Russell.

19. Gratian, *Decretum* 2, in: *Corpus iuris canonici* (1879), vol. 1, C.23.

20. Gratian, *Decretum* 2, in: *Corpus iuris canonici* (1879), vol. 1, C.23, q.8., c.24.

21. Zerbi; Leclercq, "Prophète", pp. 297-98; Leclercq, "Attitude"; Delaruelle, "Bernard".

22. Ivo, "Decretum", pt. 10, cols. 689-746; Ivo, "Panormia", bk. 8, cols. 1303-18. See: Brundage, "Holy War".

23. "Exseratur gladius uterque fidelium in cervices inimicorum" (Bernard, *De laude*, in: Bernard, *Opera*, vol. 3 (1963), p. 218).

24. "Ceterum cum uterque homo suo quisque gladio potenter accingitur, suo cingulo nobiliter insignitur, quis hoc non aestimet omni admiratione

dignissimum, quod adeo liquet esse insolitum" (Bernard, *De laude*, in: Bernard, *Opera*, vol. 3, p. 214).

25. Chodorow, pp. 58, 228. See also the criticism of this book in: Benson, "Chodorow", esp. p. 101.

26. "Nonne ut Apostolica Sedes, ita et Caput imperii Roma est? Ut ergo de Ecclesia taceam, num honor Regi est truncum in manibus tenere imperium? .... Quamobrem ACCINGERE GLADIO TUO SUPER FEMUR TUUM, POTENTISSIME, et restituat sibi Caesar quae Caesaris sunt, et quae sunt Dei Deo. Utrumque interesse Caesaris constat, et propriam tueri coronam, et Ecclesiam defensare. Alterum regi, alterum convenit Ecclesiae advocato" (Bernard, *Epistolae*, in: Bernard, *Opera*, vol. 7 (1977), letter 244, p. 135).

27. The same perception of St. Bernard is brought up in the chronicle of Odo of Deuil, *De profectione* (p. 15): "The assembly continued with the problem of the custody of the realm . . . the king . . . gave the prelates of the church and the nobles of the realm the privilege of election . . . . Led by the holy abbot, the latter said, 'Behold, here are two swords; it is enough,' pointing to Father Suger and the Count of Nevers."

28. Letter of Pope Eugenius III to the Franks, see: Letter XLVIII ['Ad Ludovicum regem Galliarum. De expeditione in Terram Sanctam suscipienda (Anno 1145, Dec 1)'], in: Eugenius III, *Epistolae* 2, cols. 1064-66.

29. "Beatam ergo dixerim generationem, quam apprehendit tam uber indulgentiae tempus, quam invenit superstitem annus iste placabilis Domino, et vere jubilaneus" (Bernard, *Epistolae*, in: Bernard, *Opera*, vol. 7, letter 363 [to the Eastern French], p. 314).

2

The Pomeranian Missionary Journeys of Otto I of Bamberg and the Crusade Movement of the Eleventh to Twelfth Centuries

Klaus Guth

The missionary journeys of Otto of Bamberg, the Apostle of the Pomeranians, as he was called by his biographer Ebo,[1] mark a short but significant period in the life of the missionary and imperial bishop. At the same time they prompt one to question the legitimacy of the conception and motivation of such conversion missions in the Western world of the eleventh and twelfth centuries. It is difficult to find a satisfactory answer which considers the interests of both the "converter" and the "convert", since there are no direct sources showing the points of view of the Pomeranians or Slavs.[2] Their reactions to conversion attempts in the East can be gathered only indirectly from missionary sources written in Latin.

The fruitful new approach to international research on the crusades, which involves analyzing the Western crusades by using Islamic source material,[3] can be applied only partially in the case of the German mission to the East. This mission was formulated in the summons to join the Wendish Crusade (1107-08) in the region of Magdeburg, and clearly defined by the Pomeranian journeys of Bishop Otto of Bamberg (1124-25 and 1128) and the Wendish Crusade in 1147. The latter, as, in part, the missionary journeys to Pomerania, should be judged in the light of papal and imperial policy, canon law, and theological reasoning, as well as the particular motives of the protagonists themselves in the period between the First (1096-99) and Second (1147-49) Crusades.

1. Heathen conversion and the crusades in the context of canon law

Extra ecclesiam non est imperium: there is no domination outside the Church.[4] With this statement the canon law of the High Middle Ages points to the close link between worldly and religious power in the German Empire.[5] The German mission to the East in the twelfth century is the expression of the official authority of pope and emperor. It finds its legitimacy above all in canon law. Here a distinction is made between the mission as the natural expression of Christian faith and the biblical message,[6] and the (military) journey against heathens and crusades to the Holy Land.

It is not without reason that a recent publication on this topic bears the title, "La croisade, obstacle à la mission."[7] The crusade, as an instrument of violent subjugation of a non-Christian area under Christian rule (in East and West), contradicts the biblical principle of voluntary conversion of free people by missionaries. According to the Bible, the missionary is an apostle, whereas the crusader remains a warrior. This distinction had already aroused strong criticism in the Middle Ages, as was demonstrated recently by an English investigation based on a wide range of sources.[8] The crusade as a war against the heathens was a firm concept in canon law. It was usually undertaken by lay knights; missions and the administration of sacraments such as baptism were the responsibility of the priests. Whereas contemporary writers, especially Benedictine monks,[9] who were not eyewitnesses to events connected with the First Crusade to the Holy Land, were inclined to speculation, the biographers of the *Ottoviten* based their work mainly on the oral narratives of the monk Ulrich of the Michelsberg and his companions when they reported the events of the two missions to Pomerania. It may be assumed that those involved, as well as the biographers, knew the canonical stipulations for the missions to the heathens.

Augustine responded to the question of the conversion of the heathen with the well-known statement from St. Luke (14:23), "Compel them to come in",[10] thus drawing a parallel with the feast (14:15 - 24). Gregory the Great had a different response.[11] It was through him that the emphasis on freedom and nonviolence in the process of missionary conversion became part of Gratian's *Decretum*.[12] In his own words:

One must therefore proceed in such a way that those to be converted want to follow us (in our faith) by reason of words of good sense and gentleness and do not flee from us . . . . Therefore, my brother, inflame their hearts with exhortations, as best you can and with God's help, so that they are converted, and do not permit them to fall again into unrest because of their own festivals.[13]

Historical reality, however, referred to Augustine's teaching to justify the "conversion" of Spanish Muslims, Jews, and Saxons by forced baptism at the time of Charlemagne. The traditional Augustinian line,[14] however, did not justify the direct missionary war, as Hans-Dietrich Kahl attempted to make plausible, "in the service of genuine extra-ecclesiastical missions against the heathens in new Christian territory",[15] but permitted the use of force in the "winning back" of former Christians,[16] i.e. recusants who had left the medieval church community. The Augustinian line of tradition, which led to the wars against heretical recusants in the High Middle Ages, but not to the crusades, was known to Burchard of Worms when he compiled his collection of decretals. Conversion must be voluntary according to Romans 9:18: "Therefore, hath He mercy on whom He will have mercy and whom He will, He hardeneth." Recusants, however were to be returned to the community of the faithful by force: " . . . it is in the order of things that even those who were won over to the faith by means of violence or compulsion have to be forced to remain faithful."[17]

This position no longer applied in connection with the summons to the Wendish Crusade (1107-08),[18] a proclamation issued in the area of Magdeburg. In this case, a campaign of war was promulgated which was intended to ensure the safety of the borders and defend the Empire. The "crusaders" could be certain of spiritual and material gains, which meant the acquisition of land and spiritual salvation. This promise was similar to that made by Pope Urban II, at the Council of Clermont prior to the beginning of the First Crusade, to those who took part in the journey to Jerusalem.[19] The idea of the Holy War against the enemies of the Church, one of the main motives for the First Crusade,[20] was also a primary consideration here. The missionary methods and motives of Bishop Otto I of Bamberg, on the other hand, originated from reasoning in the tradition of Pope Gregory the Great. Thus it says in Ebo's *Ottovita*:

It is not my task to force you to adopt this religion, for God, as I heard from the mouth of my lord and bishop, does not wish for services acquired by force, but only those that are voluntary . . . .[21]

These words were put into the mouth of the Pomeranian Duke Wratislaw. Herbord added to them in his dialogue: "Bishop Otto seeks nothing but to bind you to the Lord Jesus Christ by faith. But by what means? Not by deception or the use of violence . . . ."[22] The political and religious-*cum*-ethical conception of the missionary journey to the heathens characterizes the Pomeranian mission of the Bishop of Bamberg even more than the theological-*cum*-legal background mentioned above. Concern for people (*cura animarum*) arose from the biblical task, theological tradition, and the Benedictine zeal for reform.

2. The mission as ministry according to the monastic reform theology of the twelfth century

In the eyes of canonists in the High Middle Ages, the crusade to the Holy Land remained a pilgrimage. Canonical regulations about crusades do not, therefore, appear in the writings of Gratian and his pupils and annotators. On the other hand, the vow as a condition for taking part in the crusades, the duties and privileges which proceeded from participation, and the fact that the crusade was a Holy War, found a strong echo in canon law, particularly after the pontificate of Alexander III (1159-81).[23] At the same time, there was a change in purpose. The Holy War was no longer waged against a special group of non-Christians in any particular country, but served the religious policy of the popes at the height of the Middle Ages, especially during the time of Innocent IV (1243-54). Thus the crusade became an instrument employed by the popes in the struggle against all kinds of enemies in the known world at that time. Crusades against Baltic peoples and Slavs, against Staufen, Ghibellines, and so on, indicate a metamorphosis from the former idea of crusades. The crusades, as the arm of the world, supported the spiritual power until the end of the Middle Ages.

Although missionary journeys in the Middle Ages served a particular policy, as will be shown, they also proceeded from the biblical missionary task of the Church and the conception of "monastic reform theology" in the twelfth century. Its spiritual basis was the command to undertake missions (St. Matthew, 28:19), the expression of the biblical mission of the apostles and disciples:[24] "Go ye therefore, and teach all nations, baptizing them. . . ." Only St. Mark and St. Matthew pass on the message of an imperative missionary task. This universal mission[25] developed in the course of ecclesiastical history to become missionary history, which is still to be written for the Middle Ages.[26] In contrast to the modern mission,[27] missionary work in the Middle Ages, and more particularly in early modern times, is supported by the domination, or by the example, of converted rulers.[28] Peaceful methods of conversion and violent action against "heathens" alternate with one another. For the twelfth century, the missionary sermon of Bishop Otto I of Bamberg in Pomerania, and the Wendish crusade, following the idea of the crusade and the crusade theology of Bernard of Clairvaux, form the two fundamental models for conducting missions against the heathens in the High Middle Ages.

The missionaries east of the Elbe belonged almost exclusively to the Cluniac, Lothringian or Italian reform movements:

> The missionary to Prussia and martyr, Adalbert of Prague, belonged to the circle of ascetics around Romuald of Ravenna.

> Günther the Hermit had become familiar with the Lotharingian reform ideas in the monastery of Altaich before . . . working east of the Elbe, and Bruno of Querfurt was a Camaldulensian . . . .[29]

According to Wilhelm Berges, the mission to Wendland was the expression of the new reform movement found among the Benedictines of the Hirsau school of thought, as well as the Augustinian canons, the Cistercians and the Premonstratensians. Later the Dominicans and Franciscans joined the mission to the East. Poverty and apostolate were the reformative aims of their monastic life. The Augustinian canons and, to an even greater extent, the Premonstratensians (their special form), defended "their share of ministry and preaching against very strong opposition."[30] Mission and ministry are inseparable from one another. This inroad by the missionary reform orders of the twelfth century into what was, in fact, the sphere of responsibility of the secular clergy (something that was rejected by the older Benedictines over and over again for fear of losing the purity of the contemplative ideal), also brought changes to the communal life of those concerned in the Benedictine reform movements. Bishop Otto I, who supported the Hirsau reform movement in the monastery on the Michelsberg in Bamberg, recalled to Bamberg the nobly-born monk Wolfram, who had been educated at the Bamberg Cathedral school and had been elected prior in Hirsau, and with him five Hirsau monks. They brought with them Hirsau discipline, which resulted in the establishment of lay monks on the Michelsberg from 1112. On the death of Abbot Wolfram I (1112-13), not only had the number of monks grown from twenty to seventy, but also the church, which had been destroyed by an earthquake, had been rebuilt and the monastery buildings extended.[31] Bishop Otto supported the reform of the monasteries or founded new monastic communities both within and outside his diocese. The fifteen new monastic foundations confirm his reputation as a reviver, founder and organizer of monasteries.[32] Sponsored by Bishop Otto, Cistercians, Augustinian canons, Premonstratensians and reformed Benedictines were sent to places as far as Carinthia and to the Ostmark. The union, founded by Otto in 1131, of all the monasteries belonging to Bamberg, served to strengthen the reform movement in Benedictine monasteries and with it the strict observance (*regula strictior*): " . . . the standard of the prescribed rule [of the Order] has been restored with magnanimity."[33] This reformed rule prevailed on the Michelsberg and in those regions belonging to the Bamberg monasteries all over the Empire.

Monks from St. Michael's Monastery in Bamberg accompanied and supported Otto on his mission to Pomerania.[34] Preaching, the administration of the sacraments, and instruction were the new pillars of the reformative monastic ministry, which, like the secular clergy, was able to exist on tithes and benefices (*censualia beneficia*).[35]

The peaceful Pomeranian mission was planned and carried out from Bamberg in the spirit of monastic reform and for political reasons. It was based on a new interpretation of the monastic mission, which now recognized the right of preaching and ministry. In the middle of the twelfth century, this theologically reformative mission program was afterwards discussed in treatises. In this connection, *Dialogus inter Cluniacensem monachum et Cisterciensem*, written by the monk Idung of Prüfening in 1156,[36] *Altercatio inter clericum et monachum*, the authorship of which is still disputed,[37] and the manuscript *De vita vere apostolica*, should be remembered.[38] Even before this, however, monastic ministry formed part of the missionary work of the Benedictines.[39] During the early part of the Middle Ages, bishops and popes transferred rights of ministry to the monasteries. Gerhoch of Reichersberg admitted monks to the ministry if no regular clergy were available.[40] In fact, one cleric, Honorius Augustodunensis, wrote a tract with the significant title, "Why monks are permitted to preach."[41] Even at the time of Abbot Bernard of Clairvaux, missions against the heathen without preaching were described as being impossible. Thus he writes in about 1136/40:

How are they [the heathens] to believe something of which they have heard nothing? But how should they believe without preachers? How can there be sermons if no preachers are sent to them?[42]

The monk, therefore, remained a monk as far as his monastic vows were concerned, but was a member of the clergy insofar as he had accepted a clerical mission.[43] The reform monks with clerical status due to ordination by the bishop had a mission to preach and minister. This takes the same form for secular clergy and monks. The missionary sermon is only possible on the instructions of a responsible priest or bishop.[44]

3. Conversion by mission

As the considerations above attempt to show, the Pomeranian journeys of Otto of Bamberg are consistent with the medieval idea of nonviolent missionary work in the tradition of Gregory the Great as far as the reasons, motivation, and accomplishment are concerned. True to the missionary injunction in the Bible, the missionary journeys of the Bamberg bishop demonstrate the liberal medieval variant of group and personal conversion. Though varying in individual details from the modern idea of the mission of the churches,[45] this high medieval and modern plan of action determined the work of persuasion (preaching, discussion) in an environment free of fear, without haste, and accompanied by belief in spiritual guidance and miracles. In this way, collective medieval conversion was made easier for the "apostles", in the original meaning of the word, by the Germanic idea of allegiance and by having suitable representatives to further their work. In the case of Bishop Otto, his great qualities as a preacher and missionary with a knowledge of languages were an additional benefit.[46] The medieval form of mission without direct compulsion was, however, only intended for the conversion of non-Christians until the appearance of the crusade concept in the eleventh century. The need to win back into the Christian community former Christian peoples or tribes who had reverted to heathenism was confirmed again, particularly in the twelfth century, on the basis of theological and canonical arguments. War against heathens who threatened the borders of the German Empire was well-known in the twelfth century as a political variant of the fending-off and integration of the heathen tribes who were assisted by the Church in their Christianization. Examples from the Carolingian and Saxon periods have been cited in recent research.[47] The combination of the aims of journeys against heathens, or wars like this, with the protection of the German Empire, by means of the stabilization of conditions and by integration into the German sphere of power, using the ideals of the First Crusade as a basis, was clearly laid down in the summons to the Wendish Crusade (1147), which had originated in about 1108 around Archbishop Adalgot of

Magdeburg.[48] On this occasion, those capable of carrying arms were summoned to the "War of Christ" in the East. By their participation they could "acquire both salvation for their souls and, if they so desired, excellent land for a dwelling."[49]

Why the idea of the armed journey or crusade against the heathens was not raised in connection with Otto's Pomeranian mission may have had various reasons of convenience. The Pomeranians posed no threat to the eastern and northern borders of the German Empire. Apart from this, the region lay in the political sphere of influence of the Polish duke[50] and in the field of tension pertaining to the claims of the Church in Magdeburg and Gnesen. Did the two Church provinces prevent a mutual summons? A fruitless question, for the failure of the Wendish Crusade likens it to the Second Crusade to Jerusalem, promulgated by Bernard of Clairvaux, and reminds us of its lack of success. The personal interests of the leaders and their aspirations to establish their own domination even before their arrival in Jerusalem may explain the failure of the enterprise. For did Margrave Albrecht the Bear not go off to Pomerania at the very beginning of the Wendish Crusade and besiege Stettin?[51] Are crusades, with their secondary theaters of war, not intrinsically doomed to failure?

The Pomeranian mission of the Bamberg bishop remained unaffected by such crusade ideology. It served the peaceful establishment of a missionary church of Pomerania[52] which was first of all a subsidiary church within the concentrated bishoprics and endowments of the German Empire, and was finally consolidated as the bishopric of Wollin (1140) only after struggles involving conflicting interests. It was during the course of the Middle Ages, however, that the bishopric united the German and Slav populations in a common culture.

The connection with Bamberg was never entirely severed.[53] With the tomb of the saint and bishop, Bamberg remains today a cult center reminding us of the pastoral mission of the "Apostle of Pomerania."[54] Personal zeal for reform, acquaintance with the Polish duke, early experience of the situation in Poland, and papal and imperial authorization of the missionary journeys had strengthened Otto's resolve to go to Pomerania. The success of the mission was promoted by fortunate circumstances, the support of the pastoral work by monastic orders and the establishment of a native clergy.[55] Did Otto wish to spend the rest of his life as a missionary in the east? Only the threat by Emperor Lothar to place Bamberg's church property under imperial dominion brought Otto back to his bishopric.[56] The missions of conversion to Pomerania are granted a large share of space in the reflections of the biographers. It is certain that, through these missions, the life of the politician and reformer, the bishop and missionary, reached a decisive outward climax and inner turning point.[57] The missionary journeys also underline the fact, as do his efforts to reform and found monasteries and churches, that ministry was of prime importance in the life of the prince and bishop.

NOTES

1. *Apostolus Pomeranorum*; this title is used by Ebo 13 times. See: Petersohn, "Apostolus"; Demm, esp. pp. 83-86 (here p. 84); Petersohn, "Bemerkungen"; *Bischof Otto*.
2. Petersohn, *Ostseeraum*.
3. Prawer, *Kingdom* 1; Kedar, *Crusade*; Schwinges; Hehl; Kedar, "Muslim"; Siberry, "Missionaries".
4. Cf. Muldoon, "Canonists".
5. Weise.
6. Kertelge; Collet.
7. Rousset, *Réveils*, pp. 37-48.
8. Siberry, *Criticism*.
9. See: Riley-Smith, *First Crusade*, pp. 135-52; Guth, *Guibert*, esp. pp. 63 ff.; Guth, "Dreifache".
10. Kahl, "Compellere".
11. Gregory I, *Registrum*, letter 15, in: MGH Epist., vol. 2 (1889), bk. 13, p. 383. Lotter, p. 35; Luke 14:23.
12. Gratian, *Decretum* 1, distinctio 45, ch. 3, in: PL, vol. 187, cols. 233-34. Lotter, p. 35, n. 90.
13. Gregory I, *Registrum*, letter 15, in: MGH Epist., vol. 2 (1899), bk. 13, p. 383.
14. Kahl, "Compellere", esp. pp. 201 ff.
15. Kahl, "Compellere", p. 253.
16. Kahl, "Compellere", p. 253.
17. Burchard of Worms, bk. 4, ch. 82, in: PL, vol. 140, col. 742B; Kahl, "Compellere", p. 253, n. 265.
18. Kahl, "Ergebnis"; Kahl, "Compellere", p. 267.
19. Epist. patriarchae Hierosolomitanae ad occidentales [anno 1098], IX, 6, in: Hagenmeyer, *Kreuzzugsbriefe*, p. 148. Lotter, p. 61, n. 192.
20. Schwinges, p. 3.
21. Ebo, *Vita*, p. 105.
22. Herbord, in: MPH, n.s., vol. 7(3), p. 153; Kümmel, pp. 36 ff.; Lotter, pp. 37 ff.
23. Brundage, *Canon law*, esp. pp. 191-96.

24. Matthew 28:16-20; Mark 16:14-20, 24:26-49; John 20:19-23. Schneider, pp. 91 ff.
25. Frohnes, vol. 2.
26. See: *LThK* (1935), vol. 7, cols. 732-35; *LThk* (1962), vol. 7, cols. 462-68.
27. Kertelge; Collet.
28. Guth, "Kulturkontakte".
29. Berges, p. 321.
30. Berges, p. 325.
31. Meyer, *Oberfranken*, pp. 91-101 (here pp. 97 ff.)
32. Guttenberg, vol. 1, pp. 128-36; Meyer, *Oberfranken*, p. 100 (15 new foundations); Berges, p. 329.
33. Ebo, *Vita*, p. 7.
34. In his *Vita* which, like the *Vita* of Idung of Prüfening, was written in 1152/58, Ebo uses Udalrich of St. Ägidien (Bamberg) and other sources. His *Vita* is not, however, based on the other lives of St. Otto. See: Meyer, *Oberfranken*, pp. 101 ff.; Demm, pp. 15, 97.
35. Idung of Prüfening, "Argumentum", p. 119 and esp. p. 129.
36. Demm, p. 29.
37. Demm, p. 49. Text in: PL, vol. 170, cols. 538-42.
38. Author unknown; see: Demm, p. 49.
39. See: Demm, pp. 47-50.
40. See: Demm, p. 49.
41. *Honorius*, pp. 145 ff.
42. Bernard, *Tractatus*, in: PL, vol. 182, col. 1032.
43. Idung of Prüfening, "Argumentum", p. 129.
44. Hofmeister, pp. 255 ff.
45. See the decree about missionary activities of the church (*LThK* (1968), Suppl. vol. 3, cols. 22-124). See also: "Mission", in: *RGG*, vol. 4, cols. 973-84, 1013-15.
46. Ebo, *Vita*, bk. 2, ch. 18, pp. 86-89.
47. Erdmann, "Heidenkrieg"; Kahl, "Geist"; Guth, "Kulturkontakte", *passim*.
48. Kahl, "Ergebnis", pp. 300 ff.
49. Kahl, "Ergebnis", pp. 300-302; *Urkundenbuch Magdeburg*, vol. 1, no. 193 (p. 249).
50. Herbord, pp. 68-71 (bk. 2, ch. 5). Duke Boleslaw fought against the Pomeranians, put 18,000 of them to death, and deported another 9,000 to Poland.
51. Kahl, "Ergebnis", esp. pp. 306-13.
52. Sources in: Demm, pp. 71-82.
53. Meyer, *Oberfranken*, pp. 74-82; Südekum; Guth, "Cramers".
54. Petersohn, "Apostolus"; Demm, pp. 84-6.
55. On Otto's efforts of acculturation among the Slavs, see: Demm, pp. 60 ff., 66-73.

56. Ebo, *Vita*, pp. 136-38 (bk. 3, ch. 24); Herbord, p. 195 (bk. 3, ch. 31).
57. On Otto's missionary personality see: Berges, pp. 329-31; Kist, pp. 31-8.

3

St. Bernard and the Jurists

James A. Brundage

In a fiery passage of *De consideratione*, St. Bernard warned his disciple, Pope Eugenius III (1145-53), to be wary of lawyers and their doings. "I am astonished", he told the pope, "that you, a man of piety, can bear to listen to lawyers dispute and argue in a way which tends more to subvert the truth than to reveal it."[1] Lawyers, although clever, Bernard continued, are a morally dubious lot, for they seek to make profit out of iniquity.[2] "These men", he thundered, "have taught their tongues to speak lies. They are fluent against justice. They are schooled in falsehood." He admonished Eugenius to put an end to lawyerly babble in the papal palace, to "Cut off their lying tongues and shut their deceitful mouths."

Lawyers, according to St. Bernard, were dangerous to spiritual health not only in court, but also in the council chamber, for they were impudent and covetous as well as lying and deceitful: "The church", he cautioned, "is filled with ambitious men", many of them trained in the law. Pope Eugenius should deal with them as Christ had dealt with the moneychangers in the Temple: "He did not take time to listen, he took a whip to beat them."[3]

St. Bernard's scalding criticisms of the legal culture that was growing around, and threatened to take control of, the papal administration in the mid-twelfth century found many sympathetic ears. Other writers cf the period seconded the complaints of the abbot of Clairvaux. Gerhoch of Reichersberg was among the earliest to second Bernard's indictment of the lawyers;[4] other critics soon joined the chorus of recrimination, among them

Peter the Chanter, Walter of Châtillon, Jacques de Vitry and many others.[5] It is scarcely surprising then, that modern historians have fallen into the trap of reading Bernard's excoriation of curial advocates as a denunciation of law. They have even described St. Bernard as "one who neither knew nor cared about canon law."[6] Elizabeth Kennan has shown, however, that this characterization does a great deal less than justice either to St. Bernard or to his knowledge of and respect for twelfth-century law.[7] Bernard, she argues, was in reality attacking abuse of legal process, irregularities of practice, and procedural complexity, not law itself.[8] In addition, Msgr. Jacqueline has proposed the more startling view that Bernard, far from being ignorant of canon law, drew repeatedly from the canonical collections of Ivo of Chartres, and that his denunciation of abuses could only have been conceived and written by one who was keenly aware of the differences between canonical and civilian jurisprudence.[9] It seems more plausible, however, as Stanley Chorodow has argued, that while St. Bernard doubtless knew some law and drew upon his legal knowledge occasionally to buttress his views, he was, on the whole, not much interested in juristic topics, which he considered secondary to other, more central, concerns in Christian spirituality.[10]

What Bernard most objected to in mid-twelfth century canonical practice, as Father Congar has pointed out, was the intrusion into canonical processes of what he regarded as unnecessary procedural refinements drawn from *cognitio extraordinaria*, the elaborate system of civil procedure that had dominated post-classical Roman law and remained current in Justinian's time.[11] Like many later pontiffs, and, for that matter, legal reformers of every stripe down to our own times, St. Bernard believed that complex procedures created unnecessary delays, caused needless expense, clogged the courts, and resulted in substantial denial of justice to litigants, particularly to the disadvantaged who most needed the law's protection and instead found it an instrument of oppression.

Medieval popes — many of them trained lawyers — often shared Bernard's impatience with procedural subtleties and experimented with means to curtail the length and expense of litigation in the courts Christian. Some, such as Innocent III (1198-1216), penalized litigants who indulged in delaying tactics by making them liable for the resulting costs.[12] Others, such as Clement V (1305-14), attempted a more radical solution by authorizing summary procedure in place of a full-blown formal trial in many situations.[13] In civil matters, this seems to have meant that litigants and their lawyers were left free to speed up hearings by almost any means that was mutually agreeable to the parties and the judge in a given case.[14] In any event, St. Bernard's criticisms of procedural complexity fell squarely into the mainstream of notions about legal reform current in the central Middle Ages. Indeed, St. Bernard did a good deal to define where the mainstream lay.

Thus, rather than being scornful of canon law, Bernard tended to see the Church as an institution shaped by law, in which law and legal values played an important but secondary role. His disciple, Idung of Prüfening (fl. 1144-55), reflected St. Bernard's views faithfully, I think, when he spoke of the monastic rule as law and centered his criticisms of the Cluniacs on the argument that the Cluniac monks had improperly supplemented monastic law with unauthorized customs. The fundamental argument that runs through Idung's *Dialogue* centers on the legal force of custom as compared with written law. His defense of the Cistercian approach, in contrast to the Cluniac one, is based as much on issues of legality as of spirituality.[15]

As for St. Bernard himself, I should like to focus here on two themes, namely the use that he made of concepts drawn from canon law in his discussions of the Crusade and more broadly of sacred violence, and the influence of Bernard's ideas on the further development of the law itself. With reference to the first theme, St. Bernard was troubled by one of the central issues of medieval political theory: defining the moral limits of the power to initiate lawful violence, and in particular the question of whether the pope and other prelates are entitled under any circumstances to declare war against the enemies of Christendom. This in turn raises further issues concerning the proper relationship between priestly power and princely power. Twelfth- and thirteenth-century writers normally addressed these problems in juristic terms, and St. Bernard was no exception.

St. Bernard believed that, on the one hand, the pope must be able to determine when the use of force was justified and, in addition, that he must have some power to initiate warfare in order to protect Christendom. But at the same time Bernard also believed that the right to declare war, and *a fortiori* the right to wage war, was clearly the prerogative of secular princes. Thus Bernard wished to have it both ways: the pope, as spiritual leader, could not declare war, even against the enemies of the Christian commonwealth, but he must have the right, and even the responsibility, to determine the moral question of when it was proper for princes to go to war in defense of Christendom. Accordingly, while Bernard advised Eugenius III in 1150 to proclaim a new Crusade, he cautioned the pope at the same time not to intervene directly in its conduct, as Pope Leo IX (1049-54) had done in the ill-fated campaign against the Normans in 1053.[16] Bernard thus sought to preserve a key distinction between the proper roles of prince and priest. The pope had not only the right, but the obligation to advise secular rulers when the use of violence was morally indicated, but he did not have the right either to declare war or to take up arms himself. Princes, who did have that right, also had the obligation to exercise it as and when the pope indicated that they should.[17] Here Bernard differed pointedly from Gregory VII and his advisers: it was grossly improper in Bernard's view for the pope or any other cleric to command armies or declare war: the pope's proper role was that of prophet, not general.[18]

Bernard's discussion of this issue concerning the power to declare war relied on canonistic sources, but also reshaped conventional canonistic teaching in an original way. Bernard found support in earlier canonistic tradition for maintaining that the Church and its leaders had the right to authorize material coercion against Christendom's enemies,[19] but that at the same time the clergy themselves must refrain from personal participation in hostilities.[20] Bernard sought to reconcile those earlier teachings by setting limits on ecclesiastical power to initiate warfare. It was, as he saw things, morally proper and responsible for the pope (and perhaps other bishops) to call on princes to use force against Christendom's enemies, but it was quite improper for clerics, including the pope, to participate in the exercise of the war-making power, either by directing the conduct of armies, or even by declaring war themselves.

Bernard's reading of the canons clearly influenced subsequent canonistic discussions of public law and political theory, and influential canonistic writers in subsequent generations would adopt his views as their own.[21] Paucapalea, the earliest commentator on Gratian's *Decretum*, for example, expounded views on these issues very similar to St. Bernard's, and Master Rolandus, another influential early expositor of the *Decretum*, took much the same position.[22] Similarly, Ricardus Anglicus (1186/87-1242) incorporated St. Bernard's analysis of the role of the papacy in sanctioning the use of force into his discussion of sacred violence.[23] Ricardus' treatment, in turn, was reflected in the *Glossa ordinaria* on the *Decretum* of Gratian completed by Johannes Teutonicus (d. 1245) in 1216 and in the *Casus* of Benencasa (d.1206).[24] It was also among those reported by Bernard of Parma (d. 1266) in his *Glossa ordinaria*, the standard academic commentary on the papal legislation in the *Liber extra* which was taught in every canon law faculty in the High Middle Ages.[25] And at the beginning of the fourteenth century, when Johannes Monachus (c. 1250-1313) wrote the *Glossa ordinaria* on Boniface VIII's bull *Unam sanctam*, he not only cited St. Bernard as his authority for imposing limits on papal power to initiate war, but also quoted relevant passages from *De consideratione* in support of his argument.[26] Thus Bernard's views entered through canonistic teaching into the mainstream of discussions on this topic in the High Middle Ages.[27]

St. Bernard was understandably sensitive to issues raised by the role that monks played in recruiting crusade armies. Otto of Freising tells us that Bernard himself was reluctant to preach the Second Crusade, and refused to do so until the pope specifically commanded him.[28] His hesitancy was no doubt grounded, as Giles Constable pointed out years ago, on the long-standing canonical prohibition of preaching by monks.[29] Bernard had serious misgivings about this matter, which he expounded in one of his sermons on the Song of Songs, where he maintained that it was altogether inappropriate for monks to preach in public, or, for that matter, to undertake other kinds of pastoral ministry.[30] Here Bernard not only demonstrates once again an awareness of the canonical rules and shapes his vision of the monastic life in accordance with them, but he even seems prepared to let obedience to those rules take precedence over his own passionate and lifelong commitment to the crusading enterprise.

A third instance of the influence of juristic concepts on St. Bernard's crusade ideology concerns the corporate character of the crusading army. Bernard conceived of the various forces that he summoned to participate in the Second Crusade as collective entities, as *societates* or partnerships, bound together in a common enterprise, owing allegiance to a common leader, sharing resources for a common purpose, enjoying privileges in common, subject individually and severally to rules agreed upon by their members and ratified by sworn subscription. Each crusading army was a *coniuratio*, an association of members bound by oath to obey rules that they agreed upon in common. The language of association and collective enterprise surfaces several times in Bernard's writing about the crusade.

Bernard's model for the collective identity of the crusading army was the monastic community. This is not quite as unlikely as it may at first seem. Professor Riley-Smith has pointed out how monastic ideals and imagery permeated popular accounts of the First Crusade, which described the crusading army as a kind of fighting monastery in motion.[31] That vision, in turn, shaped the whole notion of the nature and goals of the crusading enterprise, at least during the twelfth century. The concept of consecrated knighthood, the ideal of the warrior dedicated to sacred violence, moreover, forms the central theme of St. Bernard's treatise on the Templars.[32] And the Templars comprised, of course, an ecclesiastical corporation, a body of men who lived in common, held property in common, and acted as a group under the direction of an elected leader.[33] Hence it should be no surprise that Bernard likewise thought of crusading forces as bodies with corporate characteristics that resembled those of monastic communities. Crusaders, after all, took vows as monks did — although not the same vows, to be sure.

And like monks, crusaders were bound to fulfill their vows and were subject to severe penalties should they fail to do so.[34] When he took the cross and pledged that he would join the crusade, the crusader made a *professio* similar to that of a monk and he formalized his promise in a liturgical ceremony that recalled the clothing of a monk with his habit.[35] Conversely, monks had for a very long time described their own calling in military terms as "God's knights", a metaphor dear to the hearts of Church reformers and monastic writers alike, as Professor Graboïs reminds us.[36]

Given these similarities between the crusader and the monk, then, it was not incongruous that Bernard and his contemporaries should think of crusading groups as partnerships or associations, in terms appropriate to monasteries and ascribe to them characteristics common to bodies corporate.[37] Like other corporate groups, crusading forces acted in common under the direction of leaders whom they chose and to whom they delegated authority to establish and enforce standards of conduct.[38] These standards of conduct took the form of laws or regulations for the crusaders, who took an oath to obey them — although, in the judgement of some, they did not always observe that oath very scrupulously.[39] Disputes and complaints about noncompliance might be settled by elected judges, who were not necessarily identical with the military leaders of the expedition.[40]

St. Bernard believed that regulations for crusaders, like the rules under which monks lived, should include a common dress code, and he set out the main points of such a code in his letter to Bohemian crusaders. It is no surprise to find that these regulations sought to reinforce the monastic character of the crusade and accordingly prescribed attire that was plain, modest, and unostentatious, like that expected of monks and penitents. Even the crusaders' horses were to be outfitted plainly and without conspicuous displays of wealth. The sole exception that St. Bernard admitted to the general rule of austerity in outward appearance was shrewdly calculated to take advantage of the psychological impact of nonverbal communication. Crusaders, St. Bernard thought, might properly equip themselves with shields and saddles picked out in gold and silver when they rode into battle, "so that as the sun's rays reflect from them, terror may sap the heathens' courage."[41]

Yet although Bernard thought of crusading forces as collective units analogous to monastic communities, he was aware that the analogy was imperfect and that membership in the one was by no means an adequate substitute or alternative to the other. Cistercian monks, in particular, he warned, must not embark on crusade. Any who did so were to be excommunicated.[42] This view was by no means original with St. Bernard. Indeed, it had been a standard and consistent part of crusade regulations from the time of Pope Urban II (a former Cluniac monk himself), who strongly discouraged monks of any kind from participating in the First Crusade.[43] Bernard's stricter admonitions even more closely echoed the sentiments of St. Anselm at the time of the First Crusade.[44]

Two things are apparent in all of this: first, that St. Bernard, far from despising the law, made repeated use of legal constructs and categories, particularly in his writing and thinking about the crusade and the more general theme of sacred violence. And second, St. Bernard's ideas about the relationship between sacred and secular powers on the specific issue of the right to declare war became an important source for subsequent discussions of this matter in the legal writings of late twelfth- and thirteenth-century canon lawyers.

NOTES

1. Bernard, *De consideratione* in: Bernard, *Opera*, vol. 3, pp. 408-409; English quotations are from: Bernard, *On Consideration*, p. 44. On the relationship between St. Bernard and Pope Eugenius III, see also: Jacqueline, "Pape".
2. Bernard, *De consideratione*, in: Bernard, *Opera*, vol. 3, pp. 45-6.
3. Bernard, *De consideratione*, in: Bernard, *Opera*, vol. 3, p. 45.
4. Morrison, p. 115.
5. Jacques de Vitry, p. 50; Peter the Chanter, cols. 161-62; Eldridge, p. 64; and see generally: Baldwin, "Critics".
6. White, "Gregorian Ideal", p. 337.
7. Kennan, p. 90.
8. Kennan, p. 113.
9. Jacqueline, "Yves de Chartres", and in greater detail in: Jacqueline, *Episcopat*, pp. 25-6, 29-32, 34-39; Kennan, pp. 105-106.
10. Chodorow, pp. 260-65.
11. Congar, p. 187.
12. *Corpus iuris canonici* (1879), X 2.14.5.
13. *Constitutiones Clementis Quinti*, 2.1.2, 5.11.2.
14. Johannes de Legnano; Helmholz, pp. 120-22.
15. Idung of Prüfening, "Dialogue", pp. 38, 77.
16. Bernard, *De consideratione*, in: Bernard, *Opera*, vol. 3, p. 454; Bernard, *On Consideration*, pp. 117-18; also: Bernard, *Opera*, vol. 8, letter 256, para. 1, p. 163.
17. Robinson, "Church & Papacy", pp. 304-305; Watt, pp. 372-74.

18. Congar, pp. 188-89; Russell (p. 36) maintains that St. Bernard wished to limit the role of princes solely to the conduct of fighting, but asserted that only the pope had the power to declare just war. This seems to go somewhat beyond the position that St. Bernard himself adopted.

19. E.g.: Ivo, "Decretum", part 10 (PL, vol. 161, ch. 11, col. 693; ch. 59, cols. 707-709; ch. 73, col. 713; chs. 83-85, cols. 719; ch. 91, col. 720); Stickler, "De ecclesiae" & Stickler, "Anselmo da Lucca".

20. Ivo, "Decretum", pt. 10 (PL, vol. 161, ch. 29, cols. 699-700; ch. 34-35, col. 701; ch. 45, col. 702.

21. Jacqueline (*Episcopat*, pp. 303-304) notes references to St. Bernard's view in three twelfth-century canonical collections prior to Gratian.

22. Paucapalea, p. 103 (ref. to C.23, q.8, pr.); Rolandus, p. 89 (ref. to C.23, q.3). Contrary to earlier views, however, it now seems unlikely that Master Rolandus, the canonist and author of this *Summa*, was the same Rolandus who in 1159 became Pope Alexander III; Noonan; Weigand.

23. Richard Anglicus, *Summa questionum*, quoted from Zwettl Stiftsbibliothek MS 162, fol. 147va-148vb, by Watt, p. 380, n. 26-27.

24. Johannes Teutonicus, *Glossa ordinaria*, ref. to C.23, q.3, c.10, v. *ab imperatoribus*; Benencasa, *Casus* to C.23, q.8, pr. The canonistic *Glos. ord.* and *Casus* are cited here from the *Corpus iuris canonici* (1605), vol. 1.

25. Bernard of Parma, *Glos. ord.* to X 5.7.13 v. *accinxerint*.

26. Johannes Monachus, *Glos. ord.*, ref to *Extravagantes communes* bk. 1, ch. 8, para. 1, v. *certe qui in potestate*, referring to: Bernard, *De consideratione*, bk. 4, ch. 3, para 7; Muldoon, "Boniface VIII", pp. 64-65; Jacqueline, *Episcopat*, p. 307.

27. An early and important writer on international law, Alberico Gentile (1552-1608) referred approvingly to St. Bernard's views on several problems in the law of war (see: Ullmann; but see also: Brundage, "Holy War", pp. 109-11).

28. Otto of Freising, *Gesta* 2, bk. 1, ch. 36, p. 200; Constable, "Second Crusade", p. 244.

29. Burchard of Worms, bk. 2, ch. 158, in PL, vol. 140, cols. 651-52 (= C.16, q.1, c.19); Constable, "Second Crusade", pp. 276-78.

30. Bernard, *Sermones super cantica canticorum* bk. 64, section 3, in: Bernard, *Opera*, vol. 2, pp. 167-68; similarly, Bernard's disciple, Idung of Prüfening ("Argument", pp. 176-77).

31. Riley-Smith, *First Crusade*, pp. 150-52.

32. Bernard, *De laude*, in: Bernard, *Opera*, vol. 3, pp. 205-39.

33. Bernard, *De laude*, bk.4, section 7 in: Bernard, *Opera*, vol. 3, p. 220.

34. Brundage, *Canon Law*, pp. 30-114.

35. Brundage, "Cruce signari"; Pennington.

36. Below, Ch. 5. Harnack; Erdmann, *Origin*, pp. 4-6, 201-28.

37. Bernard, *Opera*, vol. 8, letter 458 (to Bohemian crusaders [1146/47]), pp. 434-47: "Audiat ergo universitas vestra verbum bonum . . . ." (p. 435),

"[D]iligentius super hoc universitatem vestram studeat exhortari" (p. 437). *Ann. Magdeburgenses* (*anno* 1147), p. 188: "Ubi in una societate convenerant . . . armatis bellatoribus sexaginta milibus. Interim in alia societate se in unum collegerant Albero Bremensis archiepiscopus, Thietmarus Fardensis episcopus, Heinricus dux Saxonie . . . ."; Constable, "Second Crusade", p. 240.

38. Bernard, *Opera*, vol. 8, pp. 311-17, letter 363 (to the bishops and people of eastern Francia and Bavaria [1146]): "Viros bellicosos et gnaros talium duces eligere est . . . ." Bernard sent virtually identical letters to the archbishop of Cologne and to the bishop of Brescia.

39. Odo of Deuil, *Croisade*, pp. 26-7; Constable, "Second Crusade", p. 240.

40. *Lyxbonensi*, p. 56.

41. Bernard, *Opera*, vol. 8, letter 458, p. 436: "Illud quoque statutum est ne quis aut variis aut griseis seu etiam sericis utatur vestibus, sed neque in equorum faleris auri vel argenti quippiam apponatur; tantum in scuto et ligno sellarum, quibus utentur, cum ad bella procedent, aurum vel argentum apponi licebit his qui voluerint, ut refulgeat sol in eis et terrore dissipetur gentium fortitudo." Other medieval writers sometimes remarked on the psychological advantages that Christian warriors secured from the splendor of their shining shields and glistening weapons (e.g.: Henry of Livonia, 9.3 [p. 49] and 14.5 [pp. 97-8]). Scriptural allusions may have been in the minds both of Bernard and Henry; cf. Deuteronomy 32:41, Habakkuk 3:11.

42. Bernard, *Opera*, vol. 8, letter 544 (1147), pp. 511-12.

43. Urban II, letter to the people of Bologna (September 19, 1096), in: Hagenmeyer, *Kreuzzugsbriefe*, pp. 137-38; see generally: Brundage, "Transformed Angel".

44. Anselm, *Opera*, vol. 4 (1949), letter 195, pp. 85-96; vol. 5 (1951), letter 410, p. 355; see also: Brundage, "St. Anselm".

4

Crusade Eschatology as Seen by St. Bernard in the Years 1146 to 1148

Hans-Dietrich Kahl

The Second Crusade had ended a failure; indeed, it had proved to be an utter disaster. Harsh criticism was levelled against the man who had been its principal driving force, Bernard of Clairvaux. The impact of his strong personality had a lasting effect all the same. The Cistercian Order, soon after his death, in an attempt to achieve his formal canonization, was obliged to play down the degree of Bernard's commitment to the Crusade. It would not be difficult to show how the Order at Clairvaux deliberately minimized Bernard's role, creating a gap in the tradition.[1]

There are, however, historiographical notes showing what really struck Bernard's contemporaries about the general tone of his crusading sermons. These notes are important supplements to his own letters and must be added to the material on which Bernard McGinn bases his excellent study of Bernard's eschatology;[2] they fill the chronological gap left in McGinn's study between the early and late 1140s. Thus, that short period presents a rather different picture from the one given by McGinn. Of course, these testimonies need careful study, which cannot be included here.[3]

That study would show that, at least at a later stage of his activities on behalf of the great cause, Bernard must have more or less overtly embraced convictions that originated in the old so-called Sibylline prophecies.[4] He was not the only one to have done so. Otto of Freising testifies that the most exalted minds in France were susceptible to such influences, seeking to obtain a deeper understanding of their own times.[5] Thus, they believed that mankind was at the eve of the end of the world; that the last emperor had come to force the Christian religion upon what seemed to be left of the heathens in the geographically limited world known to Western man;[6] that he had come to Christianize them, and to restore both crown and empire to Christ in a solemn symbolic act in Jerusalem; after that, Antichrist was to appear. Old prophecies had it that the emperor was naturally associated with the Roman Empire (*imperium*), but held the title of "King of the Romans" (*Romanorum rex*) only. The initial letter of his name was to be a "C".[7] It so happened that there was indeed a contemporary of Bernard who met all those prerequisites, Conrad III of Germany. The general obtrusiveness of the abbot's attempts to win the emperor over to his plan for a crusade, against all political sense, has long been duly emphasized.[8] But that he had actually been successful with the emperor came as a *miraculum miraculorum* for Bernard himself[9] — a kind of emphasis never really explained hitherto. I take it that the harassing urgency with which Bernard tried to persuade the *Romanorum rex* with the initial letter "C" to accept the plan of the crusade, was the final test for Bernard, to prove to him whether or not the old prophecies could be trusted, and whether he could take them as a basis of an eschatological interpretation of his times. The remarkable fact is that the clearest testimonies in favor of a crusade sermon formed according to this kind of interpretation come from the very spheres that were not reached by Bernard's influence until after the taking of the cross by Conrad.[10]

This material is somewhat difficult to detect and to interpret, and it will also be presented elsewhere.[11] There is one text, however, that I shall submit to a closer examination here, and that is Bernard's letter no. 457 — the only one of his letters on the crusade that was conceived more or less independently from his other and older drafts. It was issued in March 1147, following the Reichstag at Frankfurt at which a special enterprise was decided upon, obviously at the instigation of Bernard, the so-called Wendish Crusade (*Wendenkreuzzug*).[12]

No particular notice has been taken of this letter hitherto in research into the crusades, because it was supposed to refer to minor events. Yet nearly half of the letter deals with nothing else but the preparations for the imminent expedition to the Orient. Again, a comprehensive analysis would be outside the scope of this chapter. However, I shall select one concept or idea which is unique to this letter among Bernard's writings on the crusade.

The issue was, he writes, one of extirpating the enemies of the name of Christ from the face of the earth, *ad . . . exstirpandas de terra christiani nominis inimicos*. The devil, gnashing his teeth, saw many evildoers, who had already been in his clutches, defecting, because of the crusade vow. "But there is an evil he fears more than anything else, originating from the conversion of the heathens, because he has heard" — and then follows an indirect quotation from St. Paul (Romans 11:25-26): "that their fullness will enter [the Kingdom of Heaven] and Israel as a whole will be saved. The time has now come, so it seems to him, *hoc ei nunc tempus imminere videtur*." That is why he strained every nerve to work against this, and why he had incited some heathens to attack the crusading army from the rear. Bernard felt that these heathens had been tolerated for much too long, but with God's help it would come to pass "that their pride will be humbled all the more quickly and that the expedition to Jerusalem will take place without let or hindrance" from the evil one.

It is apparent that a great metaphysical vision of the salvation of the world is being evoked through this text, a vision inspired by the ideas of the two Augustinian *civitates*. It is true that Bernard used the quotation from the Epistle to the Romans in other statements about the crusade,[13] but never with such a clear expression of immediate eschatological expectation as in letter no. 457.

Exstirpare de terra: a comparison with other texts shows that the whole-sale extermination of the heathens can be achieved not only by the physical destruction of human beings, but by baptism as well.[14] Then follows a reference to the Biblical promise of the final conversion of both heathens and Jews which will coincide with an expedition to Jerusalem undertaken by "kings and princes". This association is found only in the Sibylline tradition of a last emperor, so Bernard must at least have been cognizant of this tradition. All these events are seen as being imminent, *quod ei nunc imminere videtur*, but in a rather indirect way: it is to the devil that all this seems to be happening. Nevertheless, Bernard appears to identify himself with this belief. *Ad . . . exstirpandas de terra christiani nominis inimicos*: this was the objective of the crusade which was proclaimed in letter no. 457; it offers a solution to the problem of the heathens, a universal solution which encompassed the limited world known to Bernard and his contemporaries, so that they could believe that most people had been Christian for a long time.[15] Such a definitive solution to the problem of the heathen would, in accordance with Christian belief, be reserved for the end of the world (cf. Matthew 24:14 and Mark 13:10). Bernard did not view the evil one as the harmless figure of popular superstition. He was not one of the simple people who believed all the anecdotes of the triumph of human ingenuity over the great adversary. Bernard took the evil one seriously. So it is of some consequence that Bernard cites this bearer of superhuman knowledge in order to hint at what he himself wishes to say.

The text then deals with the heathen inhabitants of areas beyond the River Elbe. They are not named, to emphasize the irrelevance of ethnic observations to the great universal struggle between the two *civitates*. The crusaders are supposed to exterminate or convert them, in that order, *ad delendas penitus aut certe convertendas nationes illas*; similar words are used elsewhere in the letter. This obligation is hammered into them rigorously and severely. Such a demand is monstrous, in terms of both theology and canon law. Its counterpart, expressed in the same severe tone, is found in the traditions surrounding the Sibylline belief in the last emperor.[16] It is crucial to understand that this must not be measured by normal standards; it has nothing to do with the everyday activities of the Church, because it deals with the fine line between what could be done on the eve of the last days of the world to obey the risen Christ's command to baptize all heathens[17] and thus save souls, and the end of time, when it would be too late. Faced with this situation, everyday standards are seen as no longer relevant; only here the unusual can be allowed to happen, unusual deeds that would not even be hinted at in other situations — allowed to happen because old prophecies, believed to be authoritative, had shown the way. Possibly this is what was motivating Bernard when he preached his crusading sermons at this late stage, and what an even later tradition tried to suppress after the prophecy had been proved wrong.[18] It must be noted that the tradition of the last emperor, in any of its different forms, had not won any ecclesiastical or any other kind of official approval, nor had it been expressly repudiated. No true follower of the Church would have felt the need to renounce that tradition. The monstrosity of teaching radical extirpation at the point of a sword as a form of missionary work remains monstrous, but may now be better understood.

A look at those source texts which cannot be dealt with here would confirm the validity of this interpretation.[19] Moreover, Bernard is seen as an example of a more general development beginning around the middle of the eleventh century which is characterized by two main traits: the first, which is more striking to the reader of the sources, is a rather noncommittal, theoretical, theological discussion of the end of time, without any clear indication that it was felt to be imminent; the second is an indication that the year 1000 of the Christian era no longer had the strong intellectual and religious significance once ascribed to it, but as the years passed there had been a general and ever-increasing sense of readiness for the approaching end.

A turning point was, perhaps, the great pilgrimage, which set out from Germany for Jerusalem in 1064/65 because Easter Day 1065 coincided with the feast of the Annunciation. This coincidence was believed to be especially meaningful, and might bring with it the second coming of Christ, the Parousia; the pilgrims wanted to be in Jerusalem when this came to pass. The huge train was led by four eminent representatives of the Imperial episcopate who seemed unconcerned about leaving their dioceses vacant for a year or two: the archbishop of Mainz, and the bishops of Bamberg, Regensburg and Utrecht. The number of pilgrims must have run into the thousands.[20] Since that date, source texts on real apocalyptical expectations have multiplied. It is well known that many expectations and ideas of an eschatological nature were associated with the First Crusade.[21] One of the pre-conditions included in the widely disseminated prophecies regarding the Antichrist seemed to have been fulfilled: Jerusalem was again under Christian rule. Let me mention just one less well-known episode from the period following the First Crusade: the whole diocesan clergy of Liège was assembled in the cathedral on the vigil of Ascension Day 1117 when a thunderstorm broke out, the like of which nobody present had ever experienced. Everyone had the same idea: the time had come! Three people died of excitement. But the storm subsided and nothing had happened. It had simply been an error, and that was all.[22]

The testimony given by Otto of Freising[23] shows how the downfall of Edessa on Christmas Day 1144, the event that gave rise to the Second Crusade, stirred up expectations in the leading intellectual circles of France, expectations similar to those in the minds of the Liège clergy when the thunderstorm broke out on that vigil of Ascension Day in 1117. The general pattern of the events was the same: an incident interrupted the daily routine, certain expectations were, more or less consciously, associated with it, and the incident was then taken as a clear indication of something about to happen. It is here, then, that Bernard proves himself a true child of his time, just as we are children of ours.

Bernard's individual development has been particularly well documented by the combination of McGinn's material[24] with mine. McGinn showed that Bernard was susceptible to eschatological questions, and that in the course of the 1130s Bernard was ever more ready to interpret present times in an eschatological light, even though he did not expect the end of the world to come on a definite date. This is the interpretation that can be made of the usual source material of the theologian. But this material does not suffice on its own — it must be supplemented by what can be adduced and interpreted by the historian, whose material shows furthermore that Bernard was normally more inclined to view the end of time and problems pertaining to it in a rather academic and dispassionate way and to treat them accordingly. The actual occurrence of a particular event, however, could change his mood to one of expectation of the imminent end of time, and he did not hesitate to publicize his expectation. But when he could no longer deny that he had been wrong, he reverted to his former, more detached, way of viewing things. In other words: neither kind of development can be distinguished nicely from the other; they can gain in importance within one and the same person, each for a while, with much depending on the specific phase in which an author wrote a particular text.

Our picture of those times will possibly become more true to life if we pay greater attention to similar probabilities and tendencies in the future. The historian will do well if he thinks in terms of dynamic processes rather than static effects.

In conclusion, let us glance at the ecclesiastical and political impact of Bernard's crusade eschatology. His special plan for the so-called Wendish Crusade had been announced in Frankfurt, without the official approval of the pope, which was required because only the pope could issue and proclaim the pledge of indulgence. The Holy See was occupied at that time by Bernard's old disciple and Brother, Eugenius III, who issued a bull of his own on April 11, 1147.[25]

In this bull, the idea of the crusade conceived in Frankfurt was altered in a characteristic way. There is no sign that the pope shared Bernard's expectation of the last days, but there is, however, one idea that is taken up: the object of Christianization is to be achieved by the crusade, directed against the "heathens of the North" in order to subjugate them and force the Christian religion upon them, *eos Christiane religioni subiugare*. The bull did not express the alternatives of extermination or conversion. Treaties of peace with the heathens, who remained unwilling to be converted to the Christian religion, even by the threatened use of military force, were still considered possible. All this differed considerably from what Bernard had advocated.[26] The bull marks the first official sanction by a pope of the use of force against the heathens in order to convert them.[27] It was meant, not as an indirect move to create opportunities for consequent, peaceful, missionary preaching, according to a tradition dating back to Gregory the Great,[28] but as a direct military operation designed to achieve conversion to the new belief.

Helmut Roscher coined the term *"Missionskreuzzug"* (missionary crusade) for this kind of war, sanctioned by the Church, that Christianity waged against the heathens. It is hardly by chance that such wars against the heathens broke out on more than one front in the eastern Baltic region, not long after 1147, with or without papal pledges of indulgence. In the last analysis, these wars must be traced back to Bernard's crusade eschatology, even though none of them was occasioned by an immediate expectation of the end of the world.[29]

Appendix A

Bernard of Clairvaux
Letter 457
Frankfurt, c. 11-23 March 1147
(from Bernard, *Opera*, vol. 8, pp. 432-33;
[author's italics in text])

Dominis et Patribus reverendis archiepiscopis ceterisque episcopis et
principibus et universis fidelibus Dei, Bernardus Claravallensis vocatus
abbas: spiritum fortitudinis et salutis.

   Non dubito quin auditum sit in terra vestra, et celebri sermone vulgatum,
quomodo suscitaverit spiritum regum Deus et principum *ad faciendam*
vindictam in nationibus et exstirpandos de terra christiani nominis inimicos.
Magnum bonum, magna divinae miserationis ubertas! Verumtamen videt
hoc malignus et invidet more suo; frendet dentibus et tabescit; multos amittit
ex his quos variis criminibus et sceleribus obligatos tenebat: perditissimi
quique convertuntur, declinantes a malo, parati facere bonum. Sed alium
damnum veretur longe amplius *de conversione gentium,* cum audivit
plenitudinem eorum introituram, et omnem quoque Israel fore salvandum.
Hoc ei nunc tempus imminere videtur, et tota fraude satagit versuta malitia,
quemadmodum obviet tanto bono. Suscitavit proinde semen nequam, filios
sceleratos, paganos, quos, ut pace vestra dixerim, nimis diu sustinuit
christianorum fortitudo, perniciose insidiantes dissimulans, calcaneo suo nec
conterens capita venenata. Sed quia dicit Scriptura: ANTE RUINAM EX-
ALTABITUR COR, fiet ergo, Deo volente, ut eorum superbia citius
humilietur, et non propter hoc impediatur *via Ierosolimitana*; quia enim
verbum hoc crucis parvitati nostrae Dominus evangelizandum commisit,
consilio domini Regis et episcoporum et principum, qui convenerant
Frankonovort, denuntiamus *armari christianorum robur adversus illos, et*
ad delendas penitus, aut certe convertendas nationes illas signum salutare
suscipere, eamdem eis promittentes indulgentiam peccatorum quam et his
qui versus Ierosolimam sunt profecti. Et multi quidem signati sunt ipso loco,
ceteros autem ad opus simul provocavimus, ut qui ex christianis necdum
signati sunt ad viam Ierosolimitanam, noverint eamdem sese indulgentiam
hac adepturos expeditione, si tamen perstiterint in ea pro consilio
episcoporum et principum. Illud enim omnimodis interdicimus, *ne qua*
ratione ineant foedus cum eis, neque pro pecunia, neque pro tributo, donec,
auxiliante Deo, aut ritus ipse, aut natio deleatur. Vobis sane loquimur

archiepiscopis et coepiscopis vestris, opponite omnino, ut maximam super his geratis sollicitudinem, et quantumcumque potestis, studium adhibeatis et diligentiam, ut viriliter fiat; et secundum Deum ministri Christi estis, et idcirco fiducialius a vobis exigitur, ut negotio eius, quod ad vos spectat, invigiletis. Nos quoque plurimum id rogamus et obsecramus in Domino. Erit autem huius exercitus, et in vestibus, et in armis, et phaleris ceterisque omnibus eadem quae et alterius exercitus observatio, quippe quos eadem retributio munit. Placuit autem omnibus in Frankenevort congregatis quatenus exemplar istarum litterarum ubique portaretur, et episcopi atque presbyteri populo Dei annuntiarent, et eos *contra hostes crucis Christi, qui sunt ultra Albi,* signo sanctae crucis consignarent et armarent; qui nimirum omnes in festo apostolorum Petri et Pauli apud Magdeburg convenire debent.

Appendix B

**Confirmation by Pope Eugenius III of an expedition against the Slavs and other pagans living in northern parts.
Troyes (*in territorio Trecensi*), 11 April 1147
(from *Pommersches Urkundenbuch*, vol. 1, pp. 36-7, l. 32
[author's italics in text];
cf. Jaffé-Loewenfeld, no. 9017 [1st ed. no. 6297])**

Eugenius episcopus servus servorum Dei universis Dei fidelibus salutem et apostolicam benedictionem. Divini dispensatione consilii factum credimus, quod tanta multitudo fidelium de diversis mundi partibus ad infidelium expugnationem accingitur et *fere tota Christianorum terra* pro tam laudabili opere *commovetur.* Inter alios enim principes et potentes ipsi reges, qui ceteris nationibus dominantur, signo vivifice crucis assumpto *ad deliberationem orientalis ecclesie* preparant et *crucis Christi inimicos,* qui peccatis exigentibus in partibus illis fratres nostros aput Edessam et in aliis multis locis crudeliter trucidarunt, cum Dei auxilio *potenter expugnare disponunt.* Rex quoque Ispaniarum contra Saracenos de partibus illis potenter armatur, de quibus iam per Dei gratiam sepius triumphavit. Quidam etiam ex vobis tam sancti laboris et premii participes fieri cupientes *contra Sclauos ceterosque paganos habitantes versus aquilonem ire et eos Christiane religioni subiugare* Domino auxiliante *intendunt.* Quorum nos devotionem attendentes omnibus illis, qui crucem eandem Iherosolimam non acceperunt et contra Sclauos ire et in ipsa expeditione, sicut statutum est, devotionis intuitu manere decreverunt, illam remissionem peccatorum, quam predecessor noster felicis memorie papa Vrbanus Iherosolimam transeuntibus instituit, omnipotentis Dei et beati Petri apostolorum principis auctoritate nobis a Deo concessa concedimus eadem auctoritate sub excommunicatione *prohibentes, ut nullus de paganis ipsis, quos Christiane fidei poterit subiugare, pecuniam vel aliam redemptionem accipiat, ut eos in sua perfidia remanere permittat.* Preterea quia expedire cognoscimus, ut aliqua religiosa, discreta, litterata persona sit inter vos, que paci et tranquillitati vestre provideat et unitatem inter vos conservet et vos *de promovenda Christiana religione* commoneat, venerabil(id)em fratrem nostrum A. Hauegelbergensem episcopum, religiosum, discretum et litteratum virum, ad hoc providemus et hanc ei sollicitudinem iniunximus. Quocirca per apostolica vobis scripta precipimus, ut eum pro reverentia beati Petri et nostra et omnium vestrum salute diligatis et honoretis eiusque salubribus consiliis et ammonitionibus et preceptis humiliter pareatis, ut Deus exinde honoretur atque concordia et fraterna dilectio Domino auctore et ipsius studio annuente inter vos conservetur. Illos autem, qui ad tam sanctam expeditionem crucem acceperint, et bona eorum sub beati Petri et nostra protectione manere decernimus. Datum in territorio T[re]censi, tertio idus Aprilis, pontificatus [vero domini Eugenii III. pape anno III.].

Appendix C

For a list of preparatory works by the author with supplementary material, see the following entries in the Bibliography:
Kahl, "1147"
Kahl, "Antichristo"
Kahl, "Auszujäten"
Kahl, "Bernard 1"

Kahl, "Bernard 2"
Kahl, "Bernard 3"
Kahl, "Bernard 4"
Kahl, "*Fides*"
Kahl, "Kriegsziel"
Kahl, "Slawen"
Kahl, "Wendenkreuzzug"

NOTES

1. The present contribution is a summary of two more comprehensive papers (Kahl, "Bernard 1"; Kahl, "Auszujäten") printed simultaneously with further material. The English translation was prepared by Dr. Wolfgang Becker of the University of Giessen. For the gap of tradition mentioned above, see: Kahl, "Bernard 1", ch. 7.
2. McGinn, "St. Bernard".
3. Kahl, "Bernard 1", chs. 5-6.
4. Sackur; Adso *De ortu*; McGinn, *Visions*, with extensive bibliography; Verbeke; Fried.
5. Otto of Freising, *Gesta* 2, Prologue, pp. 114:24-116:24: "[de] scripto, quod illis in diebus in multis Gallie locis lectitabatur . . . . Quod scriptum tante auctoritatis a probatissimis et religiosissimis Galliarum personis tunc putabatur, ut a quibusdam in Sibillinis libris repertum ab aliis cuidam Armenio divinitus revelatum affirmaretur . . . quod fidem aliquam habere potuit . . . ."
6. See: Kahl, "Mittelalter".
7. [Pseudo-] Alcuin, in Adso, *De ortu*, p. 125: "Sicut ex sibyllinis libris habemus, tempore predicti regis, cuius nomen erit C. rex Romanorum totius imperii . . . exsurgunt ab aquilone spurcissime gentes . . . . Quod cum audierit Romanorum rex, convocato exercitu, debellabit eos et prosternet usque ad internecionem . . . . Omne sibi uindicet regnum terrarum. Omnes ergo insulas et ciuitates paganorum deuastabit et uniuersa idolorum templa destruet et omnes paganos ad baptismum conuocabit, et per omnia templa crux Christi dirigetur. Iudei quoque tunc convertentur . . . . Impletis autem . . . annis regni eius, ueniet Hierosolimam, et ibi . . . deposito diademate, relinquet Deo Patri et Filio eius Christo Iesu regnum christianorum." See also n. 16 below. It is well known that in medieval Europe, the Muslims were considered pagans, polytheists, and idolaters. Without further ceremony, it was thus possible to apply these prophecies against them as well as against pagans in the narrower sense of the word.

8. Theodore et al., *Annales* (*anno* 1147), p. 82: "Conradus Romanorum rex . . . sumens et ipse crucem ad eandem expeditionem . . . Bernhardo Clarevallensis abbate nimium urgente eius profectionem . . . ."

9. Philip of Clairvaux, cols. 381B-382B: "ibi enim factum est, ut ipsius verbis utar, miraculum miraculorum . . . signatus est rex . . . ."

10. Kahl, "Bernard 1", chs. 4-6.

11. Kahl, "Bernard 1", chs. 4-6.

12. The letter is reproduced in Appendix A. On Bernard's role in the origins of this special crusade, see: Kahl, "1147". The term "Wendenkreuzzug" is usual but does not correspond with the contemporary aims and objectives of this expedition (see: Kahl, "Auszujäten", ch. 1).

13. Bernard, *Opera*, vol. 8, epistle 363:6 (p. 316:12 ff.); epistle 365:2 (p. 321:24 ff.); epistle 457 (p. 432:14 ff.). Cf. *De consideratione* (written just after the crusade), bk. 3, 1, 3 (Bernard, *Opera*, vol. 3, p. 433:12 ff.).

14. Kahl, "Auszujäten", ch. 9.

15. Kahl, "Mittelalter", pp. 25 ff.

16. After the erection of the cross in the hitherto heathen temples, the traditions quoted above (n. 7) are in several texts completed by the following sentence: "Qui vero crucem Jesu Christi non adoraverit, gladio punietur." For example see the so-called *Tiburtina*, in Sackur, p. 185, and the anonymous *Mirabilis Liber*, in Radcke, p. 66 (this book contains good texts, but too much speculation). Note that these two texts seem to have been compiled and written in France during the eleventh and twelfth centuries; they thus testify to the fact that such eschatological views were current in Bernard's own country during his lifetime.

17. Matthew 28.19-20 reads τα εθνη (*gentes*). The usage makes it quite clear that the heathens only are meant here, to the exclusion of the Jews. To understand this text, one must assume the meaning of "peoples" or "nations" to be an anachronism which reaches far back in Christian history (see: Kahl, "Zusammenlebens", pp. 165 ff.).

18. See: Kahl, "Bernard 1", ch. 7.

19. See n. 3 above.

20. Hauck, vol. 3, pp. 733 ff.; Erdmann, *Origin*, pp. 302 ff., cf. pp. 291 ff.; Classen, "Eschatologische 1", p. 146 (cf. pp. 139 ff.) or Classen, "Eschatologische 2", p. 316 (cf. p. 313). Fried, pp. 465 ff. (cf. p. 461 & n. 357).

21. Erdmann, "Endkaiserglaube"; Alphandéry, vol. 1; Classen, "Eschatologische 1", pp. 144 ff. or Classen, "Eschatologische 2", pp. 315 ff.

22. *Ekkehard Chronica*, Recensio IV (*anno* 1117), pp. 334 ff.: "dum . . . universus clerus . . . intra matrem ecclesiam. . .vespertinalem sinaxim concenturi iam primum psalmum complessent, subito serenissimus aer in turbinem versus tanta simul tonitrua terribiliter et fulgura cum sulphureis ignibus excussit, ut extremum ultimi iudicii horam instare nemo qui aderat dubitaverit . . . ." immediately follows the account of a further event of some months later, felt also to be so terrible that in the same way "rerum omnium finem minitari putaretur" (p. 336:11 ff.).

23. See n. 5, above.
24. See n. 2, above.
25. See Appendix B.
26. See Appendix A.
27. Roscher, p. 192 and cf. p. 212.
28. See Kahl, "Bernard 3", pp. 139 ff.; Kahl, "Auszujäten", ch. 6.
29. On the problems in the Baltic region, cf. Petersohn, *Ostseeraum*; Nyberg; Hellmann; Colloquio, *"Livonia"*.

5

Militia and *Malitia*: The Bernardine Vision of Chivalry

Aryeh Grabois

In his treatise, *De laude novae militiae*,[1] Bernard of Clairvaux distinguished between the Templars and the entire secular knighthood. The first deserved the epithet *militia*, while the others received the pejorative classification *malitia*.[2] His praise of the "new knighthood" emphasized that its members were the sole knights to behave according to the principles of *Vita perfecta*, both of the chivalric ideals and of the monastic orders. Moreover, their dedication to a perpetual war against the Muslims and to the defense of the Holy Land was considered by the abbot of Clairvaux to be both the real expression of chivalric ideals, and an achievement of the Gregorian ideas of *milites Christi*.[3] Against this sense of the term *militia*, the lay knights not only did not deserve to be *milites*, but, because of their behavior, clothes and hairstyles, which expressed the sins of vanity and luxury,[4] represented *malitia*, or malice.

However, one may legitimately question whether this distinction between "religious" and "secular" chivalry reflected Bernard's vision of knighthood. Was he condemning the entire system of chivalry as "malicious"? Or, did he develop this dichotomy in order to emphasize the distinction between "good" and "evil" knights on the ground of qualitative criteria, connected with the implementation of moral principles of conduct proper to the ethical ideals of chivalry as they prevailed at the time? By the formulation of such questions, it is possible to perceive a gap between the practical goals that brought

Bernard to the elaboration of this treatise and a broader vision of chivalry.[5] It must be remembered that Bernard, who had been worried by the serious crisis the small company led by Hugh of Payns faced during the first decade after its foundation in 1118, decided, in the spirit of the rule he drafted for the Order, both to comfort them and to help them to recruit new members. Thus, his *Praise of the new knighthood* was written as a propaganda manifesto, aiming at the exaltation of Templar virtues and at the "conversion" of the European knights, who were invited to join the new Order in the Holy land.[6] His approach was similar to that undertaken in his appeal to the European knighthood urging their participation in the Second Crusade.

Certainly, there had been a clear distinction between the "religious" and lay chivalry. The adaptation of monastic ideas by the military orders during the twelfth century, both in the Holy Land and in Spain, led to the emergence of a symbiosis of monasticism and knighthood, previously characterized by Sidney Painter as "religious chivalry".[7] Thus, the basic distinction between "good" and "bad" knights was the result of the long-term evolution of the lay group of warriors, and had no relationship to the establishment of the military orders.

This process resulted in the transformation of warriors into a social class, characterized by its own ethical norms of behavior, education, and patterns of culture. It was achieved at the beginning of the twelfth century with the awakening of the consciousness of its superiority within Western society.[8] Thus, the violent *juvenes* of the eleventh and beginning of the twelfth centuries[9] were the same wandering knights as the contemporaries of William Marshal; as such, they might qualify for Bernard's *malitia*. However, the differing perceptions of the term "malice" in the mind of succeeding generations brought about a change in chivalric ideals, to the point that the approach to the *juvenes*, considered a social calamity until the first quarter of the twelfth century, was entirely opposite to the attitude towards the wandering knights of the second half of the same century.

Among the various factors in this evolution, the qualitative distinction between the "good" and "evil" knights, as expressed by contemporary sources,[10] played an important role in the crystallization of public opinion to the transformation of the behavioral norms of these knights. Undoubtedly, such definitions represent the attitude of their authors, all of whom were monks. But they also reflect their implantation among lay society as an outcome of its structure and of "chivalric" education.[11] Among the factors considered, the ideas of the Peace and Truce of God played a cardinal role in this distinction, particularly because they became part of the values acquired by the new generation of knights. Accordingly, the question of whether Bernard of Clairvaux invented the distinction formulated in his treatise or used notions already widespread, and adapted them to the Templars, bears special interest. Had it only been an expression of monastic ideas, the distinction between *militia* and *malitia* might be qualified as a Bernardine vision of chivalry, related to his spirituality and sociopolitical ideas.[12] In such a case, this distinction might be accepted as another expression of the ideas, later formulated in his crusade propaganda. Thus the notion of *pax christiana* has to be connected both with his crusading ideology, and with his vision of celestial Jerusalem as implemented in the cloister (*hic est Hierosolyma*),[13] reframing Augustinian and Anselmian views.

Contrary to any hypothesis which might confine the ideas of peace to the cloisters, the sources reveal that since the middle of the eleventh century such a dichotomic approach to chivalry had largely been spread by public opinion. While the movement of the Peace and Truce of God did not bring about the abolition of wars and violence, it did succeed in implanting in Western society opprobrious feelings against gangs of warriors, condemned as disturbers of the public peace and as enemies of the social order.[14] Such feeling implied the need for justification of military activities, emphasizing their defensive character as the sole reason for their legitimization. Accordingly, the "good" knights were those who fought in order to protect the churches, the poor and the oppressed. The sources consequently insist on the military activities of their heroes, who, as genuine knights, responded to the appeals of ecclesiastical authorities who were fighting for the freedom of the Church. Moreover, the defensive nature of these wars has been emphasized by attributing responsibility for them to the adversary, an aggressor and offender against peace. Thus, even though wars were considered to be illegitimate in terms of the peace movement, they might have become "just wars" under particular circumstances,[15] at least for those who were qualified as "good" knights.

The expressions of the new approach to chivalry are emphasized in the chronicle of Raoul Glaber. One of the wars recounted, namely the conflict between the counts of Blois and Anjou in 1044 over the lordship of the city of Tours, represents an excellent example of this qualitative distinction. Raoul blamed the Blois party, castigating them as aggressors and troublemakers, while the Angevin *milites*, whose manners in no way differed from those of their adversaries, are represented as champions of the faith, as defenders of the good "cause", fighting in order to free the Abbey of St. Martin which was "oppressed by the tyrant of Blois".[16] In terms of the social stratification of the period, it also reflects the transformation of the mass of warriors, the *bellatores*, into *milites*[17] and, to no lesser degree, the impact of the peace movement, legitimating the "just war" conducted against "trouble-makers". The same distinction appears in the next generation, as the chroniclers of the Norman conquest of England especially bear witness. They classified William the Conqueror's army as that of "good" knights, who left aside their own interests in order to respond to the duke's call, intending to punish the "evil" Harold and his followers, to restore the "good order" of Edward's times and, particularly, to fight for the faith and the reform of the English church.[18]

While the main characteristics of the qualitative distinction among the knighthood had been formulated during the second half of the eleventh century, its crystallization belongs to the reign of King Louis VI of France (1108-37), St. Bernard's contemporary. The monarch's efforts to pacify and restructure his kingdom have been considered by public opinion to be a constant struggle between the forces of order and peace led by the king and supported by the Church, and the malicious elements, which included those who broke up the social order, the offenders of the peace, among them those who had been convicted for violating the Truce of God. Writers, therefore, such as the authors of the Chronicle of Morigny, or Suger of Saint Denis, the king's biographer, had no difficulty applying against the "malicious" the stereotypical expressions of previous generations, classifying the king's enemies as troublemakers, as oppressors of the Church, the poor and the weak, and even as being impious.[19] On the other hand, Louis' image as a just and equitable monarch, whose sole concern used to be the punishment of "evil", fighting in order to impose peace in his kingdom, caused him to be represented as the major agent of public peace and the chief executive of the legislation of the Truce of God. The latter movement began during his reign to be transformed into the "royal peace".[20]

In that respect, Suger's *Vita Lodovici Grossi* is a mirror of this evolution of chivalric ideals, especially the distinction between the good and the bad. The perspective is, however, different from the Bernardine vision, because Suger had practically no interest in crusading ideas and was less concerned by the needs of the Latin Kingdom of Jerusalem than his friend, Bernard of Clairvaux; moreover, he never showed interest in the military orders. His focus was primarily the restoration of the royal authority in France, a process in which he had been actively involved.[21] He distinguished between "genuine" knights, who were engaged in the restructuring of society and the creation of the State, and the "others", whom he classed as brigands, even though they had been dubbed.

Accordingly, Suger combined certain criteria for "genuine" or "good" knights: they were to be descendants of noble families, valiant fighters, participants in the wars of their lords, protectors of churches and the clergy, as well as of the poor and the weak; above all, they were to be the faithful vassals of their lords. Such qualifications, already witnessed by other historical sources, and especially by the literary texts of the twelfth century, reflect in Suger's mind the implementation of new chivalric ideals.[22] While the dubbing ceremony remained essential to the "ordination" of knights, it was, according to these new ideals, only symbolic of joining the *militia*. It was a man's behavior which determined whether he was worthy of knighthood.

In this respect, the case of Hugh of Puiset is significant. He belonged to a very noble family, whose members, including his own father, distinguished themselves on crusade. His cousin became count of Jaffa, and thus a member of the highest rank of the nobility of the Latin Kingdom of Jerusalem.[23] However, in addition to his rebellion against royal authority, Hugh was an open enemy of the Abbey of Saint Denis, claiming some of its estates in the Beauce, which were at the time administrated by Suger, the abbey's provost in the area. Therefore, Suger considered Hugh to be

> a man lacking moral values, rich because of his tyranny and his ancestor's oppression; he succeeded to his uncle Guy, inheriting the honor of Puiset, because his arrogant father took his arms and went on the first expedition to Jerusalem; since his accession, Hugh did not cease to behave maliciously, as his father had done previously.[24]

Because of his personal involvement in that conflict, Suger's criticism is bitter, to the point that he did not find any excuse for the conduct of Hugh's father, even though Everard had been a crusader and was killed at the siege of Antioch and accordingly deserved the remission of his sins.

Finally, one may consider the case of Thomas of Marle, lord of Coucy, a former crusader who had acquired a bad reputation due to his cruel behavior.[25] After his return from the First Crusade, Thomas renewed his activity in Picardy, terrorizing the country. Excommunicated in 1114 by the Council of Beauvais, where he was proclaimed "enemy of the peace",[26] he was also considered as a rebel against royal authority. Suger described him as a prototype of a tyrant, "a scoundrel and enemy of God and mankind".[27] Recounting his excommunication at the Council of Beauvais, the Abbot of Saint Denis emphasized that Cardinal Conon of Praeneste, after having pronounced the sentence, in Thomas' absence, "deprived him of the knight's belt and divested him of his honors, being a scoundrel, an infamous person, and an enemy of Christianity". Suger emphasized the procedure adopted at the Council: a knight whose behavior brought on him public disapproval and who deserved to be convicted as a disturber of the peace ought to be degraded, in a way similar to the ecclesiastical procedure of degradation of ordained persons.[28] In that respect, the account is a complimentary testimony concerning the early twelfth-century transformation of knighthood into the *militaris ordo*, which was shaped under the influence of the monastic orders.[29]

Thus, Bernard of Clairvaux was not the first thinker or author to distinguish between chivalry and malice. Since it had emerged and developed during three previous generations, this distinction was already a commonplace for his contemporaries. His original contribution to the idea resided in his interpretation of this dichotomy, which he adapted to his purposes. But this adaptation, used in a narrow sense in his *De laude novae militae*, where he applied it exclusively to the Templars, contained the elements of a broader distinction between worthy and unworthy knights. Moreover, in connection with positions and attitudes adopted, either in the conflict in 1140-42 that opposed Theobald of Champagne to Louis VII, king of France,[30] or during the propaganda campaign for the Second Crusade,[31] Bernard acknowledged that there were many secular knights worthy of the qualification of *milites*. In that respect, Suger and Bernard held in common some views concerning the definition of the *militia* and the incompatibility of malicious warriors with knighthood. But Suger's pragmatic views led him to deal with more realistic definitions; these consequently prevailed in the process of the crystallization of chivalric ideals during the twelfth and thirteenth centuries, until the elaboration of the treatises on chivalry in the late Middle Ages.[32] On the other hand, despite his brilliant style, Bernard's definitions were based on his dogmatic approach to the topic and represented an utopian vision. This vision, based on his inflexible criteria and qualifications, was incompatible with the conditions of real life. Even the Templars, therefore, once the small group of founders had been transformed into a formidable Order by the recruitment of successive waves of knights, were not able to implement these ideas, deserving in their turn the criticism of the chroniclers of the Second Crusade.[33]

NOTES

1. Bernard, *De laude*, in: Bernard, *Opera*, vol. 3, pp. 213-240.
2. Bernard, *De laude*, ch. 2, in: Bernard, *Opera*, vol. 3, p. 216.
3. See: Robinson, "Gregory VII", and Leclercq, *Nouveau visage*, s.v.

4. Bernard, *De laude*, ch. 2, in: Bernard, *Opera*, vol. 3, p. 216.

5. Some examples of a broader use of this dichotomy may be found in Bernard's sermon, such as: *Sermones in laudibus Virginis Mariae*, Homilia IV, 10 (Bernard, *Opera*, vol. 4, p. 56); *In Psalmum qui habitat*, Sermo V, 2 (Bernard, *Opera*, vol. 4, pp. 402-403); *In Dedicatione Ecclesiae*, Sermo II, 4 (Bernard, *Opera*, vol. 5, p. 378); and *In Natali Sancti Victoris*, Sermo II, 5 (Bernard, *Opera*, vol. 6, p. 36).

6. This conclusion results from a comparison with Bernard's letter addressed to the Templars (see: Leclercq, "Templiers 1").

7. Painter, ch. 3: "Religious Chivalry". Since the publication of this book, significant progress has been made in research in that field. The proceedings of the 1979 Reichenau conference (Fleckenstein) opened new perspectives on this topic. For the linkage between "secular" and "religious" knighthood, see: Winter, *Rittertum*; Keen.

8. See: Wolff, "Eveil"; Duby, "Sociétés". See also: Duby, *Bouvines*; Duby, *Marriage*.

9. See: Duby, "Sociétés"; Duby, "Origines".

10. See: Cardini; Flori, *Glaive*, pp. 158-65.

11. For trends of monastic historiography, see: Ambroise, s.v. On "chivalric" education, see: Riché; Orme.

12. See: Leclercq, *Nouveau visage*; Sommerfeldt.

13. Bernard's *De conversione, ad clericos sermo seu liber*. (Bernard, *Opera*, vol. 4 (1966), pp. 69-116) should be considered as part of his polemical activity against Abelard and his Parisian students and must be interpreted in that context (Graboïs, "Quartier Latin" [rpt. with the same pagination in: Graboïs, *Civilisation*, ch. 7]). On the other hand, it expresses in a broader sense Bernard's views on the celestial Jerusalem (Konrad; Bredero).

14. See: MacKinney; Bonnaud-Delamare; Hoffmann; Cowdrey, "Peace & Truce"; Renna.

15. See: Russell.

16. Raoul Glaber, p. 129. In this context, similar attitudes had been adopted and expressed by Gerard of Cambrai and Adhemar of Chabannes, enlarging thus the geocultural area where such ideas prevailed to northeastern and western France; see their analyses by Duby (*Trois ordres*, pp. 35-61, 168-74), as well as Flori (*Glaive*, pp. 137, 161-63).

17. See: Johrendt; Van Luyn; Batany.

18. *Gesta Guillelmi*, pp. 154, 182-84. See: Douglas, pp. 185-88; Brown, *Normans*, pp. 145-51.

19. The *Chron. de Morigny* (2nd ed.) uses such stereotypical qualifications: King Louis VI is described as the ideal knight (p. 11), while the troublemakers deserved malicious terms, such as Robert of Oinville, "a malicious warrior" (p. 14), or Hugh de Crécy, "an impious knight" (p. 22).

20. See: Graboïs, "Treve".

21. The autobiographical references included in Suger's works are the best source testifying to his activity (see: Misch, vol. 3, pp. 318-23).

22. Suger, *Vita Ludovici* (1964), p. 90. For the general trend of this evolution, see: Hunt, Paterson, and particularly, Flori, *Chansons*.

23. For the genealogy of the family, see: Dion; for the participation of its members in the crusade and their role in the new Latin Kingdom of Jerusalem, see: La Monte, "Le Puiset".

24. Suger, *Vita Ludovici* (1964), p. 130. Suger's personal involvement in this conflict caused him to deal at length with this story (see pp. 128-70).

25. See: Chaurant, with a good bibliography. In the late thirteenth century Thomas became the hero of a popular epic, *La Chanson de Jérusalem*. On his literary image, see: Durparc-Quioc, "Coucy". A revised and up-dated version of this article was included in Durparc-Quioc, *Cycle*, pp. 39-44.

26. Suger, *Vita Ludovici* (1964), pp. 174-76.

27. Suger, *Vita Ludovici* (1964), pp. 30, 176. See similar qualifications by Guibert of Nogent, who was well informed about Thomas' conduct on the crusade and in Picardy (Guibert of Nogent *Vita*, p. 160). See also the English translation in: Benton, *Guibert of Nogent*, pp. 184-88, with notes by the editor.

28. Suger, *Vita Ludovici* (1964), p. 176. See: Winter, "Cingulum militiae"; Flori, "Adoubement"; Flori, "Chevalerie".

29. See: Morris, *"Equestris Ordo"*.

30. Bernard's Letter 221, addressed to King Louis VII (PL, vol. 182, cols. 386-87). See: Pacaut, *Louis VII*, pp. 42-4 and Graboïs, "Louis VII".

31. See: Constable, "Second Crusade"; Willems.

32. Among the various studies, see: Barber, *Knight*; Keen.

33. See: Demurger.

6

The Influence of St. Bernard of Clairvaux on the Formation of the Order of the Knights Templar

Marie Luise Bulst-Thiele

.

After the conclusion of the First Crusade, more pilgrims visited the Holy Land than ever before. Unprotected, many of these pilgrims were attacked, losing their property and often their lives. A murderous attack on some hundred pilgrims journeying from Jerusalem to the Jordan during Easter of 1119[1] induced a group of nine men to abandon their idle lifestyle under the shelter of the Prior of the Holy Sepulchre. They asked King Baldwin II of Jerusalem for permission to arm themselves in defense of the pilgrims.

Baldwin discussed the feasibility of the volunteers' plans with the patriarch, the clergy, and the barons, possibly at an assembly in Nablus in January of 1120.[2] According to William of Tyre,[3] the knights vowed to lead obedient and chaste lives, forswearing property (after the manner of the Reformed Canons of Jerusalem), and to protect and defend pilgrims so that their sins might be forgiven. "The king was very happy," wrote Ernoul.[4] Consequently, he gave the knights and their leader, Hugh of Payns, room in his palace, the Aqsa Mosque on the site of the Temple of Solomon, while the Canons of the Dome of the Rock provided a section of the extensive Temple precincts for the knights' workshops. The tale that nine knights remained nine for nine years, until the Council of Troyes in 1129,[5] is a legend. Neither the king nor the patriarch would have taken an interest in so small a group. Dante, among others, provides a possible explanation of the legend: nine is the holy cipher of the order of angels, three times the holy cipher three of the Trinity.[6]

The Order of the Templars, as the group came to be known, was designated as sacred and sanctified from the beginning. It had been founded for the praise and glory of God, to defend the faithful and to liberate the church of God. Though they were only one of several orders founded c. 1100, the Templars were different. While the Cistercians and the Augustinians aligned themselves with the doctrine of the Church Fathers, the aims of the Order of the Templars were startlingly new. The Templars combined monastic discipline with a fighting vocation. Only in the fervor of their vows did they resemble other orders. However, this duality of purpose created uncertainty and doubt among the Templars themselves. Some wished to live a religious life, but did not have the time for meditation. Others envied the Canons and their considerable possessions; the Templars had no share in the gifts of the faithful, nor were they mentioned in public prayers. Many of the Templars would have preferred to be in a more respected order rather than subsist on alms. A certain Hugh "the sinner", perhaps Hugh of St. Victor,[7] understood their troubles. He encouraged the knights, who adhered to monastic discipline, despite the fact that their military calling represented a way of life which others — perhaps the Canons — disputed on the grounds that religious orders were forbidden to fight. Hugh preached humility and persistence: it was the devil who instilled doubt and ambition among them. In the same way, Guigo of the Grande Chartreuse admonished the Templars first to conquer themselves; only when they were humble and obedient could they vanquish the foreign enemy.[8]

Ever since its foundation, the Kingdom of Jerusalem had never had enough defenders. The crusaders who remained in the Holy Land preferred farming to fighting. In the event of war, they were required to levy a fixed number of soldiers from among their men. A standing army did not exist, however. King Baldwin II was hard pressed for men-at-arms. Since 1119 he had been governing Antioch for Boehmund II, who was a minor. As there was no hope of booty there, Baldwin's vassals were unwilling to follow him.[9] Baldwin needed the support of the Templars. Presumably, it was he who sent Hugh of Payns to the West to gather warriors and to have Hugh's rule for the Order amended and confirmed by the Council of Troyes in January 1129, under the legate, Matthew of Albano, and in the presence of archbishops, bishops, abbots and secular princes.[10] The rule, written in the Holy Land before the death of Patriarch Stephen on June 12, 1130, refers twice to Bernard's presence at Troyes.[11] However, it is impossible to ascertain which parts of the manuscripts were composed by Hugh, the Council, the patriarch, the Chapter of the Order, or Bernard.

By this rule, Hugh of Payns might have wished to sever connections with the Canons, whose customs differed from those of the Templars. Initially, the Templars had attended the services of the Canons of Jerusalem; later, when they had their own priests, their only link with the Canons was the retention of the same service.[12]

Certainly, Baldwin wished to distance the Templars from the patriarch's influence. The rule of St. Benedict of Nursia was the model for the Templars' rule, from which many phrases were adopted. Members of the order shared simple meals of meat and wine and slept together in one room, fully clothed and belted, with a candle burning. The ban on personal property was only one of the many edicts the Templars followed with unswerving obedience; they had to live together amicably and to care for the old and the sick. Like the Cistercians, the Templars celebrated the minor office of the Virgin, and recited the first and last prayer of the day in honor of Our Lady. The rule established that "the hours for Our Lady be said every day first, except for the Compline of Our Lady which is said every day at the end . . . , for in honor of Our Lady our Order was founded and in Her honor it will come to its end whenever it pleases God." These words were spoken during a knight's initiation into the Order.[13] The service rendered by a courtly knight to his lady was spiritualized as service to Mary. The writings of St. Bernard were used as a model to underscore the tie to Mary through the use of feudal vocabulary. Mary is "queen", "advocate" and "intermediary"; she "reconciles", "represents" and "commends" "mankind to her son".[14]

The rule of the Templars governed all aspects of life. It began by outlining their religious service and the canonical hours of prayers and Paternosters. It detailed the type of alms and prayers to be said for the dead. Frugality and plainness of dress and weapons were required. The knights were allowed three horses and one shield-bearer. No worldly pleasures were permitted: no chess, hunting, or hawking.

The commemoration calendars of the Cistercians provide further proof of the close connection between the two orders. It was Cistercian practice to list only the names of those monasteries and communities within their own order. Out of 173 communities named in fourteen lists, only nineteen communities apppear on all lists, among them the Templars.[15]

The second document associating Bernard with the Templars, his *De laude novae militiae*, was written after the Council of Troyes. Hugh had encouraged him to rally support for the Templars. In his mind's eye, Bernard saw the knights as perfect in every way. All their doubts and those of their enemies were dismissed. Their militia was holy and secure. They lived by the rule: brotherly love, voluntary poverty, asceticism, abstention from amusement and respectful submission to the grand master and the Chapter. In contrast to the richly clothed, worldly knights, Bernard saw the dirty, shabby Templars as assured of eternal salvation. Though the first privilege (*Milites Templi*) granted to the Templars in or about 1135 by Pope Innocent II only specified the defense of the pilgrims, Bernard anticipated eventual combat with the heathen.[16] Bernard decried the foppish youth of his era. He hoped that his treatise would convert a generation of idle aristocrats: the younger sons of noble families who roamed France, indulging in private warfare, hunting and tournaments, with no productive or set future.[17] Bernard wished to redirect their lives, away from their *malitia* to his new vision of a *militia*. The young men did flock to the new standard, but not because Bernard seduced them. Until the dissolution of the Order, the Templars thought of Bernard as their founder;[18] the words adopted from the prologue of the Benedictine Rule by Bernard for his *De Laude*, "not for us, Lord, not for us, but to Your name may glory be given" (Ps. 113:1), served as the Templar war cry.[19]

Bernard never preached war. God, he wrote, permitted Palestine to be conquered by the heathen in order that Christians might fight for the Holy Land and gain complete remittance of their sins. The Crusade was a unique opportunity to achieve forgiveness. Even the most heinous evildoers, such as murderers, robbers, adulterers and perjurers, could be saved. However, this did not give the Templars free license to associate with the excommunicated. As outlined in the Latin Rule, contact with excommunicates was strictly forbidden. This ban was later repeated by various popes. The corresponding paragraph in the French Rule, written c. 1140, was wrongly translated; the Latin Rule clearly states that no bishop may absolve the excommunicated.[20]

The French Rule defined, for the first time, the hierarchy of the members of the Temple. Differences in rank established the divisions between knights and sergeants, just as monks and lay brethren were divided at Cîteaux. The Council of Troyes decreed that only knights were allowed to wear the white mantle and be attended by squires. Sergeants-at-arms and craftsmen-sergeants oversaw all matters of business, both in the Holy Land and in Europe. They directed the work in the house, the stables and the fields, and took an active part in commerce, banking and shipping. The undermarshals and the commanders of the house also ranked as sergeants. It was they who were accused, examined — and many of them tortured and killed — in the trials in France, England and Italy, due to the limited number of knights in Europe at the time.[21] The efficiency of the sergeants provided the capital with which the architectural strongholds and military expeditions of the Order were funded. What R. W. Southern wrote concerning the Cistercians is equally applicable to the Templars: "They were from the beginning an aristocratic movement, the product of the society of northern Europe. They had a natural disdain for the lower orders and for all stirrings of those whom St. Bernard characterized as 'rustics without learning or fitness for war'"; and

> The Cistercian ideal demands complete self-abnegation, poverty, simplicity, retirement, purity and refinement of spiritual life. But the historic role of the Order and its reputation among uncommitted contemporary observers suggests aggression, arrogance, military (or at least militant) discipline, outstanding managerial qualities and cupidity. How is this contrast to be explained?[22]

A provincial preceptor's description of the Order to an aspiring member provides a more realistic portrait:

> On the outside you see us finely clad with splendid horses and magnificent appearance, but you cannot see the austerities and the strict commands within, for when you want to remain here on this side of the sea, you will have to go overseas and vice versa; when you are tired you will have to be alert and when you are hungry there will be nothing to eat.[23]

This stands in stark contrast to Bernard's picture of the Order.

Following the Council of Troyes, Hugh of Payns travelled to England and the south and north of France, while his companions visited Spain. Hugh received so many gifts of land, men and money that the Order was obliged to organize new provinces and preceptors. The Council allowed this accumulation of power because, as paragraph 49 of the Latin Rule stated, "this new genus of religion began with God's help, that you may reconcile religion with military service, so that religion may advance with the support of arms."[24] Hugh returned from Europe with a great number of knights and men. Many were killed in the fighting around Damascus in 1129, unable to withstand the Muslim manner of fighting, the cold, and the rain.[25]

For a long time, the Templars called themselves the Poor Knights of the Temple (*pauperes milites Templi*). Grand Master Hugh lived to see the first papal gift to the Order: at the Council of Pisa in 1135, the pope and his prelates promised the Templars a yearly donation and probably awarded them the first papal charter, the *Milites Templi*.[26] This charter absolved the benefactors of the Order from the seventh part of their penance, and allowed the Templars to hold a divine service once a year in interdicted townships and to bury people who were not excommunicated. Terrified of purgatory and hell, the faithful became eager benefactors of the Templars. Orderic Vitalis' vision of the dead suffering terrible torture as punishment for their sins demonstrates contemporary fears of the afterlife.[27]

This charter may have originated in a letter from Baldwin II to Bernard, who was the pope's adviser.[28] Baldwin supported the Templar desire to become independent of the patriarch. Baldwin's successor and son-in-law, Fulk of Anjou, also wished to strengthen his position with the help of the Order. Fulk's influence was a decisive element in the election of Robert of Burgundy, the second grand master. Both had been in the Orient before, where Fulk had affiliated himself with the Order on a temporary basis, giving it an annuity of thirty pounds.[29] Robert was one of the foreigners from Anjou whom Fulk favored.[30] As the younger son of a noble family, Robert's only chance of bettering his station was an advantageous marriage or a high church office. As grand master of the Templars, he held a high rank in both worldly and spiritual affairs. Under his mastership, the Order attained the greatest extension of its power by means of the papal bull *Omne datum optimum,*[31] though its wealth was to increase further. This is the oldest general-privilege of the Order, awarded just before the Second Lateran Council on March 29, 1139. The Templars owed obedience only to their grand master, whom they elected themselves. Nobody was permitted to attack their customs. They were not allowed to leave the Order, even to join a stricter congregation, though later the grand master had the right to dispense with this restriction. The Templars were not required to pay tithes and could keep any of the booty normally divided among the victors. Templars could receive priests into the Order and dismiss them after a year of probation. They could build oratories for themselves and their clients. Solely under the protection of the pope, the Templars were not allowed to bind themselves by oath to anyone else.

The Templars were slow to exploit the liberties made possible by the papal charter, liberties which would never have received the approval of St. Bernard.[32] The Templars remained loyal to the kings of Jerusalem, to Queen Melisende and later, to Melisende *and* her son, who were at daggers drawn with each other.[33] In his letters,[34] Bernard admonished the Queen to rely on the Templars and begged his beloved uncle Andrew of Montbard, seneschal and later grand master of the Order, to maintain close ties with the queen. Ebrardus of Barris, third grand master, escorted Louis VII of France safely through the dangerous mountains of Asia Minor, having previously made peace between the Greeks and the Franks in Constantinople. He also frequently subsidized the King.[35] Though urgently needed in the Holy Land,

Ebrardus later left the Order and became a Cistercian, one of the last to pursue the purely religious goals of the Order.

Unavoidable ties with the kings of Jerusalem placed the Templars under obligation. The contradictions inherent in the Templars' credo of piety and war could not be resolved. Not all Templars were pious and peaceful men. The constant struggle with a bitter enemy did not breed kindness and gentleness. Furthermore, their unique role as monks and warriors made them arrogant. As a result, the Templars came to be envied and hated. As early as the second crusade, they were accused of causing the disaster of the aborted conquest of Damascus in 1148 through bribe and treason.[36] It was the first of many subsequent impeachments. In the end, the Order's privileges and wealth, added to its entanglement in the quarrels of the Holy Land, sealed its fate.

In 1630 Chrysostomos Henriquez compiled the *Menologium ordinis Cisterciensis*. It included the Rule of St. Benedict, the Rule of the Templars and that of other knightly orders, the *Carta Caritatis* of the Cistercians, papal charters awarded to the Templars and a potentially unauthentic form of a vow intended for the Templar-preceptor of Portugal. This collection indicates that, despite the persecution of an ambitious king, the example of the Templars remained within the great community of the orders of Cîteaux as late as the seventeenth century.[37]

NOTES

1. Albert of Aachen, bk. 12, ch. 33, pp. 712-13; Barber, "Origins", p. 224; Hiestand, "Kardinalbischof".
2. Mayer, "Concordat".
3. Wm. of Tyre, *Chronicon*, bk. 12, ch. 7.
4. *Chron. d'Ernoul*, pp. 7 ff.
5. On the Council of Troyes and its "new" date, see: Hiestand, "Kardinalbischof", pp. 303 ff.
6. Dante, *Vita nuova*, ch. 28/29 (ch. 30); Meyer & Suntrup, cols. 582 ff.
7. Leclercq, "Templiers 1" / Leclercq, "Templiers 2", where the authorship of Hugo de St. Victor is conjectured.
8. *Lettres Chartreux*, vol. 1, pp. 151 ff.
9. Mayer, "Jérusalem", pp. 722, 733.
10. Hiestand, "Kardinalbischof", p. 308; Schnürer, *Templerregel*, pp. 44-9; Schnürer, "Organisation", pp. 298 ff.; Barber, "Origins", pp. 229 ff.
11. Bernard, *Opera*, vol. 7 (1974), letter 21, p. 71; letter 39, p. 97; Schnürer, *Templerregel*, p. 112.

12. The only bond existing at the beginning of the Order of the Templars was religious service which they maintained also in the thirteenth century (Latin Rule, para. 1 [Schnürer, *Templerregel*, p. 135]; French Rule: para. 363 [Curzon, p. 206]: "ensi come nostre ordenaire, lequel fu estrais de l'ordenaire del Sepulcre, le devise" ["as our religious ordinance, which is taken from the ordinance of the Holy Sepulchre, prescribes it"]. This part of the French rule was written between 1230 and 1240. The Canons gave the Templars, at some undetermined time, an annuity of 150 Byzantines [Hiestand, "Kardinalbischof", p. 315, n. 118]).

13. Curzon, para. 306, p. 180; para. 685, pp. 349-50. This is confirmed by a confession of a French knight in Paris during the trials against the Order on January 12, 1311 (Michelet, vol. 1, pp. 349 ff.).

14. Leclercq, *Bernard*, p. 101.

15. Wollasch.

16. Hiestand, *Papsturkunden* 1, nos. 2, 8; Hiestand, *Papsturkunden* 2, s.v. Milites.

17. Duby, "Jeunes".

18. Bulst-Thiele, *Magistri*, pp. 316, 351 n. 264.

19. Benedict of Nursia, *Regula*, Prologue 30; Bernard, *De laude*, in: Bernard, *Opera*, vol. 3 (1963), pp. 238-239; see: Bulst-Thiele, *Magistri*, p. 115, no. 32.

20. Bernard, *Opera*, vol. 8 (1977), epist. 363, pp. 311 ff; epist. 458, pp. 454 ff. *De excommunicatis*: Latin Rule para. 63 (Schnürer, *Templerregel*, pp. 32-33); French Rule, para. 12 (Curzon, p. 23), para. 37 (Curzon, p. 43). Cf. Schnürer, *Templerregel*, p. 32 for both texts.

21. On March 28, 1310, during the trial of the Templars, all the imprisoned members of the Order were assembled in Paris for the first time at the bishop's palace. Of a total of 546, only 18 were knights (M.L. Bulst-Thiele, "Der Prozeß gegen den Templerorden," in: Fleckenstein, p. 388).

22. Southern, *Church*, pp. 270, 252.

23. French Rule, para. 661 (Curzon, pp. 338-39). The religious ceremonies for priests during their reception were taken from the Cistercians (cf. Curzon, paras. 274-78, pp. 167-69). The terms of reception into the Order remained the same until its end, as is shown by the confessions of Templars during their trial in France, e.g. Gerald de Caus (see note 13).

24. Bernard, *De laude*, ch. 1, in: Bernard, *Opera*, vol. 3 (1963), p. 213.

25. Wm. of Tyre, *Chronicon*, bk. 13, ch. 26, paras. 1-2; Hiestand, "Kardinalbischof", p. 320.

26. Hiestand, *Papsturkunden* 1, no. 2 (pp. 203 ff.); no. 8 (pp. 214 ff.); Bulst-Thiele, *Magistri*, p. 28, n. 40.

27. Orderic Vitalis, *History*, bk. 13 (vol. 4, pp. 236 ff.) and the visions of Othlo of St. Emmeram. The latter tells us that the dead appear to their relations or friends begging them to repair the evildoing of the deceased in order to soften their pains in purgatory (Othlo, *Liber Visionum*, vision 6, p. 65; vision 12, p. 81; vision 17, p. 91).

28. *Cart. Temple*, no. 1, p. 1; Barber, "Origins", pp. 226-27; Hiestand, "Kardinalbischof", p. 316, n. 122.

29. Mayer, "Angevins", pp. 3, 6-7.

30. Bulst-Thiele, *Magistri*, pp. 30 ff.

31. Hiestand, *Papsturkunden* 1, no. 3, pp. 204 ff.; Hiestand, *Papsturkunden* 2, pp. 67 ff., 90, 96 ff.

32. See: Bernard's epistle 42 to Archbishop Henry of Sens (Bernard, *Opera*, vol. 7 (1974), p. 128): "libertas omni servitute servilior; quid igitur vos, o monachi, sacerdotum gravat auctoritas?" ("freedom [which is] more servile than any slavery; why, you monks, does the authority of the priests encumber you?"). Cf. also Bernard, *De consideratione*, vol. 3, ch. 4, paras. 14-18 in: Bernard, *Opera*, vol. 3 (1963), pp. 441-46.

33. Mayer, "Melisende", pp. 124, 130, 144, 152.

34. See: Bernard's letters to Queen Melisende (Bernard, *Opera*, vol. 8 (1977), epist. 206, p. 65; epist. 289, p. 205; epist. 354, p. 297; epist. 355, p. 299), and his letter to the Templar Andreas of Montbard (ibid., epist. 288, p. 203).

35. Bulst-Thiele, *Magistri*, pp. 41 ff.; Melville, p. 65.

36. Constable, "Second Crusade"; Niederkorn; Hiestand, "Konrad".

37. Henriquez. For the Rule of the Templars, see pt. 1, p. 276 and pt. 2, pp. 41 ff. For papal charters to the Templars, see pt. 2, pp. 477 ff., 479 ff., 531 ff. For the vow of a Templar-preceptor of Portugal, see pt. 2, pp. 478 ff.

7

Singing the Second Crusade

Margaret Switten

Bernard of Clairvaux had a pivotal role in the Second Crusade, both because of his persuasive eloquence and his approach to crusading ideology. According to Jean Leclercq, a core notion in Bernard's concept of crusade was love: St. Bernard saw in the crusade a way of loving God and of proving it to Him.[1] Bernard thus "interiorized" the crusade and its justification, calling upon each individual conscience to take up the cross in fervent spiritual dedication. "Passionate enthusiasm and eloquence and an emphasis on the personal religious significance of the crusading vow", as Giles Constable has pointed out, "were the great contributions of Bernard of Clairvaux to the Second Crusade and to crusading theory in general."[2]

In this essay, I will address one aspect of the theme of love as it can be linked to singing the Second Crusade. One could propose, and scholars have indeed made the argument, that crusades and love songs were born for each other.[3] The crusading movement came at a moment of intense religious fervor, at a moment, moreover, when a new monastic literature of divine love was paralleled by a new secular literature of human love. While it is true that one must not draw the parallels too closely, they are nevertheless in a general way quite obvious. Metaphors of human love are used to talk about divine love; metaphors of divine love are used to describe human love. More specifically germane to our subject, departure for the crusade could bring to the poetic theme of absence a powerful spatio-temporal context. Crusading knight and poetic lover desire and long for a distant goal: the lady, Jerusalem, paradise, finally. To be sure, many differences separate crusade and love songs, and indeed, the comparisons one can or cannot make between sacred and profane love have fuelled many a scholarly debate. And yet, if there is any debate at all, it is because notions of love suffused the twelfth century, for the monks, for the crusaders, for the poet-composers. I propose here to look at one song by the troubadour Jaufre Rudel, "*Lanquand li jorn son lonc en mai*", in which the fusion of themes of crusade and themes of love is particularly rich. This song has been much discussed from the standpoint of the text; I will here emphasize the music as integral to the art of singing the crusade.

It is on the basis of texts, to be sure, that crusading songs have for the most part been classified. Music has power to stir the soul,[4] but it is the text that transmits crusading ideas and crusading propaganda.[5] There is some controversy over what constitutes a crusading song. A narrow definition would include only exhortations to join a crusade to the Holy Land;[6] a definition of crusade in geographically wider terms as a defense of Christian ideals in any area under pagan threat yields a correspondingly richer harvest of songs; and a less restrictive thematic focus allows the inclusion of songs where crusading features or references are clearly present but in a more diffuse manner. Beside geographical and thematic questions, one must also consider the term *chanson* (song). For the period covered by this essay, the term applies to epic as well as lyric genres so that the *Song of Roland* is as much a crusading song as any lyric composition. However, there is no music extant for the epic, so if we are to examine musical properties, we cannot include it. For this chapter, concentrating on one lyric composition, I have taken a wide definition of crusading song, but I will not touch on certain categories such as departure for the crusades, direct exhortation, or sharp criticism that could fall within that definition.

As Richard Crocker has pointed out,[7] the crusade songs for which we have music come to us almost entirely from the repertories of the troubadours and trouvères, that is, from secular, vernacular monophonic (single melodic line) song. Other repertories — Latin monophonic song, and, more importantly, the new polyphonic song (several melodic lines or part-singing) that was being cultivated in northern cathedrals, especially in Notre Dame de Paris, by the end of the twelfth century — contain few or no examples of crusade songs. Polyphony was composed by trained musicians, usually clerics (not monks or knights) attached to urban cathedrals. Crocker argues that "the virtual absence from the polyphonic repertory of references to the crusades reflected a lack of interest on the part of northern, urban bourgeois, intellectual and clerical circles."[8] The crusades, for Crocker, as they were sung, were rather associated with the landed baron and his entourage, with what elsewhere has been named courtly circles. The songs reflect lay aristocratic views — although composers and singers were not necessarily all aristocrats — which makes the fusion between courtly themes such as love and the crusading experience the more potent.

No vernacular lyric compositions can be securely attached to the First Crusade.[9] Singing in the vernacular takes on clear importance only at the time of the Second Crusade. From this period, we have an Old French anonymous song, one or two songs by the troubadour Cercamon, several by Marcabru, including the oft-mentioned *"Pax in nomine Domini"*, and several by the troubadour on whom this chapter is focused, Jaufre Rudel.

Very little is known about Jaufre Rudel's life except that, in all probability, he went on crusade in 1147, reaching the Holy Land in 1148. In a recent paper, Roy Rosenstein has proposed that Jaufre Rudel may have accompanied his close friend Hugh of Lusignan to hear St. Bernard preach at Vézelay in 1146 before setting out for the Holy Land the following year.[10] Rosenstein would link one of Jaufre's songs (*"Qan lo rius de la fontana"*, "When the stream from the spring") directly to Bernard's preaching.

The thematic center of Jaufre Rudel's corpus of six songs is the concept of distant love, captured by a now celebrated expression from the song I am going to discuss: *amor de loing* (love from afar).[11] This concept must have immediately become well known, and the song, *"Lanquand li jorn"*, which is its quintessential expression, must have travelled widely, if we are to judge by the number of manuscripts which have preserved it — with three versions of the melody, a relative rarity for troubadour song. Marcabru's *"Pax in nomine Domini"*, for example, which is considered by many modern scholars the most famous crusade song of all, is preserved in far fewer manuscripts, and only one has the melody. It is probable that Jaufre's songs sparked a lively exchange among troubadours on the meaning of love in a crusading context. Marcabru addressed possibly one of his last songs to Jaufre Rudel "outra mar" (over the sea), i.e. in the Holy Land, and in the song, love is a prominent theme. A troubadour of the next generation, Peire d'Alvernhe, treats the concept of distant love in a song with crusading overtones, with obvious reference to Jaufre Rudel. Scholarly opinions differ on the tone of these exchanges. Some see a criticism of Jaufre Rudel, whose distant love would have seemed too sensual; others see the three poets weaving together motifs of love and spirituality as part of crusading ideology.

The notion of distant love in Jaufre Rudel's work is ambiguous, with the wonderfully rich, probing ambiguity that characterizes so many early troubadour songs. Nowhere are multi-layered meanings more sumptuously exploited than in the song *"Lanquand li jorn son lonc en mai"*. Not only was this song widely circulated in the Middle Ages, not only did it inspire a legendary fourteenth-century *vida* (little biography) which describes Jaufre's trip to the Holy Land as a quest for the love of the Countess of Tripoli — a "far-away princess", it also, with this *vida*, became an integral piece of the nineteenth-century romantic revival, and seems now to encapsulate for many critics a central aspect of the complex phenomenon called courtly love. The considerable scholarly literature on this song chiefly addresses the major interpretive problem: the nature of the love depicted therein. Is it spiritual or sensual? Turned to God or to a lady who is never actually mentioned in the song? I have not space here either to rehearse the numerous solutions that have been proposed or to elaborate one of my own.[12] I want to focus instead, and only, on the core opposition held in balance by the repeated expression *amor de loing*: love and distance. This opposition is as central to the crusades as it is to the love song.

Let us first look at the song.[13]

<table>
<tr><td>I.</td><td>I.</td></tr>
</table>

Lanquand li jorn son lonc en mai	When the days are long in May,
M'es bels douz chans d'auzels de loing,	I like the sweet song of the birds from afar,
E qand me sui partitz de lai	And when I have departed from there,
Remembra'm d'un' amor de loing;	I remember a love from afar;
5 Vauc de talan enbroncs e clis,	I go sad and bowed with desire
Si que chans ni flors d'albespis	So that neither song nor hawthorn flower
No'm platz plus que l'inverns gelatz.	Pleases me more than icy winter.

II.

Ja mais d'amor no.m gauzirai
Si no.m gau d'est' amor de loing,
10 *Qe gensor ni meillor non sai*
Vas nuilla part no pres ni loing.
Tant es sos pretz veris e fis
Qe lai el renc dels Sarrazis
Fos eu per lieis chaitius clamatz.

III.

15 *Iratz e gauzens m'en partrai*
Qan veirai cest' amor de loing,
Mas non sai coras la.m veirai,
Car trop son nostras terras loing:
Assatz i a portz e camis.
20 *E per aisso no.n sui devis,*
Mas tot sia cum a Dieu platz!

IV.

Be.m parra jois qan li qerrai
Per amor Dieu l'amor de loing.
E s'a lieis plai, albergarai
25 *Pres de lieis, si be.m sui de loing.*
Adoncs parra.l parlamens fis
Qand drutz loindas er tant vezis
C'ab bels digz jauzirai solatz.

V.

Ben tenc lo seignor per verai
30 *Per q'ieu veirai l'amor de loing,*
Mas per un ben qe m'en eschai
N'ai dos mals, car tant m'es de loing.
Ai! car me fos lai peleris
Si que mos fustz e mos tapis
35 *Fos pelz sieus bels huoills remiratz!*

II.

Never in love shall I rejoice
Unless I enjoy this love from afar,
For nobler or better I do not know
In any direction, near or far,
Her worth is so true and perfect
That there in the kingdom of the Saracens
I would, for her, be proclaimed captive.

III.

Sad and rejoicing I shall depart
When I shall see this love from afar,
But I do not know when I shall see her
For our lands are too far.
Many are the ports and roads,
And so I cannot prophesy,
But may all be as it pleases God!

IV.

Joy will surely appear to me when I seek from her,
For the love of God, this love from afar.
And if it pleases her, I shall lodge
Near her, although I am from afar.
Then will appear fine discourse,
When, distant lover, I shall be so close
That with charming words I shall take delight in
                                        conversation.

V.

I consider that Lord as the true one
Through whom I shall see this love from afar;
But for one good that befalls me from it,
I have two ills, because she is so far.
Ah! Would that I might be a pilgrim there
So that my staff and my cloak
Might be seen by her beautiful eyes.

VI.

Dieus qe fetz tot qant ve ni vai
E fermet cest' amor de loing
Me don poder, qe'l cor eu n'ai,
Q'en breu veia l'amor de loing
40 Veraiamen en locs aizis,
Si qe la cambra e'l jardis
Me resembles totz temps palatz.

VII.

Ver ditz qui m'apella lechai
Ni desiran d'amor de loing,
45 Car nuills autre jois tant no'm plai
Cum jauzimens d'amor de loing;
Mas so q'eu vuoill m'es tant ahis
Q'enaissi'm fadet mos pairis
Q'ieu ames e non fos amatz.

VIII.

50 Mas so q'ieu vuoill m'es tant ahis . . .
Toz sia mauditz lo pairis
Qe'm fadet q'ieu non fos amatz!

VI.

God who made all that comes and goes
And established this love from afar,
Give me the power, for the desire I have,
Quickly to see this love from afar,
Truly, in agreeable places,
So that chamber and garden
Might always seem to me a palace!

VII.

He speaks the truth who calls me greedy
And desirous of love from afar,
For no other joy pleases me as much
As enjoyment of love from afar;
But what I want is so difficult,
For thus did my godfather decree my fate,
That I should love and not be loved.

VIII.

But what I want is so difficult
May the godfather be cursed
Who decreed my fate that I should not be loved.

The poet establishes a crusading context by the evocation of the Saracens (stanza II, verse 13), and especially by presenting himself as a pilgrim (V, 33) setting forth on a long and perilous voyage (III, 18-19). This context allows him to deploy a rhetoric of conflation, by means of which the central concept of distance is at one and the same time physical, temporal, psychological, spiritual, human *and* divine. The complex metaphors woven into the poem's texture express, as the poem unfolds, a love that is eternally absence and longing. From the place of his speaking, the poet turns his desire toward another place, the *lai* (verses 3, 13, 33) which is the place of possible fulfillment, the far-off land, perhaps Jerusalem itself,[14] the chamber and the garden (verse 41), the earthly or spiritual paradise. The salient feature of the text is the constant reiteration of the word *loing*. The word appears as a refrain at the rime position — thus always accented — in the second and fourth lines of every stanza, etching the theme of distance into our memories, and relating it, with the successive stanzas, to different facets of the idea. The full expression *amor de loing* occurs only once per stanza through the first five stanzas, then, to effect a kind of crescendo, twice per stanza for the last two (VI and VII) where the climax is reached, and the song then falls back to its conclusion: the fated impossibility of fulfilment, "Qu'ieu ames e non fos amatz" — to love and not be loved.

The melody that carries this text is one of the most hauntingly effective in the troubadour repertory. What devices can it be said to employ to seize the essence of distant love?

The most obvious device is structural: the notes connected to *loing*, or to the expanded *amor de loing*, are always the same. It is important that these are cadential notes, that is, they conclude phrases. This cadential repetition is a function of complete phrase repetition in the melody, with the first and second phrases being repeated for the third and fourth. So that on a very immediate level, the return of *loing* in the text is always underscored by a return of the same gesture in the melody. Further, since the melody of the last line of the stanza is similar to that of phrases 2 and 4, the stanza closes each time in the melody, though not in the text, on an echo of distance. Now, the text has another property germane to our inquiry: the last line of each stanza concludes on the sound "*atz*" that rimes only with counterparts in other stanzas. This rime is highly valorized thematically because of the key words it places in an important position. In the first stanza, the word *gelatz*, which captures the poet's anguish, is related by the melody to the notion of distance. The effect is particularly striking in the last stanza and in the tornada because there the core expression *amor de loing* is linked to *non fos amatz* in a subtle but perceptible manner if one listens carefully. Distance is thus melodically joined to the negation of fulfillment.

Let us scrutinize the melodic rhetoric more carefully. One of the chief difficulties — or attractions — of this melody is what can be called its modal (or tonal) ambiguity. One is never quite sure what note is its final note, its "home base", if I may avail myself of that metaphor. A likely candidate for this rôle is D, and indeed the general comportment of the melody would support that choice, especially if we were to consider all three versions, of which only one is given here.[15] The kind of rhetoric we can discern in this song if we take D as the final has been convincingly described by Leo Treitler.[16] The first phrase of the melody points clearly in the direction of D, with its emphasis on the notes D and F, and its cadence on D. But the second phrase, in contrast, behaves differently. Although it starts out like the first, moving from D to F, it soon veers toward a different configuration, emphasizing G, E, C, and C is the note on which it finally closes. Now compared to D as a final and thus stable note, C is unstable. As Treitler points out,

"What has occurred in the first two phrases of this song is a shift from a more settled to a less settled configuration."[17] This is the opposite of what one might normally expect: normally in the first two phrases of a melody such as this, one expects a movement from unsettled to settled, open to closed, inconclusive to conclusive. By sketching the opposite movement, from stable to unstable, the melody inscribes instability at its very center. Since the second phrase pair (lines 3 & 4) repeats the first pair (lines 1 & 2), the movement from settled to unsettled is reinforced.

The two middle phrases of the song, 5 and 6, constitute, as it were, the climax of the melody, containing its highest note and most dramatic melodic gestures. They both remain within the stable configuration, ending first on A, then on D. Then the last phrase of the song resembles the second and fourth, ending on C, thus making the point again about a shift from stability to instability. The entire melody "ends in an unresolved manner".[18] Now this unsettling cadence, the one on C, concludes the melodic gesture that carries the word *loing* in lines 2 and 4 of each stanza, and prolongs the theme of distance melodically into the last line of the stanza, as we have seen. As a result, the corrosive key words composing the rime "*atz*", and particularly the final linking of *amor de loing* to *non fos amatz*, are given greater resonance and poignance. Musical syntax and form conspire to project the commanding idea of the song: the irreducibility of distance and love. The far-away love is an inaccessible love, a love thwarted by destiny, expressed through the unrelenting reiteration of the unresolved melody.

But if the song plays out the impossibility of fulfillment, it simultaneously establishes within itself the higher value and the permanence of desire. As Julia Kristeva has pointed out, the very law of desire for St. Bernard (as indeed it had been for St. Augustine) is the longing for what one does not have.[19] Desire for God — while on a different plane — is rooted in human desire. The quest for God is initially the quest for a lacking object. Absence is inscribed at the heart of love, and in a sense this is what Jaufre Rudel's song captures. For both Saint Bernard and Jaufre Rudel, the object of love is the object of salvation; this is the source of the emotional intensity, the "interiorized" motivation of the Second Crusade. Through words and sounds, text and melody, Jaufre Rudel projects the passion and the desire, the longing and the hope for salvation that set fire to men's hearts, propelling a whole segment of the lay population toward Jerusalem.

I do not want to overdraw the parallels. To be sure, for Bernard, the desire for God is finally fulfilling because God has loved us first, and our desire for him through his love for us can become an attainment of bliss. The vernacular poet is more somber. Yet for Bernard, the quest for bliss is perhaps not without its questioning moments, its moments of inner despair. If I may be permitted to conclude this chapter by a probably unprovable but possibly provocative perception, I would propose that Bernard, too, in the context of the Second Crusade may have known somber moments. After the disastrous events of the crusade, Bernard became a target for criticism. The hopes he had aroused by treating the crusade as a means of demonstrating love of God, as a means by which a soul could find salvation, were brutally dashed. As he struggled to explain failure in his *On Consideration*, he wrote:

> ... we have entered, as you well know, a difficult period which appears to herald an end almost to our very existence, not to mention our endeavors. Clearly the Lord, provoked by our sins, seems in some way to have judged the earth before the appointed time, rightly of course, but unmindful of his mercy. He neither spared his people, nor his own name. Are they not saying among the nations, *Where is their God?*[20]

In composing these words, could Bernard, too, have wondered in his heart if some higher destiny had not willed for him: *"Qu' ieu ames e non fos amatz"*, "That I should love and not be loved in return"? Has Rudel's song captured not only the passion and desire of the Second Crusade, but also its devastating anguish?

NOTES

1. Leclercq, *Bernard*, p. 76.
2. Constable, "Second Crusade", p. 247. For the importance of the concept of love, viewed in broad terms, to the crusades, see: Riley-Smith, "Crusading".
3. For example see: Barteau, p. 23.
4. For medieval applications of this idea, see: Stevens, pp. 386-409.
5. For a discussion of song as a method of propaganda, see: Morris, "Propaganda", pp. 92-99.
6. Hölzle. For a wider view, see: Trotter, p. 173.
7. Crocker, p. 78.
8. Crocker, p. 79.
9. Probably the earliest crusade song we have comes from a manuscript of the Abbey of Saint Martial at Limoges (Paris, Bibliothèque Nationale [BN], lat. 1139). The song is in Latin, dates from about 1095, and evokes the dazzling image of Jerusalem: "Jerusalem mirabilis". It immediately follows the first known song in Old Occitan, a prayer to the Virgin; relations between Saint Martial and the troubadours have long been established by

scholars. Paris, BN, lat. 1139 reflects a mixture of profane and sacred values that will infuse the lyric, noticeably in the crusade songs.

10. Rosenstein, p. 227.

11. Bec (p. 102) argues that the notion of distant love in Jaufre Rudel includes several subthemes ("1. L'amour de loin (proprement dit) et la poétique de la distance; 2. La dame jamais vue; 3. La 'croisade' amoureuse; 4. L'amour impossible; 5. La joie douloureuse; 6. Le songe compensatoire"), of which the most important are the first three.

12. A substantial bibliography for Jaufre Rudel is provided in: Wolf & Rosenstein; Crist has attempted a synthesis of different interpretations; a recent review of approaches may be found in Bec.

13. Text and melody are taken from: Switten & Chickering, Anthology I, pp. 59-60. The melody, from ms W (Paris, BN, fr. 844), f° 189v, is here transposed down a fifth for convenience of comparison and discussion.

14. This interpretation was expounded by Frank ("Distant"). It was sharply criticized by Spitzer, but never discredited. Frank's reply (Frank "Jaufré"), constitutes one of the first arguments for a plurality of approaches to Jaufre Rudel's song.

15. All the versions are published in: Van der Werf, *Chansons*, pp. 86-8, and Van der Werf, *Melodies*, pp. 215*-17*, where a slight error in Van der Werf, *Chansons* for the cadence of line 6 in ms. W is corrected.

16. Treitler, pp. 22-5; Van der Werf (*Chansons*, pp. 85-6) provides an analysis of the structure of the melody, underscoring its ambiguity and concluding: "In my estimation it is difficult to determine whether this melody is a centric one, moving around F, or a standing one with C or perhaps even D as a basis tone." Tischler (p. 231) opts more clearly for a melody moving around F: "Jaufre's melody is organized in a regular sixth mode, based on a central F, with the co-finalis C." The important point for this essay is not so much the various possible interpretations in themselves, although I believe Treitler's reading permits the richest understanding of the song's meaning, as the fundamental ambiguity of a melody that gives rise to divergent interpretations — much, indeed, as does the textual ambiguity of *amor de loing*.

17. Treitler, p. 23.

18. For Treitler (p. 23), "This polarization of the melody away from the more stable principal configuration is the story of the melody as a whole. It ends in an unresolved manner."

19. Kristeva, pp. 157-59. [tr., 1987, pp. 159-62].

20. Bernard, *On Consideration*, p. 47.

PART II

THE CRUSADE

8

The Origins of the Second Crusade: Pope Eugenius III, Bernard of Clairvaux and Louis VII of France

John G. Rowe

One of the best moments in the study of history occurs when we attempt to deal with original evidence. It is living dangerously, and in the end, you suspect that all you have done is to construct, with some skill and much bravado, a house of cards which could be levelled by a puff of wind.

The problem of the origins of the Second Crusade will bear me out. As I see it, there are three principal sources. We are all familiar with these: Otto of Freising, Odo of Deuil, and William of Tyre. Then there is a plethora of additional notices, some of which are useful and many more which are not. I shall construct a conventional house of cards with as few hypotheses as possible. I say this because the problem of the origin of the Second Crusade has for more than a hundred years tantalized and irritated scholars.[1]

Pride of place belongs to Otto of Freising.

To find out what Otto says about the origins of the Second Crusade, we have to look at both the *Chronica* and the *Gesta*. The first section is in Book Seven in the *Chronica*, and the second may be found towards the middle of Book One of the *Gesta*. Turning to the *Chronica* which deals with the fall of Edessa towards the end of 1144, we see that Otto knows a good deal about this event.[2] He is well aware of the significance of Edessa in the Christian history of the Near East. He emphasizes the unfortunate fate of the arch-bishop of the city and his co-religionists. He is particularly interested in the shrines and relics of Edessa, concluding with the Saracen occupation of the city which defiles those shrines.

Yet, in the *Chronica*, Otto says nothing more. There is no report concerning the dissemination of this disastrous news which must have spread through Europe by March 1145. There is no mention of appeals for help. The fall of Edessa seems to be one event among other events arranged in chronological order. Otto is more concerned at this point with the vicissitudes of papal history.

The next pertinent section of the *Chronica* begins with the arrival of a delegation from Armenia, legates sent by the bishops and the head of the Armenian Church, the Catholikos.[3] They reached the pope at Viterbo at the end of November 1145, and presented their credentials at Vetralla (a few miles away) on or about December 1.[4] Otto witnesses their arrival. They had been on the road for eighteen months. Yet the exhausting labors of the journey did not prevent them from plunging at once into a profound discussion of certain moot points in liturgical theory and practice.

It is only as a kind of afterthought that Otto introduces another visitor to the papal curia at this time. Otto saw him himself. This was Hugh, bishop of Jabala in Syria. The bishop's chief concern was the rectification of an injury done to him and his church by the patriarch of Antioch and the dowager princess of Antioch. Otto makes two additional comments. The first is that, thanks to Hugh, the patriarchate of Antioch began to be fully subject to the papacy. The second is that Hugh spoke mournfully about the peril to the Church in the Latin Orient since the loss of Edessa. He even revealed that he was considering a personal appeal for help to Conrad of Germany and Louis of France.[5]

In the first case, it is hard to know precisely what Otto is talking about. The only thing we can find in the *Chronica* which may have a bearing on this matter is a report which shows that Otto was well aware of Greek designs on Antioch. He knows that on one occasion Hugh of Jabala rejected these ambitions, confronting the Emperor John Comnenus to his face with the fact that Antioch belonged to Blessed Peter and his successors, not to the Byzantine Empire and Church.[6] Thus it may be that this episode is what Otto is referring to when he makes Hugh of Jabala instrumental in bringing the patriarchate of Antioch under papal control.

What is, however, much more important to us is that Hugh brought sad tidings concerning the Latin Orient. He seems to have spoken at some length on the resurgence of Moslem power in Syria, of the threat to the entire Latin establishment. And, as I have noted, the bishop spoke of crossing the Alps to seek aid in France and Germany.

One might have thought that Otto would give more attention to the serious news brought by Hugh. We might have expected a flood of emotional observations in response to Hugh's communication. Perhaps Otto could have indicated something of the general European response to the fall of Edessa and its consequences. Yet the good bishop does none of these things. Just as in the case of the fall of Edessa, once he has mentioned this matter, Otto says nothing more.

The *Gesta* makes, as it were, a new beginning on the subject of the Second Crusade. The wishes of King Louis of France are paramount. Otto presents the monarch as having a secret desire to go to Jerusalem, thus fulfilling an oath taken by his brother Philip, who had died before he could fulfill his oath. Otto continues to say that Louis summoned certain French princes and revealed what he had on his mind. Thus, it is Louis of France who takes the initiative and makes the idea of going on crusade a public fact.[7]

It is perhaps relevant to point out that it is difficult to make all the reports of Otto fit together into a coherent whole. On the basis of what we have examined so far, we can find in the *Chronicon* the report of Edessa's capture and its sad consequences for the Christian religion. We can observe the arrival of the Armenians with their doctrinal and liturgical concerns. Then there is the visit of Hugh of Jabala, who brought alarming news about the state of the Latin Orient. None of this seems to bear on the reports in the *Gesta* about Louis' secret desire to go to Jerusalem. But then, once again, we gain no feeling for general European anxiety and concern for the Latin Orient. Nor do we perceive any appropriate papal agitation. Certainly for the months March to November 1145, the papacy seems to be doing nothing unusual on behalf of the Latin Orient. Constable pointed out years ago evidence to suggest that Eugenius III continued to work to strengthen the crusaders' enterprise.[8] Yet this does not seem anticipatory of the Second Crusade.

Other sources tell us about the arrival of messages and messengers from the Latin Orient, particularly from Antioch and Jerusalem, which depicted the Christian situation there in dire terms.[9] We can safely suppose that, although Otto is silent, the pope was well aware of the general concern in Christendom for the Latin East. A further hypothesis might be that the papacy was at something of a loss about what was to be done. Given Eugenius' cautious and suspicious nature,[10] the curia may well have done nothing, waiting on the outcome of events in the period March-November 1145.

Close attention to the narratives in Otto's *Chronicon* and *Gesta* suggest that Eugenius and his advisers were distracted by certain profound problems which cast long shadows over the papacy and its policies.

There was the old problem posed by the continued existence of Roger, king of Sicily. Otto is no stranger to Roger's cruelty and destructiveness.[11]

Then there was a relatively new phenomenon: the Roman commune. Otto was fascinated by this development and understood fully the importance of the Roman commune as a disrupting force in papal policy. What I am saying is that the welfare of the Jerusalem crusade had even now been incorporated into the general scheme of papal politics and diplomacy. Because of this, if the papacy thought at this time about a new large-scale expedition to the East (and I cannot be sure it did!), the curia realized that there were endless ramifications which such a development might have.[12]

However, the papacy finally acted. The papal register tells us, and modern scholarship confirms, that Eugenius issued his first version of the famous crusade bull, *Quantum praedecessores nostri*, on December 1, 1145 from Vetralla.[13] In saying this, we have, of course, moved far away from Otto. At the crucial point, the *Chronicon* falls silent. The papal bull, as we all know, is preserved in the *Gesta*. Yet before we say our farewell to the *Chronicon*, it is well to point out that the *Chronicon* may have told us just what finally moved Eugenius and his associates to take the decisive step of issuing *Quantum praedecessores nostri*. Perhaps the visit of Hugh of Jabala broke through papal concerns and preoccupations. The bishop brought reports so urgent that they made his proposal to cross the Alps and seek help in Germany and France seem quite reasonable. Then, too, the presence of the Armenians may have helped the curia to transcend its Italian preoccupations and remember its ecumenical obligations. As we shall see, in the *Gesta*, Otto will have a quite different explanation for the appearance of *Quantum praedecessores nostri*. With that in mind, it would be well to break off our consideration of Otto of Freising and turn to the second great source for our investigation, the *De profectione* of Odo of Deuil.[14]

Let us not be too quick to impugn Odo's veracity. While he makes no secret of his desire to magnify Louis of France, there is no reason to begin with a general assumption that Odo's reporting will be invariably inaccurate. For all his enthusiasm for Louis and the crusade, there is a sober side to Odo as a writer of history which should not be ignored.

Odo begins with the bald statement that Louis of France assumed the crusader's cross at Vézelay at Easter 1146. He then goes back to explain how this had come about. The king seems to have cherished a secret desire to go to Jerusalem. When he was determined to share this aspiration with others, he chose to do so at Christmas court (1145) held at Bourges. It was then and there that Louis made the idea of a Jerusalem crusade public. Odo's report is close to Otto of Freising, except that the bishop explains Louis' decision by reference to the oath made by his dead brother. Both agree that the crusade became visible in Louis' determination.[15]

The royal suggestion received support from Godfrey, bishop of Langres, who delivered a spontaneous homily on the devastation of Edessa, the oppression of Christians, and the arrogant success of the heathen. This speech, greeted with much lamentation, ended with an exhortation for an expedition to help the embattled Christians in the East. Did Godfrey know of the existence of *Quantum praedecessores nostri*? Odo is silent. While we might speculate that Odo is suppressing information, the better to magnify Louis' initiative, we might instead more safely conclude that Odo's silences are due to the fact that the papal letter had not yet arrived in France. There is no mention of the letter; there is no "echo" of its contents.[16]

Odo does not tell us exactly what the response of the assembled notables was. We could surmise from Odo that it was not positive. Suger's hesitations, fully noted by his biographer in the *Vita*, have long been scrutinized.[17] Odo omits this report, determined to emphasize the king's idealism. Yet he is also consciously trying to tell how events transpired. Therefore, he makes no mention of Eugenius' crusade bull. No one did at this point. The probable truth is that they knew nothing about it.

Otto and Odo are reasonably close at this point, in that they agree that Louis is acting on his own. For his part, Odo tells us that Louis now wrote directly to Pope Eugenius.[18] Otto is a little different. The French princes, confronted with Louis' proposal, hesitated and agreed only to consult St. Bernard. The princes wrote the abbot asking for his advice.[19] The letter does not survive.

The important point here in the *Gesta* is that Bernard decides the pope must be involved.[20] The matter is too serious. It must have papal direction and sanction. Note the implication of what both Otto and Odo are saying. To repeat, in all likelihood, no one has seen or heard of *Quantum praedecessores nostri*.

As I have said, in Odo, the king writes directly to Eugenius. Louis is obviously trying to get support. He will not take "no" for an answer, and the barons are constrained to agree to another meeting on the matter on Passion Sunday (March 17, 1146).[21] Otto knows nothing about this. What he is concentrating on now is the papal reaction when the embassy from St. Bernard arrives to place the entire matter before the pope. Did Eugenius think now about the sufferings of eastern Christians? Did he reflect on Urban's idealism in launching the crusade? Otto says nothing. What he does say is that Eugenius reflected on how the First Crusade had initiated a process whereby two great patriarchal churches in the East (Antioch and Jerusalem) had returned to papal obedience. The scope of papal power and protection had also been extended to the restored churches in the Latin Orient. It is these thoughts which lead the pope to agree to Louis' request that a crusade be officially approved. The pope also grants St. Bernard the task of being the official papal delegate for the preaching of the crusade.[22]

There is both similarity and dissimilarity here between the accounts of Odo and Otto's *Gesta*. Bernard does not appear in Odo's account of the inception of the crusade. Here he differs from Otto. Rather, Louis writes directly to Eugenius. Odo says nothing about how the pope arrived at a favorable decision, but he did so, sending back the most favorable letters. A summary of one of these follows, clearly a précis of *Quantum praedecessores nostri*. Eugenius commissions Bernard to preach. The pope observes that he would rather do it himself, but is locked in mortal combat with the Romans.[23]

At this point our sources suggest that many letters are circulating between Eugenius, Louis, and Bernard. How unfortunate it is that only one, *Quantum praedecessores nostri*, is known to us. For the other letters, we might hypothesize briefly as follows:

The original version of *Quantum praedecessores nostri* reached Louis and Bernard sometime around the middle of January 1146. Both Bernard and Louis sent off replies. Perhaps Louis wanted further clarification and confirmation. Bernard wanted more stringent directions included in the papal bull dealing with arms, armor, and dress appropriate to the expedition. Eugenius probably received these letters around the middle of February. On March 1, he issued a new, slightly altered, version of *Quantum praedecessores nostri*, adding, for good measure, letters authorizing Bernard to preach the crusade on behalf of the pope. When these papal documents arrived in France, all hesitations by Bernard and Suger vanished.

About the meeting at Vézelay (Easter Day, March 31, 1146), Otto knows next to nothing save that the meeting was widely attended.[24] As for Odo, his account of Vézelay in the *De profectione* is too well known to require comment.[25] It was one of St. Bernard's more glittering performances. Armed with the papal letter of authorization and reading where appropriate from *Quantum praedecessores nostri*, Bernard spoke out on behalf of the crusade as only he could speak. The response was overwhelming.

A few words on William of Tyre,[26] who is writing some thirty-five years after the event. It can be suggested that the real value of his account is that it records how people had come to see the Second Crusade in the years following the actual expedition. We must, therefore, be extremely careful as to how much of William's account is accepted as true.

William's report begins with an evocation of the rumors which spread through the West, reports arising from the fall of Edessa and continuing on to stress the danger of the Moslem threat to the entire Latin East. According to William, messengers (presumably from the Latin Orient) at this time were carrying the bad news throughout Christian Europe. They asked for vengeance, for help in redressing the great wrongs which Moslems were inflicting on eastern Christians. He adds for good measure that Latin Christendom had become fat and slack, having been at peace too long. This last is a piece of editorializing which tells something about William himself and even perhaps about attitudes current (at the time of William's writing) in the Latin Orient.[27]

The victories of the Moslems occasioned the most pronounced suffering by the Christians in the Latin East. William reported now that it was said (*dicebatur*) that Pope Eugenius felt a father's solicitude for the suffering Christians. The *dicebatur* reminds us that William is dealing here with the collective Latin memory about the beginnings of the Second Crusade. As we know, Otto of Freising tells us something about Eugenius' state of mind. The pope was concerned not with the sufferings of eastern Christians, but rather with the fact that the crusade had extended papal jurisdiction. Therefore, we should be suspicious of William's account, not only with regard to the pope's attitude, but also as touching popular concern for the Latin Orient. Perhaps William overdoes his description of the fervor and extent of popular concern about the East. Then, too, William's insistence that there were messengers from the East asking for help seems reasonable enough. After all, we should remember Hugh of Jabala. Yet, the picture of messengers blanketing Christian Europe is probably an exaggeration.[28]

In a similar vein, William tells us that Eugenius now commissioned a multitude of preachers to inform Christendom of the sufferings of the Christians as well as rouse as many people as possible to the urgent need to avenge these wrongs.[29] More exaggeration. There is nothing in what we have examined which suggests that the pope either wanted to or could have organized an extensive number of preachers to carry the word of the crusade throughout Western Europe at this time. Given the political problems of papacy, given the natural caution of Eugenius, we must, therefore, hesitate before we accept William's account. We suspect that popular imagination had invented a multitude of preachers for this early stage in the development of the crusade.

William expatiates on the sufferings of eastern Christians. This is William's rhetoric at its best, at once horrific and plausible. Yet we might say that his imagination is working to excess as he elaborated the pictures conjured up in popular emotion: horrible prisons, irons, filth, squalor, and beggary.[30] Perfectly consistent with all this is William's emphasis on the need for vengeance.

A brief conclusion. When we consider our three principal sources, we should be, I think, struck by the fact that only William of Tyre conveys any sense of widespread concern in Europe about the fate of the Latin Orient. When they are considering the origins of the Second Crusade, both Odo and Otto concentrate their attention on Louis, Eugenius, and then St. Bernard. They do not write against a general backdrop of agitation in Western Europe. Their accounts make it seem as if Louis and Eugenius are operating in a kind of vacuum, totally isolated from any generalized concern for the eastern Christians. Otto even makes it sound as if Eugenius and the papal court had heard nothing about the misfortunes of the Latin Orient until Hugh of Jabala delivered his message. This is surely another exaggeration. Seeking a balanced point of view, we might say that there was indeed concern for the Christian East, but perhaps it was not as intense and widespread as William suggests. Eugenius and his associates were aware of rumors and reports on the state of the Latin Orient since the spring of 1145.[31] Yet it would seem that these were not sufficient to impel decisive papal action. It took the reports of Hugh of Jabala (the Armenians, perhaps?) to cut through the hesitation and uncertainty. There were, of course, political dimensions in all of this. We can imagine that the papacy was concerned about who, if anybody, was going to respond positively to a papal appeal. Conrad of Germany was ruled out of consideration, for the papacy had other hopes for him. Roger of Sicily was dangerous and destructive. That left the French, who were conspicuous for their historic association with the crusade. Even so, we cannot but feel that the publication of the great bull on December 1, 1145 was something like a shot in the dark.

While this was happening at the curia, there was another independent development. We should accept the report that Louis of France had considered in his inner mind the possibility of an expedition to Jerusalem. Both Otto and Odo say this. While we can assume that the king was affected by popular agitation that something be done to help the eastern Christians, we should nevertheless believe that personal considerations were behind Louis' aspiration. It is our suggestion that *Quantum praedecessores* had not yet reached the king.

At the Christmas court at Bourges, Louis received strong support from Godfrey of Langres. Once again, we do not read in Otto and Odo of the impact of any papal letter. Perhaps the tepid reception given the royal initiative and Godfrey's exhortations all testify to the fact that at this point the papal attitude was not known.

We can safely accept Odo's report that the princes suggested a consultation with St. Bernard. Thus Bernard enters the picture quite early. Not knowing what the papal attitude was, Bernard referred the matter to Eugenius. The abbot was not ignorant of the central role of the pope in inaugurating a crusade. Nor was he unaware of the papal problems with Roger and the Romans. So by the middle of February 1146, the pope was faced with enquiries from both Louis and Bernard.

We know that the papacy reissued *Quantum praedecessores nostri* on March 1, 1146 with the changes suggested by St. Bernard. The abbot probably started at once to preach. I think we can safely disregard William of Tyre's plethora of preachers. This developed later on.

Certainly Bernard was active, and this is confirmed by a famous letter (which I would date April-May 1146) from Bernard to Eugenius.[32] It refers to papal involvement in certain matters pertaining to France and the French Church. The letter continues on with the remark that nothing should be done to discourage the development of the good work which Eugenius had begun in the kingdom. This could be taken to mean that the *sole* responsibility for inaugurating the Second Crusade rested with the pope. The letter concludes with St. Bernard's famous description of the effects of his preaching. The letters of St. Bernard are not easily handled in a truly critical spirit. The authority of the saint's utterances is often impossible to resist. Yet we should remember that the great abbot at times suffered from excessive zeal and that he was prone to telling others the real meaning of what they had said and done. Having in great degree a holy simplicity of his own, he often achieved simplicity in his exhortations, particularly when he was not fully aware of the complexity of certain events. The origins of the Second Crusade were a bit more complicated than the saint realized.

I have attempted to present an interpretation which sees the real origins of the Second Crusade in the independent actions of King Louis and Pope Eugenius set against the backdrop of a generalized concern for the Christian East, a concern which arose from the formal and informal accounts of Moslem success at Edessa and elsewhere. The Crusade appears when these realities flow together and are picked up by the matchless, magical eloquence of St. Bernard. Not for nothing in later years did many attribute the existence of the crusade to him.[33] And it is not for nothing that St. Bernard was conspicuous among those blamed for the ultimate disasters which overtook the expedition.[34]

NOTES

1. The basic article remains Casper, "Eugens III". The appendix contains an edition of *Quantum praedecessores nostri* (March 1, 1146), pp. 302 ff.
2. Otto of Freising, *Chronica*, bk. VII, ch. 30, pp. 356-57.
3. Otto of Freising, *Chronica*, bk. VII, ch. 32, pp. 360-63.
4. Jaffé-Loewenfeld, pp. 25-7.
5. Otto of Freising, *Chronica*, bk. VII, ch. 33, pp. 363-65.
6. Otto of Freising, *Chronica*, bk. VII, ch. 28, p. 354.
7. Otto of Freising, *Gesta* 1, bk. I, ch. 35, p. 45.
8. Constable, "Second Crusade", p. 248, n. 186.
9. Many sources might be cited. Attention should be paid to *Ann. Reicherspergenses*, in: MGHS, vol. 17, p. 461.
10. John of Salisbury, ch. 21, p. 51, where John speaks of Eugenius as most suspicious by nature.
11. Otto has several reports on Roger, beginning with Roger's contribution to the papal schism of 1130 (Otto of Freising, *Chronica*, bk. VII, ch. 18, p. 334). For a reference to Roger's brutality and cruelty, see: Otto of Freising, *Chronica*, bk. VII, ch. 23, pp. 346-47. There is an episode in Otto's narrative dealing with Roger's activity during the Second Crusade (Otto of Freising, *Gesta* 1, bk. I, ch. 27, pp. 352-53).
12. For the passage introducing the Roman commune, see: Otto of Freising, *Chronica*, bk. VII, ch. 27, pp. 352-53.
13. Casper, "Eugens III", with the second edition of the bull, dated March 1, 1146 (ed. P. Rassow, pp. 300-305).
14. Odo of Deuil, *De profectione*.
15. Odo of Deuil, *De profectione*, p. 6.
16. Odo of Deuil, *De profectione*, p. 6.
17. *Vita Sugerii*, p. 108 D.
18. Odo of Deuil, *De profectione*, p. 8.
19. Otto of Freising, *Gesta* 1, bk. I, ch. 35, p. 54.
20. Otto of Freising, *Gesta* 1, bk. I, ch. 35, p. 54.
21. Odo of Deuil, *De profectione*, pp. 6-8.
22. Otto of Freising, *Gesta* 1, bk. I, ch. 35, pp. 54-5.
23. Odo of Deuil, *De profectione*, p. 8.
24. Otto of Freising, *Gesta* 1, bk. I, ch. 37, p. 58.
25. Odo of Deuil, *De profectione*, pp. 8-10.
26. Wm. of Tyre, *Chronicon*.
27. Wm. of Tyre, *Chronicon*, bk. XVI, ch. 18, p. 739.
28. Wm. of Tyre, *Chronicon*, bk. XVI, ch. 18, p. 739-40.
29. Wm. of Tyre, *Chronicon*, bk. XVI, ch. 18, p. 740.
30. Wm. of Tyre, *Chronicon*, bk. XVI, ch. 18, p. 740.

31. Various sources will support this interpretation: *Chron. Mauriniacensi*, p. 88; Richard of Poitiers, pp. 415-16; *Ann. Herbipolenses*, pp. 3-8; *Ann. Reicherspergenses*, p. 461.
32. Bernard, *Opera*, vol. 8, letter 247, pp. 140-41, lines 12-16.
33. For example, *Ann. Magdeburgenses*, pp. 188-90.
34. Constable, "Second Crusade", pp. 266-76.

9

The Origin of the Second Crusade

George Ferzoco

In seeking to establish the formal origin of the Second Crusade, one finds that in Vetralla on December 1, 1145, Pope Eugenius III issued the crusading bull *Quantum praedecessores*.[1] Here, the pope addresses himself to France's King Louis VII, his princes and all the faithful living in his realm. Eugenius recalls the efforts of Franks and Italians who, inspired by his predecessor Pope Urban II, took Jerusalem from the Moslems. The pope beseeches Louis and his men to recapture the city of Edessa (present-day Urfa, Turkey), which recently had been taken by the Moslems. In return, Eugenius promises ecclesiastical protection of those family members, goods and possessions left behind by the new crusaders; he also declares the protection of debtors who participate in the crusade. The pope establishes some norms of behavior which must be followed by all who take the cross: expensive clothes, dogs and falcons are forbidden. To those who respond to this call, the pope grants the remission of sins.

Such are the basic facts contained in the crusading bull. Surrounding this small island of historical certainty, however, is a sea of discordant historical narration and interpretation concerning the initial events of this crusade.[2] For example, Ephège Vacandard, Irénée Vallery-Radot, and Virginia Gingerick Berry are among those who have written that the bull had no effect upon the court summoned by King Louis VII to Bourges for Christmas 1145. Two present the matter rather cursorily: Vacandard, in his biography of Bernard, says that the bull did not arrive in the hands of Louis (before Christmas, at least).[3] Vallery-Radot simply says that the bull was not issued until March 1, 1146; clearly he, like André Seguin, confuses the issue of *Quantum praedecessores* with that of the later bull commonly referred to as *Quantum praedecessores II*.[4] Berry's position is not unlike that of Vacandard. She states that the French nobles approached Bernard of Clairvaux for advice some time after the Christmas court, and that this would indicate that the court had not received the bull, for if the pope's letter had indeed reached its addressee, it would seem natural for the French to have made immediate contact with the pope himself and no one else.[5] In contrast to the above positions stand those expressed by historians such as Eugène Willems, Steven Runciman and Joshua Prawer, who simply assert that Louis had indeed received the bull by the Christmas 1145 assembly.[6]

The cause of such diverse interpretations and presentations of the same historical "fact" is, in the end, to be found in these historians' readings of the original sources. We have at our disposal two important primary sources which contain details concerning the origin of the Second Crusade: Otto of Freising's *Gesta Friderici primi imperatoris* and Odo of Deuil's *De profectione Ludovici septimi in orientem*.[7] If these two works are to be viewed as chronicles of precisely the same events, they conflict far more than they complement each other, and such apparent conflict has been the cause of the differences in recent historical accounts.

What is it that Otto and Odo appear to tell us about the origin of the Second Crusade? According to Otto, Louis told some of his nobles of his secret desire to go to Jerusalem. He asked for their advice, which was to call upon Bernard for his opinion. The abbot of Clairvaux counselled the princes to seek the advice of the pope. Eugenius, after receiving the embassy from the French court, seized the opportunity to call for a new crusade, and issued *Quantum praedecessores*. Not long afterward, Bernard preached successfully to so many people that a general assembly was called for Vézelay, at which Louis and many other French nobles took the cross from Bernard.

Odo's account, unlike that of Otto, does not begin before the Christmas 1145 assembly. It is at Bourges that Louis first revealed to the bishops and magnates of France his fervent desire to go to the Holy Land. Godfrey, the bishop of Langres, spoke of the importance of a crusade to retake Edessa. But the audience remained unswayed, so it was decided that they would all meet again in a few months in Vézelay. Soon Louis sent messengers to the pope, who sent them back with letters concerning the launching of the crusade. The pope realized he would be unable to be present at Vézelay for the initial blessing of the crusade, and delegated the task to Bernard, who so brilliantly succeeded in his role that he was forced to tear his own garments in order to provide crosses to the many who wished to participate in the crusade.[8]

Both accounts begin with Louis revealing his secret desire, but apart from this, the conflicts between these two accounts are striking. However, if the events they narrate are viewed in a different context, they may be seen to fit each other very closely indeed. This newfound correspondence can be noticed once it is assumed that the *Gesta* and the *De profectione* do not always deal with precisely the same historical events. Reconstructed, the history of the origin of this crusade loses much of its apparent confusion and abruptness. This reconstruction is effected by considering Otto's account of Louis' first meeting with his princes as taking place *prior to* the Christmas 1145 assembly, instead of actually *being* that same assembly.

According to this viewpoint, sometime before December 1145, Louis had for some time been anxious to make a pilgrimage to Jerusalem, on account of an unfulfilled vow made by his late brother Philip. The king summoned some of his princes and asked for their advice.[9] Together they called upon Bernard for his opinion. Bernard's response was that his own opinion should not decide the issue, and that the nobles should turn to the pope himself. Acting upon Bernard's advice, an embassy was sent, and Eugenius, wanting to follow the example set by his predecessor Urban II in calling a crusade to spread the Christian faith, consented to the request. He granted Bernard "the authority to preach and to move the hearts of all", and wrote a letter to Louis and his princes. This letter was the crusading bull *Quantum praedecessores*, issued on December 1, 1145.

From this point, the narrative may be followed sensibly if one shifts to Odo's chronicle. At Bourges on December 25, 1145, Louis, solemnly wearing his crown, "revealed for the first time to the bishops and the magnates of the realm, whom he had purposely summoned in greater numbers than usual for his coronation, the secret in his heart."[10] It should be stressed at this point that when Otto mentions Louis revealing his secret, it is to *some* of his princes ("*quibusdam*") and not, as Odo relates, to his bishops and magnates, and also not *in greater numbers than usual* ("*generalius solito*").

Odo continues his narration by telling how the bishop of Langres, Godfrey de la Roche, formally spoke to the assembly concerning the sack of Edessa and the oppression of the Christians who lived there. He urged his audience to aid their fellow Christians by fighting on their behalf for Christ, the King of all mankind; this was to be accomplished by fighting under Louis, their temporal king.

Due to political considerations (and also likely because no response had yet been received from the pope following the embassy described by Otto), no immediate action on the crusade was taken. It was decided that less than three months later, all were to reassemble at Vézelay, on the Sunday before Palm Sunday. Those present at Vézelay, who would receive divine inspiration during the last two weeks of Lent, would then proceed to take the crusading cross on Easter Sunday.

Soon after the Bourges assembly, Louis sent messengers to Pope Eugenius in Rome, who sent them back home "bearing letters sweeter than any honeycomb". According to Odo,

> [these were letters] which enjoined obedience to the king and moderation in arms and clothing, which promised those taking the easy yoke of Christ the remission of all sins and the protection of their wives and children, and which contained certain other provisions that seemed advisable to the pope's holy wisdom and solicitude.[11]

This description would indicate that the letter in question is *Quantum praedecessores II*, written by Eugenius on March 1, 1146. Odo explicitly refers to the pope's command regarding "moderation in arms and clothing"; as Erich Casper and Peter Rassow have demonstrated, the only significant difference between the two crusading bulls is that the second stresses moderation in clothing and is the only bull which demands that no attention be given to "gilded or silvered arms".[12]

Due to great political instability in Rome, the pope was unable personally to launch the crusade by granting its initial blessing at Vézelay. It is for this reason that he formally delegated this task to Bernard. And it is at the Vézelay assembly that the separate accounts of Otto and Odo may be seen to converge.

The above presentation of the crusade's origins from late 1145 to March 1146 almost completely removes the seeming discrepancies between the accounts of Otto and Odo. As to why Odo would not have mentioned the pre-Christmas events narrated by Otto, it may be argued that one of Odo's intentions in presenting his chronicle is to portray Louis as positively as possible. Accordingly, the opening event in the *De profectione* spotlights the French king in a dramatic setting as the sole initiator of this grand and holy project. The account, if it had told of the deliberations which necessarily would have taken place before an event such as this, would be less appealing to Odo's readers (and less in keeping with the author's narrative strategy).

This is not to say that what Odo explicitly recounts is untrustworthy, despite his propagandistic approach to the episode. On the contrary, as Virginia Gingerick Berry declares, the *De profectione* "is the only history wholly devoted to the subject, and is the most important single source of information for the Second Crusade."[13] Odo had a privileged position in observing the activities of the French crusaders: he was, after all, the chaplain of the king himself. Given that Otto did not have such a vantage point, his *Gesta* cannot serve as a final court of appeal in establishing the facts concerning the crusade's origin when his account differs from that of Odo.

The single point which seems to remain most problematic in reading these accounts concerns the role of Bernard of Clairvaux. Otto states that Bernard was granted the authority to preach the crusade at the time *Quantum praedecessores* was issued. Furthermore, after presenting the text of the bull, Otto says:

> [Bernard] made no misuse of the authority of the Apostolic See that had been granted to him. He valiantly girded himself with the sword of the Word of God; and when he had aroused the hearts of many for the expedition overseas, finally a general assembly was summoned at Vézelay . . . .[14]

Thus Otto makes it very clear that the summoning of the general assembly at Vézelay was due directly to Bernard's successful and persevering preaching. And since this preaching resulted in calling the Vézelay assembly, it would have to have been accomplished before Christmas 1145; Odo makes it very clear that the summons to Vézelay was made at the Bourges Christmas assembly.

Concerning this, one should note that it seems that no contemporary chronicle mentions Bernard as present at the Christmas assembly; in particular, Odo makes no reference to Bernard's presence at Bourges. As it is virtually inconceivable that Bernard's presence at the Christmas court would have been passive or unnoted by the primary sources, it is reasonable to assume that Bernard was not there. Furthermore, in all probability, Bernard did not preach the crusade before Easter 1146. No such sermons exist today, and, with the sole exception of the *Gesta*, such preaching is not mentioned authoritatively by any contemporary chronicles.

The most damaging evidence against Otto's assertion regarding Bernard's preaching comes from the pen of Bernard himself. As he grew older, Bernard spoke more freely of his desire to remain in the cloister. Around the end of 1143, just two years before the issue of *Quantum praedecessores*, he had written to Peter the Venerable, saying:

I have decided to stay in my monastery, and not to go out, except once a year for the general chapter of abbots at Cîteaux .... I am broken in body and have a legitimate excuse for not going about as I used to.[15]

More to the point, early in 1146, pressured by those who wanted him to support openly and to preach the Crusade, Bernard wrote to Pope Eugenius, tersely stating his wishes:

... if anyone suggests to you that more might be put on me, know that as it is I am not equal to supporting what I carry. Inasmuch as you spare me, you will save yourself. I believe that my desire never to leave my monastery is not unknown to you.[16]

It is obvious that with the passage of time, Bernard felt ever more determined to be a monk — a stable, contemplative monk — and no more "the chimaera of his age".[17] As a monk, he deeply loved his monastery; indeed, it is no overstatement to say that he loved Clairvaux like a spiritual Jerusalem.[18]

Most historians of the Second Crusade appear to have neglected both these letters and this aspect of Bernard's mentality. Some have added useful considerations which have not been taken up here; for example, Giles Constable says that prior to the pope's command to preach, Bernard did not become involved with the crusade due particularly to canonical restrictions with regard to preaching by the regular clergy.[19]

However, Hans Eberhard Mayer's account appears to rest solely upon perceived political motives. He states:

Understandably enough the abbot of Clairvaux was not at all inclined to support an expedition which looked as though it might have been instigated by the king. This would have meant that control over the crusade had been taken out of the hands of the Church. The papacy would have to face a considerable blow to its prestige if it could not maintain its position as overlord of the crusading movement. Bernard therefore tried to give the initiative back to the pope. He declared that he could not consider so important a question without first consulting the pope.[20]

Certainly Bernard would have considered the situation's political aspects. But Mayer's presentation would seem to be inaccurate insofar as it places politics as the basic factor in Bernard's considerations concerning the crusades.

Bernard's view of himself with regard to papal authority both during the early optimistic weeks of the crusade and after its tragic failure remain constant. This fact underlines the necessity of examining Bernard's motivations as an aid to determining the course of events before Easter 1146. On May 1 of that year, Bernard wrote to the pope, reporting the tremendous success in gaining crusaders: "towns and castles are emptied, [and] one may scarcely find one man among seven women, so many women are there widowed while their husbands are still alive." This report is immediately preceded, however, by the statement: "You have ordered and I have obeyed, and your authority has made my obedience fruitful", clearly indicating the pope as the cause of such success.[21]

Similarly, even after the crusade's failure, Bernard wrote in the *De consideratione* of his bewilderment at the negative outcome: "We rushed into this, not aimlessly but at your command, or rather, through you at God's command."[22] It is likely this statement which led Mayer to state:

> Bernard's self-defense always ended with his taking cover behind the commission to preach the crusade which he had received from the pope. That he should try to evade responsibility for the crusade after it had failed reveals a side of his character which is not very attractive.[23]

Such a judgment gives little weight to the fact that Bernard tried his hardest "to evade responsibility for the crusade" before it began and even while it was generally held to be so very successful. Ultimately it is the character and actions of Bernard which provide the key to resolving the evasive historical problem of just how the Second Crusade had its origin: an origin marked by the very confusion that would characterize its events and doom it to failure.[24]

NOTES

1. The text of the bull is in Otto of Freising, *Gesta* 1, pp. 55-7 (Eng. ed.: Otto of Freising, *Deeds*, pp. 71-73 & Brundage, *Documentary*, pp. 86-88).
2. The following examples are representative of positions taken in accounts of the origin of the Second Crusade; they clearly are not intended to include all scholars or publications.
3. Vacandard, vol. 2, p. 275.
4. Valléry-Radot, p. 319; Seguin, p. 394.
5. Berry, p. 468.
6. Willems, p. 124; Runciman, vol. 2 (1952), p. 252; Prawer, *Histoire*, vol. 1, p. 347.
7. On the present subject, see Otto of Freising, *Gesta* 1, pp. 54-58 (Eng. ed.: Otto of Freising, *Deeds*, pp. 70-74). For Odo's chronicle, see: Odo of Deuil,

De profectione, pp. 6-11 (Eng. tr. also in: Brundage, *Documentary*, pp. 88-90).

8. "Et cum earum fascem praeparatum seminasset potius quam dedisset, coactus est vestes suas in cruces scindere et seminare" (Odo of Deuil, *De profectione*, p. 8).

9. " ... Lodewicus dum occultum Hierusalem eundi desiderium haberet, eo quod frater suus Philippus eodem voto astrictus morte preventus fuerat, diutius protelare nolens propositum, quibusdam ex principibus suis vocatis, quid in mente volveret, aperuit" (Otto of Freising, *Gesta* 1, p. 54, lines 11-15). For a complete study of Louis' motivation see: Graboïs, "Louis VII".

10. "In natali Domini praecedenti [that is, the Christmas before the Easter 1146 assembly at Vézelay] cum idem pius rex Bituricas curiam celebrasset, episcopis et optimatibus regni ad coronam suam generalius solito de industria convocatis secretum cordis sui primitus revelavit" (Odo of Deuil, *De profectione*, p. 6).

11. "Rex interim, pervigil in incoepto, Romam Eugenio papae super hac re nuntios mittit. Qui laetanter suscepti sunt laetantesque remissi, referentes omni favo litteras dulciores, regi oboedientiam, armis modum et vestibus imponentes, iugum Christi suave suscipientibus peccatorum omnium remissionem parvulisque eorum et uxoribus patrocinium promittentes, et quaedam alia quae summi pontificis sanctae curae et prudenti visa sunt utilia continentes" (Odo of Deuil, *De profectione*, p. 8).

12. For the text of Eugenius' second crusading bull, see: Rassow & Caspar, "Eugens III". For an Eng. tr. of the bull, see also: Riley-Smith, *Idea & Reality*, pp. 57-59.

13. Odo of Deuil, *De profectione*, p. xx.

14. " ... Bernhardus abbas venerabilis concessa sibi apostolicae sedis auctoritate non abusus gladio verbi Dei fortiter accingitur, ac excitatis ad transmarinam expeditionem multorum animis, tandem curia generalis aput Verzelacum Galliae oppidum, ubi beatae Mariae Magdalenae ossa recondita sunt, indicitur ..." (Otto of Freising, *Gesta* 1, p. 58, lines 2-7).

15. "Decretum est mihi ultra non egredi monasterio, nisi ad conventum abbatum Cistercium semel in anno .... Fractus sum viribus, et legitimam habeo excusationem, ut iam non possim discurrere ut solebam" (Bernard, *Opera*, vol. 8 (1977), letter 245, p. 99, lines 14-15, 18-19; tr.: Bernard, *Letters*, pp. 375-76).

16. " ... si suggestum vobis a quopiam fuerit de me amplius onerando, scitote vires mihi non suppetere ad ea quae porto. Quantum mihi, tantum parcetis et vobis. Propositum meum monasterium non egrediendi credo non latere vos" (Bernard, *Opera*, vol. 8, letter 245, p. 136, lines 16-19; tr.: Bernard, *Letters*, p. 396). Vacandard (vol. 2, p. 276, n. 2) suggests this letter may have been written soon after Louis' emissaries left to consult the pope.

17. This celebrated phrase was coined by Bernard in describing himself: "Clamat ad vos mea monstruosa vita, mea aerumnosa conscientia. Ego enim quaedam Chimaera mei saeculi, nec clericum gero nec laicum."

(Bernard, *Opera*, vol. 8, letter 250, p. 147, lines 1-3). On this, see: Fracheboud.

18. See: Bernard, *Opera*, vol. 7 (1974), letter 64, pp. 157-58; here he equates Clairvaux with Jerusalem.

19. Constable, "Second Crusade", p. 224.

20. Mayer, *Kreuzzüge*, pp. 97-8 (Eng. ed.: Mayer, *Crusades*, p. 94).

21. " . . . mandastis, et oboedivi, et fecundavit oboedientiam praecipientis auctoritas. Siquidem annuntiavi et locutus sum, multiplicati sunt super numerum. Vacuantur urbes et castella, et paene iam non inveniunt quem apprehendant septem mulieres virum unum, adeo ubique viduae vivis remanent viris" (Bernard, *Opera*, vol. 8, letter 247, p. 141, lines 16-20; tr.: Bernard, *Letters*, p. 399).

22. Bernard, *Opera*, vol. 3 (1963); see p. 411, lines 8-9 (tr.: Bernard, *On Consideration*, p. 48): "Cucurrimus plane in eo, non quasi in incertum, sed te iubente immo per te Deo."

23. Mayer, *Kreuzzüge*, p. 109 (Eng. ed.: Mayer, *Crusades*, p. 105).

24. Research on this subject was begun during course work in the Master of Arts program of the History Department of Trent University, Peterborough, Ontario, Canada. This work was developed in: Ferzoco, esp. pp. 20-35, 121-27; and this has since been elaborated. I would like to acknowledge gratefully the generous support and advice I have received from Professor John Gilchrist, who was my director of studies at Trent.

10

Family Traditions and Participation in the Second Crusade[1]

Jonathan Riley-Smith

To take the cross involved committing oneself to an expensive and dangerous enterprise, but the decision cannot have been made in isolation from all kinds of pressure, including the expectations of a family that traditionally supported the crusading movement. Such traditions of commitment built up very quickly, and their strength was recognized by Pope Eugenius III when, proclaiming the Second Crusade, he called on sons to emulate their fathers.

> It will be seen as a great token of nobility and uprightness if those things acquired by the efforts of your fathers are vigorously defended by you, their good sons. But if, God forbid, it comes to pass differently, then the bravery of the fathers will have proved to be diminished in the sons.[2]

In fact, many of those who took the cross in 1146/47 followed, or intended to follow, in the footsteps of fathers or grandfathers, but some families contributed so large a number of crusaders that one is bound to ask whether there was in them some sort of collective response: the Bernards of Bré in the Limousin, for instance, who had already sent three men to the First Crusade, produced four second crusaders.[3] The minds of men and women living so long ago are, of course, closed to us, and we can never discount individual initiatives, or, within a circle of relatives, the force of some strong personality, or of loyalty to a particular lord. But the evidence for concentration in certain kin-groups is so striking that I am inclined to believe that some families may have been predisposed to respond favorably to appeals to crusade.

A good example is the family of the counts of Burgundy.[4] William Tête-Hardi of Burgundy had six sons. Odo appears to have died young. Raymond married the heiress of Leon-Castile, and so migrated to Spain, which was itself proto-crusading territory. Of the others, Rainald II,[5] Stephen I,[6] and Hugh[7] were on the First Crusade, and Guy, as Pope Calixtus II, proclaimed the crusade of 1122.[8] Two of William's grandsons in the male line, William IV of Mâcon[9] and Alfonso VII of Leon-Castile,[10] took part in the Second Crusade. William also had four daughters. Three were married before 1095 to men who were to become first crusaders: Clemency to Robert II of Flanders,[11] Gisela to Humbert II of Savoy,[12] and Sibyl to Odo I of Burgundy.[13] The fourth daughter, Ermintrude, was the mother of a first crusader,[14] as indeed was Sibyl.[15] Among the sons and grandsons of these sisters were no less than eight second crusaders: Louis VII of France himself and his brother Robert I of Dreux, Amadeus III of Savoy, William V of Montferrat, Rainald I and Stephen of Bar-le-Duc,[16] and Guy II[17] and William of Ponthieu.[18] The Burgundian sisters' daughters and granddaughters were married to a further four men who took the cross for the Second Crusade: Archimbaud VII of Bourbon,[19] Humbert III of Beaujeu,[20] Alfonso I of Portugal,[21] and William III of Warenne.[22] So the input of the comital house of Burgundy into the early crusading movement, and particularly the Second Crusade, was immense, the most notable contribution coming from the descendants of the women of the family, who were remarkable in other respects: Clemency and Ermintrude were responsible for the spread of Cluniac influence and attachments.[23]

An evident predisposition is one thing. Why it should have come into being is another. Comital Burgundy, in fact, was a family in which some of the traditions that might incline it to crusading can be traced. First: pilgrimage to the East. William Tête-Hardi's mother was Adelaide of Normandy, whose brother Duke Robert I had died in 1035 as he returned from a famous pilgrimage to Jerusalem.[24] Second: patronage of Cluny. Count Odo William (981-1026), William Tête-Hardi's grandfather, had helped to reform St. Bénigne of Dijon and had been a benefactor of Cluny; his heirs kept up the association, and William's cousin Guy entered the community.[25] Third: attachment to the reformed papacy. In 1074 Pope Gregory VII had called on William Tête-Hardi to fulfill an oath William had taken solemnly before St. Peter's tomb to defend St. Peter. It is clear that Gregory considered William to be a leading *fidelis sancti Petri*, since he was to transmit the summons to campaign on the pope's behalf to Raymond IV of St. Gilles, Richard of

Capua and Amadeus II of Savoy, and to Beatrice and Mathilda of Tuscany. The pope added that once the Normans in southern Italy had been pacified, he would personally lead the force William had helped to assemble to Constantinople to help the Christians against the Muslims.[26] William's attitude to papal reform is confirmed by the marriages of his daughters to Humbert II of Savoy, Robert II of Flanders, and Thierry II of Montbéliard, all three being from families of *fideles sancti Petri*, and to the duke of Burgundy, whose brother had entered Cluny and had also been considered by Pope Gregory VII as a supporter.[27]

The comital house of Burgundy shows another feature. There is strong circumstantial evidence that in it, as in some other family environments, women were positively influencing the responses of men to crusade appeals. Constance Bouchard has noticed that women played an important rôle in the transmission of support for monastic reform from one family to another.[28] The same process was at work in crusading. Sometimes, of course, women may be found reinforcing an existing predisposition, for instance among the Warennes. William III of Warenne, who was already married to Sibyl of Burgundy's granddaughter Adelaide,[29] his half-brother Waleran of Meulan[30], and his cousins Roger of Mowbray[31] and Drogo II of Mouchy-le-Châtel[32] all took the cross for the Second Crusade. The commitment of William and Waleran can perhaps be traced to the influence of their mother Isabel of Vermandois, a daughter of the first crusader Hugh the Great of France;[33] Isabel's brother Simon of Vermandois also took the cross for the Second Crusade.[34] But it should not be forgotten that, like the Burgundian counts, the Warennes had an attachment to Cluniac monasticism: in 1078-80, William I of Warenne had established the first Cluniac priory in England at Lewes.[35] And William III's aunt, Edith of Warenne, Drogo's mother and Roger's grandmother, had been married in turn to two first crusaders, Gerard of Gournay-en-Bray[36] and Drogo I of Mouchy-le-Châtel.[37] A similar case is that of the family of the counts of Nevers,[38] which was to have a major rôle in the history of crusading. This began with the participation of the brothers William II and Robert in 1101.[39] The family had no long tradition of support for the church,[40] and a first reaction is to see behind the brothers' decision the influence of their mother, Agnes of Beaugency, whose own two brothers went crusading in 1096;[41] one of them, Ralph, was married to Hugh the Great's daughter, Mathilda.[42] But, in fact, the Nevers family may itself have had some predisposition favorable to crusading, which had already been exported by one of the men to Anjou. The great uncle of William II and Robert, Robert I Burgundio, had settled in Anjou in the middle of the eleventh century.[43] He must have been an old man when he took the cross for the First Crusade with his neighbor Rainald III of Château-Gontier.[44] Two of his grandsons, Henry[45] and another Robert, who was to become the second Grand Master of the Templars,[46] were on the crusade of 1128; and a great- and a great-great-grandson, Geoffrey of Sablé-sur-Sarthe and Maurice II of Craon, may have taken the cross for the Second Crusade with two of their cousins, Rainald IV of Château-Gontier and Hugh I of Matheflon. By this time, the Burgundios had been integrated into a network of Angevin families which shared an enthusiasm for crusading.[47]

Nevertheless, feminine influence appears to be regularly at work and one often finds a woman at the junction between a family, her own, which produces many crusaders, and another, the one she marries into, in which only her husband and/or son crusades. One nexus is that of the linked families of Montlhéry and Le Puiset. If one includes husbands and wives, the two generations active at the time of the First Crusade produced twenty-three crusaders and settlers, of whom six became major figures in the Latin East, one being a king and another a patriarch of Jerusalem;[48] four Montlhéry sisters, whose procreativeness was mentioned with awe by William of Tyre,[49] bred no less than ten crusaders and settlers, with the traditions continuing among their grandchildren and great-grandchildren, who included the 1128 crusader Guitier of Rethel[50] and the second crusaders William Aiguillon II of Trie[51] and William of Courtenay[52]. Even allowing for the possibility that some of these were motivated by their relatives' successful careers in the eastern settlements, there must have been something special about the Montlhéry sisters. And a great-nephew was the Burgundian second crusader Humbert III of Beaujeu, whose mother, Lucienne of Roche- fort, was also a Montlhéry, being the daughter of the first crusader Guy II of Rochefort;[53] the Montlhéry sisters were her aunts. Humbert has already been mentioned in connection with the comital house of Burgundy, since he was married to a daughter of Amadeus III of Savoy (and granddaughter of Gisela of Burgundy). His wife would have inherited traditions from the houses both of Savoy and Burgundy, but Humbert himself was heir to a massive family commitment through his mother. It is noteworthy that at the time of the crusade, he was warned in a vision not to join his father-in-law's force, but to travel to the East independently. While in Jerusalem he joined the Templars, even though married, but soon gave this up and returned home.[54]

The forces that inclined the Montlhérys to crusading must have been particularly strong, but it is possible that the Le Puiset family, associated with them through the marriage of Alice of Montlhéry to Hugh I of Le Puiset, had its own pre-crusading traditions, since Walter[55] and Everard III of Breteuil,[56] the son and grandson of Waleran I of Breteuil, Hugh of Le Puiset's brother, took part in the First and Second Crusades, and that these were transmitted to yet another family by a woman. The descendants of Roger II of Montgomery and Mabel of Bellême included one first crusader,[57] one pilgrim to Jerusalem in c. 1119,[58] and two second crusaders, William VI Taillefer of Angoulême[59] and Philip of Gloucester.[60] Little in the lives of Roger and Mabel[61] point to a sympathy for those movements of opinion that would lead to crusading. But Orderic Vitalis reported that, after Mabel had been murdered, Roger married a pious and gentle woman, who persuaded him to be generous to monasteries. Her name was Adelaide of Le Puiset and she was Hugh I's sister.[62] In the same way, it is possible that traditions entered the family of Upper Lorraine, which provided five men — Thierry I of Flanders, Henry of Alsace, Hugh I of Vaudemont, Henry I of Toul, and Matthew I of Lorraine[63] — for the Second Crusade, through Thierry II of Upper Lorraine's second marriage to Gertrude, the sister of the first crusader, Robert II of Flanders.

The story of Adela of England, who persuaded her husband Stephen of Blois to take the cross in 1101 after he had deserted the second wave of the First Crusade, is well known,[64] but it is, as far as I am aware, unusual. The sources, ecclesiastical and popular, give the impression that women, distraught at the departure of husbands, sons, and lovers, were inhibiters, while men, for their part, were distressed and reluctant to leave the women.[65] There can be no doubt that the prospects for women left behind to manage estates in their husbands' absence were grim.[66] But I am being led to the conclusion that the sources are misleading us. The evidence from the genealogies is that some women transmitted an enthusiasm for crusading to the families into which they married. This helps to account for the concentrations of crusaders in certain kindred. It may, in fact, have been central to motivation in general, at least in the early decades of the movement.

NOTES

The author is indebted to the British Academy for providing travel funds to Kalamazoo, Michigan, where this chapter was read in May 1990.

1. This paper was written on the basis of family trees generated by my computerized prosopographical database of crusaders. I am grateful to Dr. G.R. Kingston, who adapted a relational database management package for

my use. Throughout the paper I treat the "1101 Crusade" as the third wave of the First Crusade.

2. Rassow, p. 303. He was echoed by St. Bernard. "How may sinners have obtained forgiveness in Jerusalem, confessing their sins with tears, after the filth of the pagans was banished by your father's swords?" Bernard, *Opera*, vol. 8, p. 313.

3. The Bernards of Bré are being studied by one of my research students, Mr. Marcus Bull.

4. See: Bouchard, pp. 261-79.

5. Albert of Aachen in: RHC Oc., vol. 4, p. 583; and possibly *Gesta Francorum*, p. 69; Peter Tudebode, p. 111; *Chanson d' Antioche* vol. 1, pp. 440, 480; Meyer, "Fragment", p. 489.

6. Albert of Aachen, pp. 563, 565, 568-69, 582-83, 591, 593-94; Orderic Vitalis, *History*, vol. 5, p. 324.; Guibert of Nogent, *Gesta*, in: RHC Oc., vol. 4, p. 244; Fulcher, *Historia* 2, pp. 430, 438, 443; Bartolf of Nangis, *Gesta*, in: RHC Oc., vol. 3, pp. 532-34; Henry of Breitenau, in: RHC Oc., vol. 5, p. 205.

7. Calixtus II, *Epistolae*, in: PL, vol. 163, cols. 1107, 1237.

8. See: Riley-Smith, "Venetian Crusade", pp. 337-50.

9. Odo of Deuil, *De profectione*, p. 110; *Cart. Mâcon*, p. 377; Peter the Venerable, *Letters*, vol. 1, p. 409.

10. *Cart. Temple*, vol. 1, pp. 297-98.

11. For Robert on the Second Crusade, see: Riley-Smith, *First Crusade*, passim; and Clemency's charter in Hagenmeyer, *Kreuzzugsbriefe*, pp. 142-43.

12. See: Guichenon, vol. 6, Preuves, p. 27. They were married c. 1090.

13. Bouchard, p. 259; Cate, in: Setton, *Crusades*, vol. 1, pp. 349-50. They were married c. 1080.

14. Louis of Mousson, see: Albert of Aachen, pp. 317, 422, 464; *Chanson d'Antioche*, vol. 1, p. 441; William of Tyre, *Chronicon*, vol. 1, pp. 330, 410; *Chron. Albrici*, in: MGHS, vol. 23, p. 804.

15. Florina of Burgundy, see: Albert of Aachen, p. 377.

16. For Louis, Robert, Amadeus, William, Rainald, and Stephen, see: Berry.

17. William of Tyre, *Chronicon*, vol. 2, pp. 713, 749; *Historia Ludovici*, p. 126; *Cart. Temple*, vol. 1, pp. 384-85.

18. *Cart. Temple*, vol. 1, pp. 298-99; Sauvage, p. 374. This list does not take account of settlers like Count Raymond II of Tripoli.

19. Odo of Deuil, *De profectione*, pp. 28, 54, 138; *Historia Ludovici VII*, p. 126; *Chartes Bourbonnais*, p. 39. Married to Agnes of Savoy in 1130/37.

20. Peter the Venerable, *Mirac.*, in: PL, vol. 189, cols. 902-903; Peter the Venerable, *Letters*, vol. 1, pp. 407-13. Married to a daughter of Amadeus III of Savoy.

21. *Lyxbonensi*, passim; *Cart. Temple*, vol. 1, p. 275. Alfonso was also a *confrater* of the Templars: *Cart. Temple*, vol. 1, p. 17. Married to Mathilda of Savoy in c. 1146.

22. See: Berry, p. 469. Married to Adelaide of Ponthieu in 1138.

23. Bouchard, p. 146.
24. Douglas, pp. 35-7.
25. Bouchard, pp. 153-55.
26. Gregory VII, *Register*, vol. 1, pp. 70-1. See: Erdmann, *Origin*, p. 216; Cowdrey, "Pope Gregory", pp. 29-31.
27. See: Robinson, *Authority*, pp. 101-102; Erdmann, *Origin*, pp. 206 n. 30, 216, 273; Robinson, "Gregory VII", passim. For Duke Hugh I's entry into Cluny, see: Gregory VII, *Register*, vol. 2, pp. 423-24; Bouchard, p. 258.
28. Bouchard, pp. 142-48.
29. For the family, see: Cokayne, *Complete Peerage*, vol. 12 (1), pp. 493-97. For William's crusade, see above n. 22.
30. Robert of Torigni, *Appendix* in: RHGF, vol. 13, p. 291.
31. Cokayne, *Complete Peerage*, vol. 9, pp. 369-70.
32. Drogo crusaded as a penance for engaging in an incestuous marriage, from which he had been absolved by St. Bernard. *Historia Ludovici*, p. 126; Suger, *Epistolae*, in: RHGF, vol. 15, pp. 485, 500 (letter from Louis VII). See also: Bernard, *Opera*, vol. 7, p. 398.
33. See: Riley-Smith, *First Crusade*, passim.
34. *Historia Ludovici*, p. 126.
35. Douglas, p. 328.
36. Orderic Vitalis, *History*, vol. 6, p. 192 n. For references to Gerard's crusade, see: Albert of Aachen, p. 316; Baldric of Bourgueil, in: RHC Oc., vol. 4, p. 33; Orderic Vitalis, *History*, vol. 5, pp. 34, 58; *Chanson d'Antioche*, vol. 1, pp. 94, 441. After the crusade, he and Edith made a pilgrimage to Jerusalem, during which he died (Wm. of Jumièges, *Gesta*, p. 278).
37. For the marriage, see: Orderic Vitalis, *History*, vol. 6, p. 192 and n.; Wm. of Jumièges, *Gesta*, p. 278. For Drogo I's crusade, see: Albert of Aachen, p. 422; William of Tyre, *Chronicon*, vol. 1, p. 330; Orderic Vitalis, *History*, vol. 5, p. 30; *Chanson d'Antioche*, vol. 1, pp. 70, 307.
38. For the family, see: Bouchard, pp. 340-51.
39. Bouchard, p. 346; Cate, passim.
40. Bouchard, pp. 131, 216-17, 239-40.
41. For Ralph and Odo of Beaugency, see: Riley-Smith, *First Crusade*, pp. 45, 76, 78, 121. Ralph also went on a pilgrimage to Jerusalem in 1125: Röhricht, *Regesta*, no. 110. Their father, Lancelin of Beaugency, had been on a pilgrimage to Rome in 1080 (*Cart. Vendôme*, vol. 2, p. 5).
42. *Stammtafeln*, vol. 3, table 55.
43. Halphen, pp. 113, 146, 298, 300-301, 305, 328.
44. *Cart. d'Azé*, p. 55; *Cart. Marmoutier*, vol. 2, pp. 87-91, 456. See for Rainald: *Cart. Saint-Aubin*, vol. 2, p. 175.
45. Röhricht, *Regesta*, no. 130; Mayer, "Angevins", p. 7.
46. He had already been in the East before 1128. Mayer, "Angevins", pp. 6-7; Bulst-Thiele, *Magistri*, pp. 30-40.

47. *Chron. de Parcé*, p. 12, in what is, admittedly, a very mythical-looking account. For something of the relationships between the families of Château-Gontier, Matheflon, and Champagne de Parcé, see: *Atlas Anjou*, vol. 1 [text], pp. 118-20.

48. For an incomplete study of the Le Puiset family, see: La Monte, "Le Puiset".

49. Wm. of Tyre, *Chronicon*, vol. 1, p. 547.

50. Röhricht, *Regesta*, no. 121.

51. *Historia Ludovici*, p. 126.

52. *Historia Ludovici*, p. 126. I have not included the many settler families with Montlhéry blood.

53. Suger, *Vita Ludovici*, p. 38; Albert of Aachen, pp. 563, 568, 573; *Chron. de Morigny*, pp. 40-1.

54. Peter the Venerable, *Mirac.*, cols. 902-903; Peter the Venerable, *Letters*, vol. 1, pp. 407-13. Humbert's father, Guichard, ended his days as a monk at Cluny. Bouchard, pp. 292-93.

55. Albert of Aachen, pp. 278, 281, 286, 288.

56. *Historia Ludovici*, p. 126; Suger, *Epistolae*, p. 496 (letter from Louis VII); Odo of Deuil, *De profectione*, pp. 52, 122; *Chron. de Morigny*, p. 84.

57. Philip the Grammarian of Montgomery: Orderic Vitalis, *History*, vol. 4, p. 302 & vol. 5, p. 34; Wm. of Malmesbury, vol. 2, p. 460.

58. William III Taillefer of Angoulême, see: *Historia pontificum*, in: RHGF, vol. 12, p. 394.

59. *Ex anonymi chronico*, in: RHGF, vol. 12, p. 120; *Historia pontificum*, p. 399.

60. *Gesta Stephani*, pp. 126-27; a vow made after an illness.

61. See especially: Orderic Vitalis, *History*, vol. 2, pp. 48, 54, 66, 122; vol. 3, pp. 134-38.

62. Orderic Vitalis, *History*, vol. 3, p. 138.

63. For Thierry I of Flanders, Hugh I of Vaudemont, and Henry I of Toul, see: Berry, passim. For Henry of Alsace, see: Odo of Deuil, *De profectione*, p. 50. And for Matthew I of Lorraine, see: Theodore, *Annales*, MGHS, vol. 16, p. 82. Henry of Toul's grandfather, Reinhard III of Toul, had been on the First Crusade.

64. Orderic Vitalis, *History*, vol. 5, p. 324.

65. For instance see: Bédier & Aubry, pp. 32-5, 101-104, 112-14, 126-29, 181-84, 191-94, 202-204, 210-212, 271-73, 283-85, 290.

66. For instance see: Tyerman, pp. 208-15.

11

Louis VII and the Counts of Champagne

Theodore Evergates

One of the more dramatic political realignments of the twelfth century, the *rapprochement* between the Capetians and the counts of Blois-Champagne, passed unremarked by contemporaries, perhaps because it was more a process of evolving relationships than a notable event. Moreover, the decisive transformation occurred beyond the kingdom of France during the Second Crusade.

Count Thibaut II of Blois-Champagne (1103-52), whose lands encircled the royal domain, long maintained an uneasy relationship with King Louis VI (1108-37). Although vigilant against royal encroachments, Thibaut possessed a very fine sense of his role as count-palatine and rallied to his king in defense of the realm.[1] The count was a generous benefactor to the Cistercians and a personal friend of Bernard of Clairvaux, who depicted him as an ideal prince: pious, solicitous of the weak and poor, generous to the Church, devoted to justice, and above all, a man of honor.[2] Abbot Suger of Saint Denis, whose influence as royal adviser grew steadily in the 1120s and 1130s, was likewise impressed with the count's generosity and repute, and it must have been Suger's counsel that prevailed in November 1135 when Louis VI, struck by dysentery and fearing the worst, appointed Count Thibaut and the royal seneschal, Count Ralph of Vermandois, as guardians of the fifteen-year-old prince Louis.[3]

Thibaut's chagrin at losing the English throne to his own brother Stephen in December 1135 no doubt brought him even closer to the ailing king in the next eighteen months.[4] In the summer of 1137, the count escorted prince Louis to Bordeaux for his marriage to Eleanor of Aquitane, and shortly after their return and Louis' accession to the throne, Thibaut accompanied the new king to eastern France as far as Langres to receive homages.[5] The seventeen-year-old Louis VII regarded Thibaut, who was then in his late forties, as a trusted guardian of royal interests.[6] Abbot Suger boasted of having encouraged the relationship so that Thibaut's reputation would rub off on the inexperienced king.[7]

In the spring of 1138, however, that relationship began to unravel. In response to communal revolt at Poitiers, Louis called on Thibaut to render *consilium et auxilium* because, he said, "I consider you to be my own and my kingdom's protector, and if you do not help me when the kingdom is in such danger, the onus will fall on you."[8] The count replied that he could do nothing without the advice of his barons,[9] and even Suger considered the summons illegitimate — Poitou belonged, after all, to Eleanor, not to Louis. In anger, Louis raised his own forces and violently suppressed the commune. Although two years later, in April 1140, Louis and Thibaut joined forces to suppress the commune of Rheims,[10] within months the count again refused the king military service on the queen's behalf, this time for an expedition to Toulouse. Contemporary chroniclers thought this second refusal marked the beginning of Louis' animosity toward Thibaut.[11] Shortly afterward, Suger retreated to Saint Denis, perhaps as a consequence of his support for the count.[12]

In 1141, two convoluted events further embroiled Louis and Thibaut. The first resulted from Louis' refusal to recognize the duly elected archbishop of Bourges; at the pope's request, probably on Bernard's recommendation, Thibaut offered the archbishop refuge in Champagne. The second event was the royal seneschal's sham divorce from Thibaut's niece and remarriage to Queen Eleanor's sister; the count protested to the pope.[13]

Legally and morally, Thibaut's position was unassailable, and in view of his own character and reputation it must have elicited considerable sympathy. The king's stance, on the other hand, was clearly reprehensible. Innocent II called him "a boy who must be instructed" and interdicted his lands.[14] In early 1142, a papal commission reaffirmed the seneschal's first marriage, excommunicated both him and Eleanor's sister, and suspended the three prelates who had performed the divorce.[15] The young king had been humiliated both by the Church and by his most powerful vassal.

Louis struck back by prohibiting episcopal elections within his *regalia*,[16] and in late May 1142, he ordered his brother Robert to occupy the see of Châlons-sur-Marne after the death of its bishop.[17] It was from Châlons late that year that Louis attacked Thibaut's castle-town of Vitry, no doubt encouraged by the royal seneschal in the absence of Suger. Bernard claimed that the attack was unprovoked, unannounced, and contrary to convention because Thibaut had neither been accused of, nor summoned to account for any misdeed.[18] Vitry fell to royal troops in January 1143 after a protracted siege during which the town and fifteen hundred innocent people were consumed by fire. The king is said to have wept at the sight, but he was not sufficiently remorseful to make peace.[19] The devastation of Champagne in 1142/43 reflected the king's deep anger toward his former guardian.

Bernard's first attempt at mediation failed, but with the accession of a more conciliatory Pope, Celestine II (September 1143), and the recall of Suger (early 1144), renewed negotiations yielded a solution with the papacy in March 1144. A settlement with Count Thibaut, however, proved more difficult, and was reached only after the June 11 dedication of the new choir of Saint Denis. There Queen Eleanor had sought Bernard's help on a personal matter: she had been married seven years, she said, but since her miscarriage the first year she had failed to conceive and was beginning to fear infertility. Bernard promised her a child if the king would make peace with Count Thibaut. Louis, by all accounts consumed with love for Eleanor, agreed to a settlement, but warned Bernard to carry out his part.[20] The following March or April 1145, about the time when news of Edessa reached France, Eleanor gave birth to Marie. Although this story appears fanciful, all recent historians of Eleanor's life accept it.[21] In the context of Louis' relationship with Thibaut, it would explain why Louis finally made peace with someone whom he had turned against after feeling betrayed and had treated unjustly both as a king and feudal lord.

The two men did not, however, renew their former relationship, and it is doubtful whether Thibaut attended the king's Christmas Council at Bourges (1145) where Louis announced his pilgrimage to the Holy Land.[22] Most barons there were unwilling to follow Louis, at least in part because of his treatment of Thibaut. Only after the Cistercians had transformed that expedition into a more acceptable, full-fledged crusade did they yield.[23] When they joined the king at Vézelay the next Easter (March 31, 1146) to take the cross, it was Thibaut's eldest son Henry who represented Champagne. That was the face-saving solution. Given Thibaut's long friendship with Bernard, it was unthinkable that a count of Champagne would not participate in the Cistercian Crusade. Moreover, Thibaut held substantial lands in fief from Godfrey, bishop of Langres and Bernard's confidant and chief collaborator in promoting the crusade.[24] And the new Cistercian bishop of Troyes, Henry (1145-69), was a close relative — perhaps the brother — of the countess of

Champagne.[25] Yet the presence of Thibaut's son at Vézelay in no way implied a *rapprochement* with Louis at that time.[26] In fact, some bitterness must have lingered, for Thibaut was pointedly omitted from the crusade regency formed in February 1147, although as count-palatine and former regent he was the natural choice. In light of the recent events, young Henry's relationship with Louis before the departure of the crusade in June 1147 might best be described as "correct".

The twenty-year-old Henry, who had been associated with his father since 1145,[27] set out with his chaplain, Martin, and a sizeable contingent of Champenois barons and knights. He carried a letter of introduction from Bernard to Emperor Manuel Comnenus asking the emperor to dub the young man so that, in Bernard's words, he would have an experience to remember the rest of his life.[28] Henry must have presented that letter shortly after the French arrived in Constantinople on October 4, perhaps during the elaborate reception Manuel held for the French king.[29] If Manuel did, in fact, knight Henry, the event must have taken place when the French barons paid homage to the emperor before marching into Asia Minor. Perhaps on that same occasion Manuel gave Henry a piece of the true cross.[30]

The disasters of the next three months are well known, but two events are relevant here. The crossing of the Maeander River was successful largely due to the spirited charge by Counts Henry, Thierry of Flanders and William of Mâcon, who crashed through a line of Turkish archers poised to destroy the French as they emerged from the swollen river. That assault was reported widely as one of the few military successes of the crusade.[31] The second event was Louis' failure as general commander: during the four-month overland march to Constantinople, discipline collapsed, and by the time the army reached the Byzantine capital, serious internal conflicts had surfaced. Odo of Deuil states that at Metz, Louis had issued an order of march which the barons swore to observe but did not.[32] Subsequent loss of command control at Mount Cadmus, followed by the virtual annihilation of the army, left Louis no option but to surrender command to the Templars, who were able to hold the French forces together until they reached the port of Attalia.

Louis and his barons — Henry among them — abandoned their men at Attalia and sailed directly to Antioch, where Louis' failed leadership exacted further toll. His brother Robert began to plot against him,[33] and his marriage unravelled when Eleanor, unburdening herself to a sympathetic uncle, Raymond of Antioch, decided to separate from Louis because of their consanguineous marriage.[34] Bernard had raised the question of consanguinity in 1141, in response to Louis' cynical abuse of the issue to obtain his seneschal's divorce.[35] It was indeed a cruel twist that Louis, unable to bear prolonged separation from Eleanor, now faced divorce on those same grounds.

It was precisely during this unhappy period of failed leadership, a crumbling marriage, and disaffection by his own brother, that Louis' attachment to Henry becomes evident. According to William of Tyre, Henry appeared at the great crusader council at Acre (June 24, 1148) as Louis' son-in-law. Although William's remark has been challenged as a later insertion,[36] there is good reason to accept it. William, who was studying in the West at the time of the crusade, began to collect information for his history only after returning to the Levant in 1165.[37] For recent events, he relied primarily on oral testimony, but he was extremely well informed and careful not to insert later information into earlier periods.[38] Of the four French barons he cites with Louis at that June meeting, William names first the king's brother, Robert, with his then-correct title, count of Perche,[39] then Henry, whom he describes as "son of lord Thibaut the Elder, count of Troyes, son-in-law of the lord king, and a young man of fine character."[40] William wrote these words in the mid-1170s and reviewed them without revision in the early 1180s after he had met Henry in person.[41] Had William updated that entry, he would have more correctly called Henry the king's brother-in-law rather than son-in-law, and he would not have identified Henry — by then a distinguished count in his own right — as son of Count Thibaut. In short, William reported what had been common knowledge in crusader circles in 1148: Louis had promised his infant daughter in marriage to Henry of Champagne, the youngest and still unmarried baron.

When Henry returned home in late 1148 or early 1149, Louis wrote an extremely laudatory letter to Count Thibaut, speaking of the close friendship (*amor*) he felt for Henry, who had displayed, he said, "devotion at all times" and whose "loyal service" earned the king's gratitude and affection.[42] Louis displayed a genuine desire to be reconciled with the old count by calling Thibaut his custodian of the realm — which, of course, was not the case at all in 1148 — and seeking his help in checking subversion in France.

Henry's friendship with Louis laid the foundation for a complete reversal of royal-comital relations in 1152, after Henry's succession as count of Champagne (January) and Eleanor's divorce (March). Henry's first significant act as count was to join Louis' attempt to seize and redistribute Plantagenet lands.[43] The next year Henry was formally betrothed to Louis' eight-year-old daughter, Marie, who thereafter was regarded as countess of Champagne, but who was placed in the convent of Avenay until her marriage.[44] Apparently there was a double betrothal in 1153, for Louis gave his second daughter by Eleanor, the three-year-old Alice, to Henry's younger brother Thibaut V, count of Blois (1152-91).[45] Thibaut, then in his early twenties, seems not to have participated in the crusade, but his appointment as royal seneschal in 1154 proves Louis' attachment to the two brothers.[46] Thereafter, the new seneschal regularly attended Louis and witnessed all important decisions, while Count Henry was consulted on political matters.[47] The two brothers would provide Louis unswerving moral and military support against their common enemy, Henry Plantagenet.[48]

The close tie between the two counts and Louis was obvious in 1160 when the forty-year-old king, newly widowed and still without a son after twenty-three years of rule, married their youngest sister, Adela. *Rapprochement* reached its culmination in 1164-65: Henry and Thibaut finally married Louis' daughters, their youngest brother William was elected bishop of Chartres, and Queen Adela delivered the child that would assure the Capetian succession.[49] While the significance of these events on Louis and his reign have yet to be explored, it is clear that the aging king increasingly came under the influence of the Champagne family, whose overbearing presence in the 1170s evoked deep resentment in the future Philip II.

Louis VII and Count Henry, with fond memories of their crusade experience and reception in Constantinople, planned a second voyage in 1177.[50] The king's deteriorating health, however, prevented his departure.[51] In May 1179, at the age of fifty-two, the count set out for Marseilles, then took passage to Brindisi where he met William of Tyre.[52] Henry's companions included the king's brother, Peter of Courtenay, and the king's nephew Philip, bishop-elect of Beauvais, who were escorting Queen Adela's daughter Agnes (Henry's own niece) to Constantinople for marriage to Emperor Manuel's son, Alexis II.[53] Henry seems to have proceeded directly from Brindisi to Acre to revisit the holy sites. Captured in Asia Minor in 1180, he was ransomed by the very Emperor Manuel who had knighted him in 1147. By August 1180, Henry was in Constantinople.[54] He probably witnessed Manuel's death (September 24, 1180) and Agnes' accession as empress — all within days of Louis VII's death in France. Shortly after returning to Champagne, Henry died in mid-March 1181.

NOTES

1. Suger, *Vita Ludovici*, pp. 224-26, ch. 28.
2. Bernard, *Opera*, vol. 7, letter 38, pp. 96-97.
3. Luchaire, *Louis VI*, p. 254, no. 559.
4. See: Arbois de Jubainville, vol. 2, pp. 321-23.

5. Lair, p. 590.

6. Orderic Vitalis, *History*, vol. 6, p. 490.

7. Lair, p. 590.

8. Quoted by Suger (Lair, p. 591).

9. Suger paraphrased Thibaut's reply (Lair, p. 591).

10. Bur, p. 290 and n. 24.

11. *Cont. Praemon.* in: MGHS, vol. 6, p. 452 [1140]; *Chron. Turonensis* in: RHGF, vol. 12 (1781), p. 472 [1141]. The break came after September 1140 (Arbois de Jubainville, vol. 2, p. 326).

12. Benton, "Suger", p. 10, n.32.

13. For these complicated events, see: Pacaut, *Elections épiscopales*, pp. 94-100.

14. Wm. of Nangis, vol. 1, p. 34.

15. Vacandard (1927), vol. 2, p 185; Arbois de Jubainville, vol. 2, pp. 346-7.

16. Sometime between January-February and June 1142 (Pacaut, *Elections épiscopales*, p. 98, n.2).

17. According to Bernard, Louis and Thibaut had an understanding about the royal occupation of Châlons (Bernard, *Opera*, vol. 8, letter 222, pp. 86-7).

18. Bernard, *Opera*, vol. 8, letter 222, pp. 86-9.

19. Arbois de Jubainville, vol. 2, pp. 348-50.

20. The story is related by Bernard's secretary, Geoffrey of Auxerre (*Vita 3*, col. 527, no. 8). A similiar account is given in: Philip of Clairvaux, col. 332, no. 18. The *Cont. Praemon* (p. 452 [1144]) confirms Bernard's mediation.

21. Labande, p. 180, n. 25; Brown, "Eleanor", p. 13; Laube, pp. 34-5.

22. There is no firm evidence that Louis and Thibaut ever met after their falling out in late 1140. Louis' act reporting a court hearing, "*videntibus et audientibus comite Teobaldo*" and others (dated by Luchaire to March 30 – November 1141), seem to report an earlier hearing (perhaps of late 1140), see: Luchaire, *Louis VII*, no. 73, pp. 361-62. Nor is there evidence that Louis and Thibaut attended the consecration of the abbey-church of Vauluisant in 1143 (as claimed in: *GC*, vol. 12 (1770), p. 231).

23. Graboïs, "Crusade", pp. 97-8.

24. Wurm, chs. 1-2.

25. Pacaut, *Elections épiscopales*, p. 141.

26. There is no evidence that Henry was betrothed to Louis' daughter Marie before June 1147, as Arbois de Jubainville claims (vol. 3 (1861), p. 13, n. 1). In fact, in the spring of 1147, the count of Anjou sought Marie's hand for his own son Henry, only to be checked by the ever-vigilant Bernard on the grounds of consanguinity (Bernard, *Opera*, vol. 8 (1977), letter 371, pp. 330-31; letter dated by Arbois de Jubainville himself [vol. 3, p. 12, n.3] to 1147, between Easter and June).

27. *Recueil Clairvaux*, no. 10, pp. 16-17; no. 12, pp. 19-20.

28. RHGF, vol. 15 (1808), pp. 607-608.

29. Kinnamos, pp. 68-9.

30. Odo of Deuil, *De profectione*, pp. 62-3 and n. 4, mentions the relics in the chapel in Constantine's palace which he and Louis must have seen. In 1153, Henry, at the request of his chaplain Martin, "who served me so well in the crusade to Jerusalem," gave to Toussaints-en-l'Ile of Châlons a rent commemorating the discovery of the Holy Cross, "part of which, by God's grace, I donated" (Barthélemy, vol. 2, pp. 407-408).

31. Odo of Deuil, *De profectione*, pp. 110-11; Wm. of Tyre, *Chronicon*, vol. 2, pp. 749-50 (bk. 16, par. 24); Niketas Choniates, pp. 39-42.

32. Odo of Deuil, *De profectione*, pp. 20-21.

33. Wm. of Tyre hints at Robert's disloyalty in naming the French barons at the council at Acre (June 1148): Count Henry was "a young man of fine character," Count Thierry of Flanders was "a magnificent count," Count Ivo of Soissons was "a wise and faithful man," but Robert was simply "count of Perche and the king's brother" (Wm. of Tyre, *Chronicon*, vol. 2, pp. 760-61 [bk. 17, ch. 1]).

34. John of Salisbury, pp. 52-3.

35. Bernard, *Opera*, vol. 8, letter 224, p. 93.

36. Fourrier, p. 301.

37. Edbury & Rowe, pp. 25-6.

38. Thus Frederick, duke of Swabia, who attended the council of Acre, "later succeeded Conrad as Emperor" (Wm. of Tyre, *Chronicon*, vol. 2, p. 760).

39. That title was correct until 1152, when Robert received the castellany of Dreux (Lewis, p. 146).

40. Wm. of Tyre, *Chronicon*, vol. 2, p. 760.

41. For Wm. of Tyre's composition, see: Edbury & Rowe, pp. 26-8.

42. RHGF, vol. 15 (1808), no. 53, p. 502.

43. Robert of Torigni, *Chronicles*, p. 165.

44. Fourrier, pp. 306-308, argues that Henry and Marie were canonically married in 1153 because a *desponsatio* constituted "consent of marriage" rather than simply a "promise of future marriage" (a betrothal).

45. *Historia Ludovici VII*, p. 128, among others, links the betrothals, suggesting that they were in part Louis' response to Eleanor's remarriage.

46. Thibaut assumed the office between August 1 and November 24, 1154 (Luchaire, *Louis VII*, p. 47).

47. Of the barons who sealed the Establishment of Soissons (10 June 1155), only Henry was named in the document (RHGF, vol. 14 (1806), pp. 387-88; see also: Graboïs, "Trêve", pp. 594-95). At the same time, Louis wrote to Pope Adrian IV that he had discussed the conflict between the bishop and chapter of Soissons "with Count Henry of Champagne and others" (RHGF, vol. 16 (1814), no. 62, p. 14).

48. See: Pacaut, *Louis VII*, pp. 179-202, esp. p. 189.

49. Fourrier, pp. 301-303.

50. Louis did not share the anti-Byzantine bias of Odo of Deuil. In a letter of 1169, he addressed Emperor Manuel as his "venerable brother and dearest

friend" whose honorable reception in 1147 "I have never forgotten" [RHGF, vol. 16 (1814), no. 451, pp. 149-50].

51. Pacaut, *Louis VII*, p. 203.
52. Wm. of Tyre, *Chronicon*, vol. 2, p. 1003.
53. *Chron. St.-Pierre-le-Vif*, p. 210, juxtaposes Henry's pilgrimage with Agnes' own voyage.
54. Arbois de Jubainville, vol. 3 (1861), p. 109.

12

The Crusaders' Strategy Against Fatimid Ascalon and the "Ascalon Project" of the Second Crusade

Martin Hoch

I

When the crusaders of the First Crusade reached Palestine in the spring of 1099, the ancient Philistine city of Ascalon was in the hands of the Fatimid Caliphate of Egypt.[1] In August of the same year, following the capture of Jerusalem, the crusaders joined battle with a Fatimid expeditionary force near Ascalon.[2] The Egyptians were routed and the governor of Ascalon offered the surrender of the city to Raymond of St. Gilles. Due to a quarrel between Raymond and Godfrey of Bouillon, however, this offer was not taken up, and no attempt to capture Ascalon was made at that time. Occasional spells of peaceful coexistence with the Frankish neighbor notwithstanding,[3] the Fatimid stronghold was henceforth to prove "a thorn in the flesh of the [crusaders'] kingdom."[4] For more than half a century, the so-called "Ascalon strip"[5] became the battleground of frequent clashes between the forces of the Latin Kingdom of Jerusalem and their Saracen adversaries, and of countless raids by both sides. In 1148 Ascalon became, for a short time, the focus of attention of the Second Crusade, but no action against it was taken. By far the last of the seaports in the Levant to fall, Ascalon was not captured by the crusaders until 1153.

This case study is an attempt to analyze the conflict over Ascalon between the Fatimids and the crusaders in the first half of the twelfth century. Several aspects will be dealt with in particular: section II will investigate in what ways Ascalon posed a threat to the Latin Kingdom, and section III how the crusaders responded to that threat. The Frankish strategy to subdue Ascalon may help to explain the outcome of the "Ascalon Project", a rather neglected interlude of the Second Crusade (section IV). Finally, the conclusion will look at some of the implications of the crusaders' course of action for our knowledge of the military history of the Latin Kingdom of Jerusalem (section V).

II

From the crusaders' point of view, Fatimid Ascalon constituted a dangerous enemy bridgehead on their side of the Sinai desert.[6] Egyptian invading forces frequently crossed the desert in safety, and used Ascalon as a convenient staging area, an operational base, and a place of refuge close to the field of battle.[7] Since the Egyptian outpost was freely accessible both by sea and by land, hostile troops could easily assemble in dangerous proximity to the heartland of the Frankish possessions in the East. As it was, important Frankish centers, such as Jaffa and Jerusalem itself, were within striking range of Ascalon. Egyptian invasions and raids by the garrison frequently took place when the military forces of the Latin Kingdom were committed on other fronts, and few troops were left for the defense of its southwestern frontier; this was the case during the invasion of Galilee by the armies of Maudud of Mosul and Tughtegin of Damascus in 1113, and twice during the siege of Tyre by the crusaders in 1124.[8] Occasionally, as in the course of the invasions of 1105 and 1118, Egyptian forces were supported by the Syrian enemies of the crusaders.[9] Ascalon was protected by formidable defensive works; its garrison was relieved several times a year, and clashes between Egyptian troops deployed in that city and Frankish forces were commonplace events.[10] Ascalon was an element of Egypt's naval defense and alert system, and a base of the redoubtable Fatimid navy which increased the operative range of the fleet.[11] Egyptian invasions were frequently supported by naval forces; in complex operations the Fatimid fleet repeatedly landed — and subsequently evacuated — soldiers and siege machines on the beaches of the Latin Kingdom.[12]

After a series of full-scale invasions of the Latin Kingdom in the first decades of the twelfth century had ended in defeat for the Egyptians, Ascalon was used primarily as a staging base for hit-and-run operations by its garrison.[13] These raids ravaged the southwestern parts of the kingdom and severely impaired the efficient administration and colonization of this area.[14] Occasionally, as in 1113 and 1124, raids penetrated as far as the environs of Jerusalem and beyond to Magna Mahumeria (Bira).[15] Moreover, the raids harassed the traffic on the Jaffa-Jerusalem route, the principal highway for pilgrims in the Latin Kingdom, and even challenged crusader control over this crucial line of communication.[16] The founding of the military order of the Knights Templar about 1120 was due in part to Ascalonite raiding activities.[17] William of Tyre's report of the beginnings of the Order indicates that the Templars' foremost task was the protection of the pilgrimage routes in the face of ambushes set up by highwaymen (*latrones*) in addition to those of raiders (*incursantes*).[18]

The proximity of Ascalon to the heartland of the Latin Kingdom proved troublesome in yet another respect. In the course of the revolt of Hugh of Jaffa and a number of other nobles in 1133 or 1134 against King Fulk, Hugh defected to Ascalon and concluded a treaty of alliance with its governor, thereby encouraging Ascalonite raids all the way to Arsuf (Tel Arshaf).[19] Even though it was this very move which caused the collapse of Hugh's rebellion, the dangers of involving the enemy in the internal conflicts of the Latin Kingdom were evident. Not surprisingly, just a few years later King Fulk was to take measures both to prevent a possible repetition of this revolt and to subdue Ascalon.[20]

In addition to invasions and raids, Fatimid Ascalon constituted a serious problem for the westward expansion of the Latin Kingdom. The crusaders had cast a covetous eye on Egypt already in the early years of their dominion,[21] well before the rich land of the Nile became the objective of the "battle of Egypt"[22] that was to ensue in the 1160s after the fall of Ascalon. As long as Ascalon was in hostile hands, however, the crusaders were unable to take advantage of the progressively ruinous state of the Fatimid empire toward the middle of the twelfth century.[23] The paramount geostrategic importance of Ascalon for the defense of Egypt was clearly perceived by contemporaries; William of Tyre relates that

> the aforementioned lord [i.e. the ruler of Egypt] and his princes exercised great and utmost care for this city. They reasoned that if they lost the city to us, there would be no alternative but that our princes would descend freely and without hindrance upon Egypt and that the kingdom would be conquered by force.[24]

III

In reaction to the threat from Ascalon, the Jaffa-Jerusalem route was protected by the construction of a number of small forts during the first two decades of Frankish rule.[25] In 1110 and 1123/24, when Western fleets were at the disposal of the Latin Kingdom, it was debated whether the capture of Ascalon should be attempted. Even though there was widespread support for such action on both occasions, at length it was decided to attack Sidon and Tyre respectively.[26] An encounter between the garrison of Ascalon and crusader forces in 1125 almost resulted in the capture of the city.[27] Raids by the Fatimid garrison were still a problem in the 1130s, for William of Tyre states that when the fortress Castellum Arnaldi (Yalu) was constructed about halfway between Jaffa and Jerusalem in 1132, this was done for the purpose of protecting the pilgrims on this route from the habitual sudden attacks of the Ascalonites.[28]

In order to put an end to these raids and to set the stage for the capture of Ascalon, the crusaders embarked on an impressive and eventually efficacious course of action. In 1136, in the reign of King Fulk (1131-43), it was decided by the kingdom's magnates "to construct strongholds in a circle around [Ascalon]".[29] Such castles, the so-called *Gegenburgen*[30] or "blockading fortresses",[31] were not uncommon in the Latin East. The *Gegenburgen* confronting Ascalon had several purposes: one, to check Ascalonite raids; two, to be nuclei of lordships and centers of colonization; and three, to serve as logistic and operational bases for attacks upon Ascalon.[32] Nearly all of these fortresses were of a relatively small and square design, the so-called *castrum* type.[33] Partners in the construction were the crown as well as the secular and clerical nobility of the Latin Kingdom: the *arrière-ban* was regularly proclaimed when one of the fortresses was to be raised.[34]

In the year 1136 the crusaders built the *castrum* Bethgibelin (Bet Guvrin) at a geographically advantageous site at the foothills of the Judaean mountains. By common consent, Bethgibelin was entrusted to the Order of St. John, and the ten nearby *casalia* were added for good measure.[35] Incidentally, this is one of the earliest instances in which the Hospitallers are associated with strictly military responsibilities.[36] Five years later, in 1141, another *castrum* was constructed near the highway from Ascalon to Ramle/Lydda at a place called Ibelin (Yavne); this castle was given to Balian the Elder, a loyal supporter and vassal of King Fulk, who subsequently took his surname from this fortress.[37] The first two Frankish *Gegenburgen* confronting Ascalon apparently produced the desired effect of checking the Ascalonite raids.[38] Accordingly, in the year 1142, the crusaders decided to build the third *Gegenburg*, the *castrum* Blanchegarde (Tel Tsafit), on a promontory of the Judaean mountains in order to increase the pressure on Ascalon; after its completion, the fortress remained in the king's possession.[39] And finally, in the spring of 1150, the last of the *Gegenburgen* was constructed in the ruins of the town of Gaza; this stronghold was entrusted to the Templars.[40]

The *Gegenburgen* were located on or close to the main roads leading from Ascalon to Jaffa and Ramle/Lydda, to the Valley of Ayalon and Jerusalem, to Hebron and Bethlehem, and to Egypt respectively, and their garrisons could react quickly to the passage of hostile forces on those routes.[41] At a distance of circa thirty kilometers from Ascalon, about halfway between that city and the highways connecting Jaffa, Jerusalem and Hebron, the first three fortresses had a primarily defensive purpose in that they denied Ascalonite raiders access to the roads and cities in the southwestern region of the kingdom. The castle at Gaza, on the other hand, was offensive in nature, and directly menaced the security of Ascalon by cutting the overland lines of communication between that city and its hinterland Egypt.[42]

After the fortification of Gaza, the Egyptian army ceased to approach Ascalon by land for fear of ambushes set up by the garrisons of the *Gegenburgen*.[43] The Frankish efforts paid off in 1153 when Ascalon was surrendered after a seven-month siege and naval blockade by crusader forces.[44]

IV

Quite possibly the crusaders' strategy of building a system of fortresses to confront Ascalon was a major factor in the outcome of the Ascalon Project of the Second Crusade in August 1148, when the system was yet incomplete.[45] Immediately after the abortive siege of Damascus in the course of the Syrian Campaign of that expedition, the three kings, Baldwin III of Jerusalem, Conrad III of Germany and Louis VII of France, convened an assembly of nobles with the intention of bringing the hitherto hapless crusade to a successful conclusion after all.[46] There was a debate in which a number of people proposed to lay siege to Ascalon. They argued that the city was not far away, and that it could be captured easily and quickly (the latter, however, seems hardly a defensible assertion).[47] In light of the troublesome relationship between Fatimid Ascalon and the Latin Kingdom throughout the previous five decades, the capture of that city was certainly a reasonable objective. Apparently some agreement to attack Ascalon was concluded; in the end, however, most of the Jerusalemite nobles refused to join the Westerners in the campaign, which was thereupon discontinued.[48]

In the absence of any explanation for the foundering of the Ascalon Project in the sources, it can be argued with some plausibility that the noncompliant Jerusalemite barons may have viewed the continuation of their long-standing strategy of containment as more promising than an impromptu assault on the Saracen stronghold. Significantly enough, no attempt to capture Ascalon is reported for the period in which the *Gegenburgen* were built. In 1148, prior to the fortification of Gaza, crusader forces blocking the road from Egypt to prevent reinforcements and supplies from reaching Ascalon would have been dangerously exposed. During the siege of Ascalon in 1153, crusader reconnaissance detachments to the west of Ascalon were indeed deployed close to their base at Gaza.[49] In addition, there is no indication in the sources that in 1148 a fleet was available to impose a naval blockade on Ascalon. Under these circumstances it would have been next to impossible to invest the city completely, and the Ascalon Project could have resulted in little more than a daring but rather desperate attempt to take the strongly fortified and well-defended city by storm.

Even though the Ascalon Project was largely inconsequential, one must not overlook the fact that even after the dismal failure of the Syrian Campaign — then, as now, widely blamed on the Jerusalemites — the Western participants in the ill-fated Second Crusade were still willing to join in an operation for the benefit of the Latin Kingdom. Following the events of the Ascalon Project, however, the majority of the Westerners changed their minds and departed from the Holy Land in a mood of frustration and resentment against their former hosts in the East.

V

In order to accomplish their purpose of engaging the enemy and suppressing Ascalonite raiding activities, the garrisons of the Frankish *Gegenburgen*, as a rule, joined forces. In describing the *modus operandi* of the troops of Blanchegarde, William of Tyre states that the garrison encountered the enemy "sometimes alone but more often reinforced by men-at-arms from the other strongholds which had been constructed for the same purpose."[50] This account is borne out by a passage in the memoirs of Usamah ibn Munqidh, a nobleman in the service of the Fatimids who participated in raids on Bethgibelin and Ibelin in 1150. According to Usamah, the crusaders used to have horsemen standing by in the *Gegenburgen* in order to be ready at all times for an attack upon Ascalon and to intercept Ascalonite raiders; these Frankish units combined forces against the Saracen raiding parties.[51] Some of the *Gegenburgen* were visible from one another, and fire signalling may have facilitated communication and coordination among the garrisons.[52] It is evident that the *Gegenburgen* of the Ascalon strip were not merely a cluster of discrete strongholds; on the contrary, the four castles confronting Ascalon constituted the elements of an interdependent system of fortifications in the sense of the dictum that "the whole is stronger than the sum of its parts".[53] The operation of these fortresses entailed a certain degree of discipline and close cooperation among the lords of the fortresses and their men in order to ensure the success of the system as a whole.

Evidently, in 1136, the crusaders reached a decision about their course of action against Ascalon which they pursued firmly over a considerable period of time. This course of action involved substantial efforts, enormous resources and the continuous support of a great number of people. In light of the controversy over the evidence of the concept of "strategy" in the Middle Ages,[54] it can be argued that the facts about the Frankish *Gegenburgen* confronting Ascalon strongly suggest that in this particular instance the crusaders developed a complex strategy — in the original, military sense of the word — in order to respond to the threat Ascalon posed to their security.[55]

What is most remarkable about the crusaders' strategy against Ascalon, however, is that this strategy of containment was implemented at a time when the Latin Kingdom of Jerusalem was subject to internal strife of no small proportions on account of the struggle for power between King Fulk and Melisende, and Melisende and Baldwin III, respectively.[56] The constitutional crisis of the kingdom was resolved only in the civil war of 1152. And yet in these troubled times, in which various factions within the ruling élite of the kingdom promoted their particular and conflicting interests, evidently there was adopted a long-term strategy which required the unreserved cooperation of these very factions in the construction and the day-to-day operation of the *Gegenburgen* for the benefit of the realm as a whole. Failure, however brief, of the lords of these castles to cooperate would have endangered the entire project to subdue Fatimid Ascalon, and could have proved extremely harmful and even dangerous for the kingdom itself. In that sense, the Frankish system of *Gegenburgen* confronting Ascalon is not only an example of a successfully implemented crusader strategy, but also an indication of the far-reaching commitment of the ruling élite of the Latin Kingdom of Jerusalem to the external security of the Christian commonwealth in the East toward the middle of the twelfth century.[57]

NOTES

1. On Ascalon and its history in general, see: Benvenisti, *Crusaders*, pp. 114-30.

2. On these events, see: Prawer, *Histoire*, vol. 1, pp. 252-53; Richard, *Latin Kingdom*, vol. A (1979), pp. 19-20.

3. Ibn al-Qalanisi, pp. 108-110.

4. Prawer, *Kingdom* 2, p. 21.

5. Prawer, *Crusader Institutions*, p. 478.

6. Prawer, *Kingdom* 2, pp. 21-22. For the crusaders' concept of security in this region, see also: Prawer, *Crusader Institutions*, pp. 477-78.

7. Prawer, *Histoire*, vol. 1, pp. 246-47; cf. Smail, p. 126.

8. Fulcher, *Historia* 2, bk. 2, ch. 49 [12], pp. 572-73; bk. 3, ch. 28 [2-4], pp 697-98; bk. 3, ch. 33 [1-3], pp. 731-32; and Wm. of Tyre, *Chronicon*, bk. 11, ch. 20, p. 525; bk. 13, ch. 8, p. 595; bk. 13, ch. 12, pp. 599-600.

9. For 1105, see: Fulcher, *Historia* 2, bk. 2, ch. 31 [1], pp. 489-90; Ibn al-Qalanisi, pp. 70-71. For 1118, see: Fulcher, *Historia* 2, bk. 3, ch. 2 [1], pp. 617-18; Wm. of Tyre, *Chronicon*, bk. 12, ch. 6, pp. 552-53.

10. Wm. of Tyre, *Chronicon*, bk. 13, ch. 17, pp. 606-608; bk. 14, ch. 22, pp. 659-61; bk. 17, chs. 22-23, pp. 790-93. See also: Benvenisti, *Crusaders*, pp. 121-30.

11. Ehrenkreutz, "Naval History", p. 102; Ehrenkreutz, *Saladin*, p. 19. On the operations of the Fatimid fleet and the naval base at Ascalon, see also: Pryor, pp. 114-16, 124-25.

12. For example, Fulcher, *Historia* 2, bk. 2, ch. 33 [1], pp. 501-502; bk. 2, ch. 53 [4], p. 585; bk. 3, ch. 2 [1], pp. 617-18; bk. 3, ch. 17 [1-5], pp. 661-63; and Wm. of Tyre, *Chronicon*, bk. 11, ch. 3, pp. 498-500; bk. 11, ch. 24, pp. 531-32; bk. 12, ch. 21, pp. 571-73.

13. Smail, p. 84; Richard, *Latin Kingdom*, vol. A, pp. 22-24.

14. Wm. of Tyre, *Chronicon*, bk. 14, ch. 22, pp 659-61; bk. 18, ch. 1, pp. 809-810. See also: Pringle, *Red Tower*, p. 127. On raiding in general, cf.: Gillingham, "Richard I", pp. 83-86.

15. Fulcher, *Historia* 2, bk. 2, ch. 49 [12], pp. 572-73; bk. 3, ch. 28 [2-4], pp. 697-98; bk. 3, ch. 33 [1-3], pp. 731-32; and Wm. of Tyre, *Chronicon*, bk. 11, ch. 20, p. 525; bk. 13, ch. 8, p. 595; bk. 13, ch. 12, pp. 599-600.

16. For example, Fulcher, *Historia* 2, bk. 2, ch. 37 [2-5], pp. 514-18; Usamah, p. 158; see also: Barber, "Origins", pp. 220-21.

17. Cf.: Barber, "Origins", pp. 224-25.

18. Wm. of Tyre, *Chronicon*, bk. 12, ch. 7, pp. 553-55.

19. Wm. of Tyre, *Chronicon*, bk. 14, ch. 16, pp. 652-53; see also: Mayer, "Melisende", pp. 102-111; Mayer, *Crusades*, pp. 83-85.

20. Tibble, pp. 49-51.

21. Smail, p. 22; Prawer, *Crusader Institutions*, p. 472.

22. Ehrenkreutz, "Naval History", p. 102. On the struggle for the control of Egypt, see: Ehrenkreutz, *Saladin*, pp. 35-54, 79-80; Mayer, *Crusades*, pp. 117-22.

23. On the decline of the Fatimid empire, see: Ehrenkreutz, *Saladin*, pp. 12-18.

24. Wm. of Tyre, *Chronicon*, bk. 17, ch. 22, p. 792, lines 39-44: "multam enim et maximam tam predictus dominus quam eius principes pro eadem urbe gerebant sollicitudinem, arbitrantes quod si illa deficeret, in nostrorum veniens dicionem, nichil restaret aliud quam ut libero et sine difficultate accessu nostri principes in Egyptum descenderent, regnum violenter occupaturi." See also: bk. 14, ch. 22, pp. 659-61; bk. 17, ch. 22, pp. 790-92.

25. Fedden & Thomson, p. 24.

26. For 1110, see: Fulcher, *Historia* 2, bk. 2, ch. 44 [1-4], pp. 543-47. For 1123/24, see: Fulcher, *Historia* 2, bk. 3, ch. 27 [1], pp. 693-94; bk. 3, ch. 28 [1], pp. 695-96; Wm. of Tyre, *Chronicon*, bk. 12, ch. 24, pp. 575-77.

27. Fulcher, *Historia* 2, bk. 3, ch. 46 [2-7], pp. 773-4; Wm. of Tyre, *Chronicon*, bk. 13, ch. 17, pp. 606-608.

28. Wm. of Tyre, *Chronicon*, bk. 14, ch. 8, pp. 639-40; Benvenisti, *Crusaders*, pp. 314-16.

29. Wm. of Tyre, *Chronicon*, bk. 14, ch. 22, line 21, p. 660: "municipia in circuitu per girum edificari."

30. Smail, pp. 209-213.

31. Fedden & Thomson, p. 24.

32. Wm. of Tyre, *Chronicon*, bk. 14, ch. 22, pp. 659-61; bk. 15, ch. 25, pp. 707-709. See also: Prawer, *Crusader Institutions*, pp. 102-107, 119-26; Pringle, *Red Tower*, pp. 12-14.

33. On the *castrum* and these fortresses in particular, see: Smail, pp. 230-36; Benvenisti, *Crusaders*, pp. 173-75, 280-82; Prawer, *Kingdom* 2, pp. 22-23, 280-82.

34. Wm. of Tyre, *Chronicon*, bk. 14, ch. 22, pp. 659-61; bk. 15, ch. 25, pp. 707-709; bk. 17, ch. 12, pp. 775-77.

35. Wm. of Tyre, *Chronicon*, bk. 14, ch. 22, pp. 659-61; Röhricht, *Regesta*, no. 164, pp. 40-41; Benvenisti, *Crusaders*, pp. 185-88.

36. Riley-Smith, *Knights*, pp. 52-53, 435-37.

37. Wm. of Tyre, *Chronicon*, bk. 15, ch. 24, pp. 706-707; Benvenisti, *Crusaders*, pp. 207-209. On Balian, see: Wm. of Tyre, *Chronicon*, bk. 14, ch. 16, pp. 652-53; Tibble, pp. 45-46.

38. Wm. of Tyre, *Chronicon*, bk. 15, ch. 25, pp. 707-709.

39. Wm. of Tyre, *Chronicon*, bk. 15, ch. 25, pp. 707-709; Benvenisti, *Crusaders*, p. 205.

40. Wm. of Tyre, *Chronicon*, bk. 17, ch. 12, pp. 775-77; bk. 20, ch. 20, pp. 937-39; and Usamah, pp. 34-35. Benvenisti, *Crusaders*, pp. 189-94; Mayer, "Melisende", p. 143.

41. See the maps in Prawer, *Histoire*, vol. 1 (1969), pp. 331, 662.

42. Prawer, *Kingdom* 2, pp. 22-23, 282.

43. Wm. of Tyre, *Chronicon*, bk. 17, ch. 12, pp. 775-77.

44. Wm. of Tyre, *Chronicon*, bk. 17, chs. 21-30, pp. 789-805; Ibn al-Qalanisi, pp. 314-17.

45. On the concepts of "strategy" and "system," see section V of this chapter.

46. Wm. of Tyre, *Chronicon*, bk. 17, ch. 7, pp. 768-69. On the Ascalon Project, see also: Kugler, pp. 201-204; Berry, p. 510.

47. Wm. of Tyre, *Chronicon*, bk. 17, ch. 7, pp. 768-69.

48. *Urkunden Konrads*, no. 197, pp. 356-57; *Cont. Praemon.*, p. 454.

49. Wm. of Tyre, *Chronicon*, bk. 17, ch. 23, pp. 792-93.

50. Wm. of Tyre, *Chronicon*, bk. 15, ch. 25, lines 31-33, p. 708: "frequenter per se, frequentius adiunctis sibi ex aliis municipiis, ad usus similes edificatis, militibus."

51. Usamah, pp. 41-42.

52. Cf. Fedden & Thomson, p. 12; Benvenisti, *Crusaders*, pp. 269-70.

53. Cf. Benvenisti, *Crusaders*, p. 282.

54. Cf. Gillingham, "Richard I", pp. 78-79.

55. Cf. Prawer, *Kingdom* 2, p. 22.

56. On these events, see: Mayer, "Melisende", passim.

57. I am indebted to my preceptor Dr. Andrew S. Ehrenkreutz, professor emeritus of the University of Michigan, for his comments on a draft of this study, and for much more.

PART III

THE AFTERMATH

13

The Cistercians and the Aftermath of the Second Crusade

Brenda M. Bolton

The failure of the Second Crusade made demands upon the resilience of those who had been its spiritual leaders. A close examination of a brief entry in the *Continuatio Premonstratensis* of Sigebert of Gembloux,[1] composed before 1155 in the diocese of Lyons or Rheims, will reveal some evidence of the consequences of this concern for Bernard and for the Cistercians. The chronicler refers to councils that were held throughout the Kingdom of France. Three were proposed, but only two seem to have taken place. The assembly at Chartres on May 7, 1150 was the largest and most solemn.[2] Present were King Louis VII of France, one of the military leaders just returned from the Holy Land, and a great collection of senior churchmen, most notably Suger, abbot of St. Denis, and Bernard of Clairvaux. The Cistercian pope, Eugenius III, although not present in person, appears to have dominated the proceedings with his letter, *Immensum pietatis opus*, dated April 25, 1150 and circulated to the whole assembly.[3] Eugenius, aware of all the difficulties, counselled extreme caution and stressed that nothing should be done without the tacit support of the king of France.

The purpose of the council seems to have been the consideration of a new or third crusade, arising from correspondence between Bernard, now recovering from his despair at the failure of the Second Crusade,[4] and Suger, who seems to have been the driving force behind the discussions. Suger had gone to Laon in early April 1150 after the news broke of the siege of Antioch and of the grave dangers which were to follow.[5] These dangers were not only to the king of Jerusalem and the Templars but also, more importantly, to the Relic of the True Cross. To Suger, the need for the assembly at Laon with some of the archbishops and bishops — and even the lord king himself — with the nobles of the realm was of vital importance. The assembly of Laon judged that, after the recent misfortunes, any proposal for a new crusade could only usefully be discussed with the attendance of each and every one of the spiritual leaders of the French Church — bishops and abbots from every province. Such a meeting was called, this time at Chartres.[6] It was equally essential that Bernard should be there, although any further absence of this abbot from his monastery would not have pleased the monks of Clairvaux. Indeed, many times during previous years while Bernard was on his various preaching campaigns, they had importuned him by writing pleading letters saying how desolate they were without him.[7] Bernard was always promising to return. Now that he was back with them at Clairvaux, they were loathe to let him go. But go he did!

In spite of having been subjected to constant requests to preach and advise on the crusade, Bernard's reluctance is stated eloquently before 1146 when, in a blunt letter to Eugenius he writes, "If someone has suggested to you the thought of imposing a new burden on me, I warn you that I am already overloaded beyond my strength. You know that I have taken the decision not to leave my monastery. I believe that I have never hidden this from you."[8] Bernard, however, was always willing to concede that the word of God should take precedence over all else. As the pope spoke for God when he launched a crusade, should the pope wish him to participate in the *Negotium Dei*, then he would surely do so.[9] Bernard's own experience in 1145 with his preaching campaign in Languedoc may well have helped him to overcome his stated reluctance because the need was so great. Much work still to do, had been his verdict when he returned![10]

The Cistercian Order itself could not give full attention to the matter, distracted as it was by the demands of its own major internal reorganization. The phenomenal growth of the Order in its first fifty years had caused grave concern in many quarters. Whether or not it was this concern which lay behind the abdication of Stephen Harding in 1133 may never be clear, but whatever the cause, in the ensuing crisis and deposition of Guido, fourth abbot of Cîteaux, the Cistercians demonstrated their ability to close ranks, expunging from their records all traces of this brief but disastrous abbacy.[11]

The year 1150 was to mark a very considerable break with what had gone before. The policy of almost unrestrained expansion had led to a major quarrel with the Premonstratensians, thus breaking the pact of 1142.[12] The length and humility of Bernard's letter to Hugh, abbot of Prémontré, reveals this to have been a far deeper and more serious quarrel than was generally allowed by the Cistercians.[13] In the same year, when Abbot Reynald died and was succeeded by Gozewin, abbot of Bonnevaux in the affiliation of Cîteaux, the general chapter seems almost immediately to have taken the opportunity to reverse the former policy towards new foundations.[14] The process of retrenchment was taken most seriously. The very first chapter celebrated by Gozewin in 1151 requested that the pope himself should reconfirm the origins on which the Order was based.[15]

In 1152, in the bull *Sacrosancta*, Eugenius gave papal approval to the regular institutions of the Cistercians in the *Carta caritatis*, and may well have been concerned with the propagandist *Exordium parvum* in draft form.[16] The initiative for the reorganization of the Order seems to have come entirely from within. There was a clear wish that those monasteries recently incorporated would show that vigor and stability of which the Cistercians were so proud. It was more important to consolidate the strength of the Order than to allow unrestricted growth. To this end, it has been suggested that the Cistercians may well have rewritten their decrees to make them seem simpler, more primitive, and therefore more original.[17] While this point may never be fully established, it is important to note that the Cistercians were not averse to tampering with their documents — sometimes for the best of motives.[18] Unfortunately, such an approach means that when we would have wished them to say more, their records remain stubbornly silent.

With so much on their minds, the Cistercians had little interest in the Council of Chartres and the prospect of a new crusade. Not Bernard! In a letter to Suger, he expresses his delight at the news that he has received from the Master of the Temple.[19] Bernard further explains that he has promised Godfrey, bishop of Langres, that he would be present at the council. In addition, he would be happy to accompany the bishop to the assembly, for his presence there would be of great value.[20] This was encouraging information for Suger, whose circular letter *Orientalis ecclesiae calamitatem* of April 1150 had been the calling notice for the Council of Chartres.[21] In spite of this notice being sent to all concerned, we know of at least three absentees from the Council. The first absentee, Peter the Venerable, abbot of Cluny, had been particularly invited and beseeched by Suger to attend in the name of God — "for the matter involved not only prison but death."[22] Bernard also made a special plea for him to be present.[23] But come he did not![24] This in spite of the fact that the abbot of St. Denis had made quite sure that neither he nor any other potential absentee could allege that they had not been warned in good time. The replies of Peter the Venerable and of the archbish-ops of Lyons and Bordeaux make interesting reading. Peter writes:

> I am sorry and grieve more than I can say not to be present at the Council of Chartres where the lord king will proclaim your wisdom and that of others. Believe me, dear friend, believe what I say. I really am unable to come and because I cannot, I am sad. Who would not grieve to miss such a meeting, where the only person to gain thereby — by a new crusade — is none other than Christ Jesus![25]

He regrets that even before the beginning of Lent, and before he had received Suger's letter of invitation, he had already summoned a general chapter of the Cluniacs for precisely the day proposed for the meeting at Chartres.

Humbert, archbishop of Lyons, had received two letters: one directly addressed to him,[26] and the other transmitted through Peter the Venerable on Suger's explicit instructions.[27] Humbert said in his reply that although he wished to attend the Council of Chartres in his primatial capacity and be in the presence of the lord king and the magnates, he was unable to do so as the archbishop of Sens persisted in refusing to recognize the primacy of the See of Lyons. "Furthermore," he added, compounding an already weak excuse, "Hilo, abbot of Saint-Just, just outside the walls of the city, was gravely ill and getting worse each day."[28] As the *castra* and fortifications of the Church of Lyons were Hilo's responsibility, the archbishop felt that he simply could not come in person and leave his church thus exposed. He did, however, delegate Stephen, formerly archbishop of Vienne, to come in his place. He added that once peace had been brought to the churches of Lyons and Sens, then he, as archbishop, would definitely declare himself ready to give advice and help in God's cause. Suger had by no means underestimated the ability of this archbishop to evade his duty!

Geoffrey, archbishop of Bordeaux, also excused himself. He was rather ill, he said.[29] Furthermore, Lord Theodoric Galeranni, on behalf of the lord king and the bishops of the diocese of Bordeaux, had convened a meeting for Good Shepherd Sunday, the second after Easter, at St. Jean d'Angely in order to bring peace to the area. Clearly it must have been pointed out to him that he would have ample time to reach Chartres by May 7. He did indeed set out, but another letter to Suger was soon to appear. "Geoffrey has fallen ill at Fontevrault and must remain there. Brother 'N' will come in his place."[30] Hardly a satisfactory substitute!

Those who managed to attend the Council of Chartres would have been in no doubt as to the recriminations which abounded after the failure of the Second Crusade, including the fact that it was all Bernard's fault.[31] Some of the complainants had even gone so far as to suggest that money donated for the *Negotium Dei* should be returned to those who had given it. A report of a lost sermon, although not contemporary, is nonetheless revealing of Bernard's actions in response to these protesters.[32] On their return from the Holy Land, he immediately hastened to the king and the French troops to give a message to the disaffected, the disgruntled and the plainly shocked. Taking as his text "God has cast off and put us to shame and goest not forth with our armies", he reminds the soldiers not to forget the truth given in Deuteronomy:[33] if their faith in one rock and one God is firm, they should prevail, even against overwhelming odds. He says that the psalmist would have understood that the troops felt cast off by God but, rather than mourning over their defeat, they should not abandon hope. And when they all had heard him, the king and the barons were wonderfully comforted by Bernard's preaching, and much strengthened in their faith. Even if this account is not strictly contemporary, it has a ring of truth about it and accords well with what we know from Bernard's own accounts of his preaching and its great effectiveness.[34]

For the church as a whole, the failure of the Second Crusade was a matter of the utmost seriousness. For Bernard in particular, it might have seemed like a personal judgment, but one which he had to overcome. In Book II of *De consideratione*, Bernard represents the failure as an example of the mysterious ways in which God works. "The judgments of God are just," he wrote, "but this is so great a blot that I can only declare blessed whomsoever is not scandalized by it."[35] Others advanced various reasons for the catastrophe — from Old Testament comparisons where God had punished those who had failed to perform his will, to the New Testament approach more favored by Cistercians such as John of Casamari who stressed, in a letter to Bernard, that all those who had made the sacrifice would be saved.[36] Bernard took the view that those who survived would be made stronger by this humbling experience — perhaps an understanding which was a direct result of his own involvement in the disaster. With such all-round demoralization, the question of who was to lead any future crusade would be crucial, particularly if churchmen were to bear in mind St. Paul's view that in a sinful world, man cannot easily govern events. Thus leadership of any new crusade, while on the agenda, was overshadowed by the main talking point of the Council of Chartres: the letter received from Eugenius III which damned the project with faint praise.[37]

The pope's approval for any new expedition to the Holy Land was vital. Should it be given wholeheartedly, it would exercise great influence over the decision of the assembly at Chartres. Eugenius, however, expressed serious reservations. He had already seen the disastrous failure of one crusade. He had no wish to be associated with another. In his letter of April 25,[38] fifteen days before Chartres, he equivocated. "He had," he said, "many fears about this project inspired by King Louis, and dared not take the initiative in advising a crusade, deploring as he did the recent loss and bloodshed of so many thousands of brave men who had perished." However, so as not to upset the project, he asked Suger to have prior discussions with the king and his barons. If they found themselves disposed towards restarting this perilous undertaking, then he would offer the usual counsel, advice and remission of sins as he had granted five years previously. The last thing that the pope wanted was to be seen to upset any such plan once it had been agreed.

In the event, and with no successful military leader being available, an exceptional but understandable decision was reached by the council. Spiritual and military leadership were to be embodied in one person under the guidance of the Holy Spirit.[39] No one could fulfill this role better than Bernard, whose every action seemed to follow such guidance. Having made this decision by a unanimous vote, the council members rapidly dispersed to deal with other pressing matters, leaving Bernard to ponder their decision. As Watkin Williams suggests, his first reaction must have been to dismiss the whole suggestion as a laughing matter, *une chose pour rire*.[40]

There were various reactions among those most affected by this extraordinary and unprecedented proposal. The king was more excited than the barons, whose reactions were, at best, lukewarm. The Templars and the ordinary soldiers might have been expected to approve, especially as Bernard had so characteristically thought to console them at the moment of their deepest humiliation. But what of those who had not attended the Council of Chartres? What of Bernard himself — and bearing in mind their earlier strictures, what of the monks of Clairvaux and the whole Order of Cîteaux?

First, those who did not attend. In spite of their protestations, we might assume that, like the archbishop of Lyons, they perhaps knew what was afoot, and wished to save themselves the embarrassment of being present to voice their fundamental objections. So far as the pope was concerned, we have to take into account the dilemma Eugenius faced by having already agreed to support decisions made at the council and by upholding the tradition, so clearly expounded by Urban II, that the participation of monks in crusades should be restricted.[41] The attitude of Bernard himself would be crucial. If Bernard was in favor of the proposal, the pope could raise doubts. If Bernard was against, Eugenius could support the decision without too much harm arising. Papal damage-limitation at its best!

In the last part of his letter no. 256 addressed to Eugenius, Bernard refers to the decision of the council to appoint him as military leader of the new crusade — just like a commander or prince.[42] On a matter such as this, Eugenius had to take soundings before coming to a decision to approve or not. He was helped by Bernard's initial reaction. Although the unanimous election by the council was a compliment, powerful reasons prevented Bernard from accepting immediately. His response is that expected of a Cistercian monk. "You may rest assured," he tells Eugenius, "not only that such a proposal was made contrary to my advice and my wishes and that I am still of the same mind with regard to it, but that to give it effect is quite beyond my powers in so far as I am able to judge them. Who am I," he asks rhetorically, "to lead an army into battle, to march at the head of the troops? What could be further from my profession, even if the strength and necessary skills were not lacking in me?"[43] Here, Bernard places himself in the hands of Eugenius to know God's will. "Do not abandon me to the will of men," he begs, "but since it is your particular mission, try to know the plans of God and have his will done on earth as it is in Heaven!" Eugenius eventually confirmed the decision of the council but, mistakenly, did not modify the proposal. There were dangers in allowing Bernard, a sixty-year-old monk in such ill health, to be in supreme military command. It would indeed have been something at which to laugh or to ridicule. However, the extension of his spiritual preaching to his physical presence at the front of the army might well have led to untold benefits. Bernard had by no means lost the power to attract and hold the attention of a crowd and lead them where they should go!

This problem of leadership was inextricably linked to the question of morale. Who else could overcome the absence of this essential quality in the knighthood of the time but Bernard himself?[44] Had not Reynald, abbot of Morimond, on Bernard's own orders, been inspired to call together the lords of Bassigny to take the Cross on Ascension Day 1146?[45] In a letter to Peter the Venerable, written in May-June 1150 Bernard repeats these orders, stressing again the desperate need for men to do God's work.[46] Although Peter had been absent from Chartres, his letter had been by no means unfavorable.[47] Bernard reflects that the hearts of the princes are tepid. "They bear their swords without a cause and the knights have defected. As you know," he writes, "at the Council of Chartres, *little or nothing was done* and much had been hoped and expected from your presence. I beseech you to be with us at another council, arranged to be held at the royal palace at

Compiègne on July 15, where what is right and proper should be done, as necessity requires — and the necessity is great indeed!"[48]

It seems that Eugenius had not fully listened to Bernard. Suger must also have felt the need to tell him what had occurred at Chartres, but we do not have a copy of the letter he wrote. The pope, in his reply from Albano dated June 19, 1150,[49] praised and thanked Suger for all his concern to get aid for the Holy Land. "This affair," he said, "troubles me greatly. I cannot refuse my consent to the demand that you and the others who have written to me have made, although it costs me dearly to do any harm to that person chosen unanimously and whose infirmity I know"[50] — obviously here referring to Bernard. Eugenius, still prevaricating, recommended that Suger should act with prudence and discretion. Perhaps this new council of the church at Compiègne would consider the matter and, incidentally, also deal with the reform of the highly irregular canons of St. Corneille who seemed to be in occupation there.[51] Subsequent documents reveal much activity over the reform of the canons, replaced by monks from St. Denis, but nothing more about Bernard's position nor indeed any further details of the Council of Compiègne, set for July 1150. It seems probable that it never took place at all and that the question of Bernard's leadership was to be quietly dropped.

The final piece of evidence is found in that brief extract from the *Continuatio Premonstratensis* already cited. The chronicler says that the pope had enjoined Bernard to place himself at the head of the crusaders to encourage the others. Then, in the next line, he states laconically that the entire proposal was completely wrecked by the attitude of the Cistercians.[52]

Cistercian sources are silent on this matter. They contain no record of a council at Chartres, nor is any mention made of Bernard's election — with one voice — as the leader of the new crusade. Surely we cannot blame this important yet solitary entry on Premonstratensian hostility alone. The Cistercians themselves had good reasons for wishing to halt this project. These may have combined a concern for the welfare and health of Bernard, a desire that Clairvaux should have the services of its outstanding abbot for as long as possible, and that members of the Order should be discouraged from taking on tasks beyond those for which it was originally formed. In all this, given the outstanding qualities of Bernard, it may have been his health and his age which were the deciding factors. Yet, in spite of both, Bernard had, it seems, at Chartres, once more preached a great crusading sermon, irresistibly provoking men to turn towards Jerusalem. But the Cistercians already recognized that they had a saint on their hands — and no saint could be allowed to risk becoming a laughing stock! Is it possible therefore that Eugenius, former monk and Bernard's pupil at Clairvaux, with the full knowledge and encouragement of the Cistercian Order, prevaricated — as we have seen — and in the end withheld his consent? As it happened, it was all for the best, because Suger died early in 1151 and Bernard on August 20, 1153. Nearly sixty years later, when Pope Innocent III, who was accustomed to using the Cistercians in a wide range of activities, made a sharp change in papal policy,[53] a St. Bernard of the day, in a position of leadership, would have been received very differently. Innocent and Bernard together would have made an irresistible combination — as Innocent himself recognized through the very special veneration he gave to the abbot of Clairvaux![54]

NOTES

1. *Cont. Praemon.*, p. 455.
2. Brial.
3. Jaffé-Loewenfeld, vol. 2, no. 9385; Eugenius III, *Epistolae*, in: RHGF, vol. 15, letter 67, p. 457.
4. Vacandard, vol. 2, pp. 442-50; Seguin; Willems; Delaruelle, "Bernard"; Constable, "Second Crusade." I have not seen: Pognon.
5. Suger, *Epistolae*, letter 107, in: RHGF, vol. 15, p. 523.
6. Peter the Venerable, *Sel. Ltrs*, pp. 87-8.
7. Geoffrey of Auxerre, *Vita 1*, cols. 411-12; Moore.
8. Bernard, *Opera*, vol. 8, letter 245, p. 136.
9. "Mandastis et oboedivi" (Bernard, *Opera*, vol. 8, letter 247, p. 141).
10. Geoffrey of Auxerre, *Vita 1* (PL, vol. 185, col. 412).
11. An excellent recent summary of the controversy is given in: Auberger. See also: Lekai, p. 42.
12. *Statuta Cisterciensis*, vol. 1, pp. 35-7.
13. Bernard, *Opera*, vol. 8, letter 253, pp. 149-55.
14. Lekai, pp. 34-47, esp. p. 42.
15. *Statuta Cisterciensis*, vol. 1, pp. 41-2.
16. Manrique, vol. 2, *anno* 1150, pp. 205-206.
17. Constable, "Study," esp. pp. 37-9.
18. Idung of Prüfening, *Cistercians*, pp. 51-3.
19. Bernard, *Opera*, vol. 8, letter 380, p. 344.
20. Bernard, *Opera*, vol. 8, letter 380, p. 344.
21. Suger, *Epistolae*, letter 107 (RHGF, vol. 15, p. 523).
22. Ibid.
23. Bernard, *Opera*, vol. 8, letter 364, pp. 318-19; Peter the Venerable, *Sel. Ltrs*, letter 163, pp. 87-8.
24. Peter the Venerable, *Sel. Ltrs*, letter 164, pp. 89-91; Brial, p. 516, n. 1.

25. Brial, p. 516, n. 1.
26. Suger, *Epistolae*, letter 108 (RHGF, vol. 15, pp. 523-24).
27. Suger, *Epistolae*, letter 107 (RHGF, vol. 15, p. 523).
28. Suger, *Epistolae*, letter 108 (RHGF, vol. 15, pp. 523-24).
29. Suger, *Epistolae*, letter 109 (RHGF, vol. 15, p. 524).
30. Suger, *Epistolae*, letter 110 (RHGF, vol. 15, pp. 524-25).
31. Constable, "Second Crusade", pp. 266-76; Willems, pp. 146-49.
32. Constable, "Lost Sermon".
33. Deuteronomy 32:30; Constable, "Lost Sermon", p. 52.
34. Constable, "Lost Sermon", p. 49.
35. Bernard, *De consideratione*, in: Bernard, *Opera*, vol. 3, pp. 413-14; Bernard, *On Consideration*, bk. 2, pp. 47-52, and esp. p. 48.
36. Bernard, *Opera* (PL) in: PL, vol. 182, letter 386, cols. 590-91.
37. Brial, p. 517, n. 1.
38. Brial, p. 517.
39. Bernard, *Opera*, vol. 8, letter 256, pp. 163-65.
40. Williams, p. 287.
41. Constable, "Second Crusade", pp. 269-70, n. 290.
42. "Quasi in ducem et principem" (Bernard, *Opera*, vol. 8, letter 256, pp. 164-5; Willems, p. 143).
43. Bernard, *Opera*, vol. 8, letter 256, pp. 163-65.
44. Constable, "Lost Sermon", p. 52.
45. Willems, p. 138.
46. "Negotium Dei" (Satabin, p. 321).
47. Peter the Venerable, *Sel. Ltrs*, pp. 164, 89-91.
48. "Nostis quod in Carnotensi conventu de negotio Dei aut parum aut nichil factum est" (Satabin, p. 323).
49. Eugenius III, *Epistolae*, letter 71 (RHGF, vol. 15, pp. 458-59).
50. "Propter imbecillitatem personae in qua omnium vota, Domino favente, concurrunt" (Brial, p. 521).
51. Constable, "Suger", esp. p. 15.
52. "Anno 1150, habitis per Franciam conventibus, jubente etiam Eugenio papa, ut abbas Clarevallensis Jerosolymam ad alios provocandos mitteretur, grandis iterum sermo de profectione transmarina celebratur, sed per Cistercienses monachos, totum cassatur" (*Cont. Praemon.*, p. 455).
53. Brundage, "Transformed Angel", esp. p. 57.
54. For Innocent's collect in honor of the abbot of Clairvaux, see: Innocent III, *Opera* (PL, vol. 214, cols. 1032-33).

the lower church of St. Clement are generally dated between 1149 and 1151, just after Arnold's return.[5]

The lower church is best known for its richly detailed cycle — originally twenty scenes in all — depicting Ezekiel's vision of the destruction and rebuilding of Jerusalem (fig.1). Sixteen scenes, fourteen of which survive today, are devoted to the destruction of the city; they appear in four quadri-partite vaults, one over each arm of the cruciform church. An additional four scenes, at the crossing, complete the cycle by depicting the rebuilding of the city. Christ in glory appears in the apse. In the semidome of the west end of the church is the Purification of the Temple (fig. 2). To the left, Christ was originally depicted entering the Temple — only fragments of the figure survive today — and on the right he drives the moneychangers from the Temple. Below, to the right, is a large figure of St. Michael, holding a sword. In the south end is the Transfiguration, and in the north, the Crucifixion (fig. 3). In the embrasures of two windows, virtues, wearing helmets and chain mail and wielding swords and lances, do battle with vices (fig. 4). Finally, in the niches of the north and south arms are four kings.[6]

The iconographic program just described is unprecedented in medieval art. The Purification of the Temple, here one of only three New Testament scenes, appears relatively rarely outside of densely illustrated manuscript cycles.[7] Furthermore, here it occupies the most prominent of the three semidomes, that in the west end of the church. Still more unusual is the meticulous account of Ezekiel's vision. Though eschatological imagery plays an important role in Romanesque art, the vision of Ezekiel is presented so elaborately in no other Romanesque monument. At Schwarzrheindorf, the vision occupies twenty scenes. Most of these are very unusual subjects; they appear elsewhere in only a handful of extant cycles, all manuscripts. But even the most comprehensive of the manuscripts includes no more than ten of the twenty scenes depicted at Schwarzrheindorf.[8] Thus, at least among extant Ezekiel cycles, the Schwarzrheindorf ensemble seems to stand alone. Something more than the widespread interest in eschatology must have influenced the program.

Despite its distinctiveness, the singular nature of the program has at times been overlooked. Krönig, for instance, simply called it a typical combination of Old Testament and New Testament scenes.[9] Demus acknowledged that aspects of the program are "puzzling",[10] but did not comment further. Other scholars recognized the idiosyncratic nature of the program, and examined it more closely. Neuss described the frescoes as unique in Romanesque painting and proposed that Rupert of Deutz's commentary on the Book of Ezekiel was the source of the program.[11] Most later writers similarly acknowledged the influence of Rupert.[12] Königs also associated the cycle with contemporary outbreaks of anti-semitism in the Rhineland.[13]

Given the complexity of the program, it seems probable that several layers of meaning were intended here. Königs' proposal that the cycle has anti-semitic overtones is almost certainly correct. Though Königs did not cite the work of Rupert of Deutz in this context, Rupert's *Commentary on the Minor Prophets* reflects his concern about the Jewish communities in the Rhineland, who he viewed as "enemies of Christ and His Church", and at one level, the program at Schwarzrheindorf may well have been intended to depict Christianity's victory over Judaism.[14] Certain details, such as the Judenhut worn by the merchants in the Purification of the Temple, would seem to confirm such a reading.

However, these anti-semitic elements are far from incompatible with the suggestion that the cycle also reflects the crusades. A close relationship between anti-semitism and crusading fervor has been well documented; Muslims were likewise viewed as "enemies of Christ and His Church", and German crusaders were equally vehement in their animosity toward both groups.[15] In several important ways, the Schwarzrheindorf frescoes appear to be specifically linked with crusading ideology. First, the subject of the Ezekiel frescoes, with their emphasis on Jerusalem, the punishment of the wicked and the ultimate triumph of the righteous, seems singularly appropriate for a returning crusader: though the Second Crusade had failed, the frescoes make clear that those violating the holy places will be punished in the end. In fact, in tenor, themes and even, at times, language, Ezekiel's vision of the destruction of Jerusalem anticipates the crusading rhetoric of the late eleventh and twelfth centuries. From Urban II to St. Bernard, those preaching the crusades repeatedly sounded the same themes: the holy places (sanctuaries, altars, and so on) are being polluted (violated, threatened, defiled, and so on) by the enemy.[16] This is precisely the theme of much of the vision of Ezekiel that is illustrated here. At times even the specific language used by Urban and Bernard seems to evoke Ezekiel. "Polluerunt templum sanctum meum", stated Urban at Clermont, according to Baldric of Bourgueil.[17] The phrase recalls similar phrases that recur repeatedly in Ezekiel: "polluerunt sanctuarium meum" (Ez. 23:38), or "polluerunt sanctuaria mea" (Ez. 22:26), or "polluerunt nomen sanctum meum" (Ez. 43:8).[18] Both Urban and Ezekiel referred to "abominations" perpetrated by those defiling holy sites.[19] St. Bernard used similar language in his exhortations to potential crusaders: he repeatedly decried the danger to the holy places, which would be "polluted" by the sacrileges of the enemy. Thus in his letters we find "polluerunt templum sanctum tuum" or "et polluant loca sancta"[20]

— echoing Urban and, ultimately, Ezekiel. The last quotation comes from a letter addressed to the East Franks and Bavarians, which Otto of Freising quoted at length.[21]

These echoes of Ezekiel in crusading rhetoric may help us understand the remarkably detailed treatment of Ezekiel's vision in the chapel of a returning crusader. And the specific aspects of the vision emphasized here seem to confirm its meaning: consistently the scenes evoke the passages from Ezekiel that stress the defiling of the holy places, the massacre of the godless and the vindication of the blessed — all of which would presumably have given comfort to the defeated crusaders. A closer examination of the specific subjects and passages illustrated here will suggest their relevance to crusading ideology.

The cycle begins with the vault in the east end of the church (fig. 1). Of the two scenes still visible, one merely sets the stage by illustrating an early passage of Ezekiel's vision, the wheel within a wheel (Ez. 1:15). The other, however, establishes the militaristic tenor of the frescoes by depicting the siege of Jerusalem, from Ez. 4: 1-3. The choice of a siege, which will here end in triumph, may have had special resonance for Arnold and Conrad, whose similar efforts had failed. Even in Ezekiel cycles, this subject is most unusual.[22]

The south arm (fig. 1) illustrates Ez. 5: 1-5: the prophet is instructed to shave his head and divide his hair into thirds, then burn a third, cut up a third, and scatter a third to the wind. As seen in Ez. 5:11, these actions prophesy the ultimate destruction of the enemy: "As I live, says the Lord God, because you have defiled my holy place with all your vile and abominable rites, I in turn will consume you without pity . . . . One third of your people shall die by pestilence . . . one third shall fall by the sword . . . and one third I will scatter to the four winds . . . ."

The west arm (fig. 1) depicts the specific "vile and abominable rites" deplored by the Lord. Within the city gate of Jerusalem, the wicked kneel before an idol and worship reptiles and rodents perched on an altar (Ez. 8:6-8). Thus here we find a graphic demonstration of the defiling of the holy places that so inflamed crusaders' passions from Urban II to St. Bernard. The Turks were described repeatedly in crusader rhetoric as "sacrilegious" or "idol-worshippers". According to Baldric of Bourgeuil, Urban II denounced the "idols" of the Turks: "But why do we pass over the Temple of Solomon, nay of the Lord, in which the barbarous nations placed their idols . . ."; according to Robert the Monk, he lamented the altars "defiled by the uncleanness" of the Turks.[23] Again, these themes are extremely unusual in Christian art.[24]

The cycle of the destruction of Jerusalem culminates in the north arm (fig. 1) with frescoes illustrating Ez. 9:1-11. The first depicts six axe-wielding men, "those appointed to punish the city" (Ez. 9:1). Next, from Ez. 9:4-6, is the marking of the elect with the Tau; the executioners are directed to mark and spare all who have not taken part in the "abominations". The Tau was identified with the cross in medieval exegesis; here, the Crucifixion appears just below the scene, making the connection explicit (fig. 3). Verdier has published a group of twelfth-century enamels, some produced around Cologne, depicting the marking with the Tau; several bear inscriptions designating those marked as "signati".[25] The meaning of this scene for crusaders, who also described themselves as "signati", signed with the cross, must have been inescapable.[26] At times, in fact, crosses were said to have appeared specifically on foreheads as portents of the crusades, and one crusading abbot is said to have burned a cross on his forehead.[27] Thus the crusaders, signed like those spared in Ezekiel's vision, were again reassured that their taking of the cross meant ultimate salvation. Most gratifying of all must have been the last fresco of the group, where the godless are hewn down by executioners following the directive of the Lord: "Kill without pity."

In the crossing (fig. 1) the scene shifts to the reconstruction of Jerusalem (Ez. 40-44), the final vindication of the faithful. A man measures the city to begin the rebuilding, and in pointed reference to those who had defiled the holy places, priests sacrifice to the Lord on a newly purified altar. In another scene, the Lord appears on the reconsecrated altar. Thus the full cycle of the Ezekiel scenes forcibly makes its themes clear: the wicked have defiled the holy places; they will be punished mercilessly; Jerusalem will be restored to the just; the righteous will triumph in the end.

Almost all of the other frescoes of the lower church can also be interpreted in the context of the Second Crusade. The most prominent of the three semidomes, that in the west end of the church, depicts the unusual theme of the Purification of the Temple (fig. 2). It is probably not coincidental that St. Bernard, who personally persuaded Conrad III to join the Second Crusade, wrote at length about just this episode in his *De Laude Novae Militae*, written to the master of the Knights Templars:

> ... the zeal of these knights for the house of God burns with the self-same fervor as that of the Leader of the knights who, violently angered, entered the temple, scattered the coins of the changers, and overthrew the tables of those selling doves .... For he thought it disgraceful that the house of prayer should be sullied by merchants of this type. Moved by the example of their King, this devout army, recognizing that it is far more disgraceful and far more insupportable for the holy

places to be polluted with infidels than to be infested by merchants, now remain in the holy house . . . .[28]

The New Testament accounts of the Purification of the Temple do not include references to the "polluted" holy places, but the phrase is so evocative of Ezekiel's vision that Leclerc and Rochais cite Ez. 22, 26 as Bernard's source.[29] Thus, this passage appears to fuse the Purification of the Temple with elements from the vision of Ezekiel, just as the frescoes at Schwarzrheindorf bring together these two biblical texts. To make the connection still clearer, the Purification of the Temple is placed immediately below the group of four scenes depicting the worship of idols, reptiles, etc. (fig. 2) — that is, the "pollution" decried by Bernard. Finally, though this scene occurs only rarely outside manuscript illumination, it does appear at Saint-Gilles du Gard, which housed the Templars. O'Meara has clearly demonstrated the crusading content of the scene there, and indeed of much of the program.[30]

Just below the Purification is a bust-length image of St. Michael (fig. 2). Though the archangel has no immediately obvious connection with that scene, his inclusion in the cycle and especially his placement next to the Purification makes sense in the context of the crusades. Michael, the patron of soldiers, served crusaders as guide and heavenly protector, and occasionally appeared in crusader epics to announce victory.[31]

The other two semidomes, depicting the Crucifixion (fig. 3) and the Transfiguration, also may be interpreted in light of the crusades. The Crucifixion works in the program on a number of levels; in particular, it gives special prominence to the cross, symbol par excellence of the crusaders. The Transfiguration has long been interpreted as prefiguring the second coming of Christ; according to Matthew 16, 27, just before the Transfiguration, Christ states, "For the Son of man shall come in the glory of his Father with his angels; and then he shall reward every man according to his works."[32] Thus this scene may have again been a reassuring reference to the ultimate triumph of Christ and his defenders.

Even the secondary scenes may reiterate the same themes. First, the four seated rulers may represent, as Demus has suggested, the four emperors Augustus, Constantine, Theodosius and Charlemagne.[33] The emperors, especially Constantine and Charlemagne, were revered as military exemplars by the crusaders, as Constable and others have shown.[34] Finally, the battle of the virtues and vices (fig. 4) again celebrates the ultimate victory of the just, and its relevance here seem fairly clear; both Seidel and Norman have already associated this theme with the struggle against Islam.[35]

This dual theme, then — the final victory of the just, the final defeat of the enemy — seems to have been chosen to reassure the defeated crusaders of the righteousness of their mission and the ultimate triumph of the virtuous. When they gathered for the consecration of St. Clement in 1151, Arnold and his patron Conrad III must have been pleased.[36]

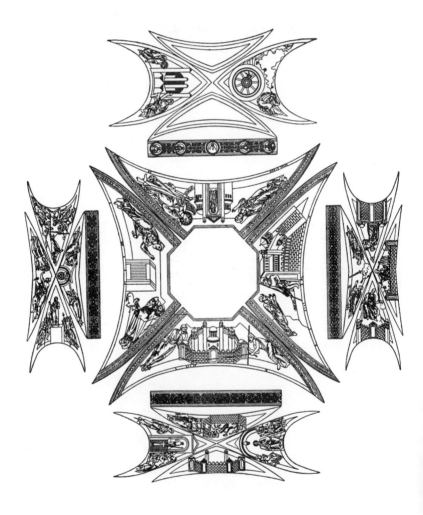

Fig. 1. The Vision of Ezekiel, lower church, St. Clement, Schwarzrheindorf (from Verbeek)

Fig. 2. The Purification of the Temple, lower church, St. Clement, Schwarzrheindorf (from Neu).

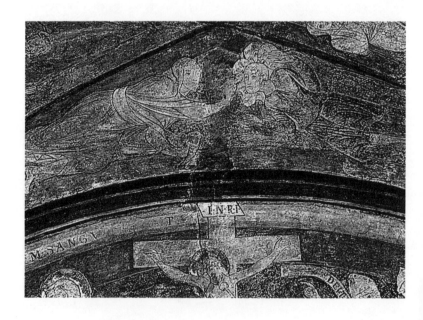

Fig. 3. The Crucifixion, lower church, St. Clement, Schwarzrheindorf (from Königs)

Fig. 4. Virtues and Vices, lower church, St. Clement, Schwarzrheindorf (from Verbeek)

NOTES

I am endebted to Jaroslav Folda and Louis Jordan for their careful reading of this paper and their perceptive comments. Thanks are also due to Ulrike Kölch, Julia Miller, Joanne Norman, Jonathan Riley-Smith, and William Tronzo. The research for this paper was supported by a grant from the Hood College Board of Associates.

1. See: Folda, "Painting", with extensive bibliography. He is currently preparing a monograph on crusader art.
2. See: Katzenellenbogen; O'Meara; Seidel, *Songs*; Seidel, "Images"; Seidel, "Holy Warriors"; Denny.
3. On the church and its frescoes see: Neuss, *Ezechiel*, pp. 265-97; Verbeek; Kunische; Demus, pp. 604-606; Neu; Frizen; Königs. The frescoes, which were once covered by whitewash, have been extensively repainted, but their outlines, at least, are an accurate reflection of the original compositions (Neuss, *Ezechiel*, pp. 267-68; Verbeek, pp. xxxvi-xxxix; Demus, p. 604). The frescoes in the upper church are generally believed to date from the 1170s.
4. For the full text of the inscription, see: Verbeek, pl. 1.
5. But Demus (p. 606) has suggested that they were executed in the 1160s, after Arnold's death, when the church belonged to the Benedictine nunnery founded by Arnold's sister.
6. For a photograph of the Transfiguration and of one of the kings, see: Demus, fig. 249.
7. The scene is generally confined to fairly comprehensive cycles. The Index of Christian Art cites only two other twelfth-century fresco cycles that include it: one, now destroyed, from the Cathedral of Peterborough, the other from St. Martin, Zillis. Both were vast programs; the Index lists over one hundred narrative scenes at both sides. One of the few other monumental examples from the twelfth century is a relief at St. Gilles-du-Gard (see O'Meara).
8. The group consists of three manuscripts, all from the eleventh century: the Roda Bible (Paris, Bibliothèque Nationale, lat. 6); the Farfa Bible (Vatican Library, lat. 5729) (on both see: Neuss, *Bibelillustration*, pp. 10-15 [Roda], pp. 16-28 [Farfa]); and the commentary on Ezekiel by Haymo of Auxerre (Paris, Bibliothèque Nationale, lat. 12302; on which, see: Neuss, *Ezechiel*, pp. 298-307). Of the twenty scenes from Ezekiel at Schwarzrheindorf, eight appear in the Roda Bible, six in the Farfa Bible and ten in Haymo's Commentary. From the mid-thirteenth century, a few other comprehensive Ezekiel cycles have survived, one in a Bible Moralisée in Paris (Bibliothèque Nationale, lat. 11560; see: Laborde, vol. 3 [1915], pls.

408-27), and another in a window of the Sainte Chapelle (see: *Corpus Vitrearum*, vol. 1, pls. 408-27).

9. Krönig, p. 162.
10. Demus, p. 606; see also p. 36.
11. Neuss, *Ezechiel*, pp. 285-89.
12. Verbeek, p. liv; Kunisch, pp. 45, 93; Neu, p. 51.
13. Königs, pp. 27-8.
14. See: Van Engen, pp. 241-48. I owe these observations to Louis Jordan.
15. For instance see: Riley-Smith, "Persecution"; Riley-Smith, *First Crusade*, pp. 54-55.
16. For the importance of this general theme, see the numerous references to crusading chronicles in Riley-Smith, *First Crusade*, p. 147. See also: Rousset, *Origines*, pp. 58-9, 156.
17. RHC Oc., vol. 4, p. 14. Baldric's introduction includes a similar phrase: "pollutum est...sanctum Dei templum" (vol. 4, p. 11).
18. Very similar themes and language do occur elsewhere, such as in the Psalms; see esp.: Psalms 74 and 79. But a Latin concordance reveals that *polluo*, to pollute, and *violo*, to defile, occur in Ezekiel far more often than in any other book of the Bible. I am grateful to Louis Jordan for this observation.
19. Urban, from Baldric of Bourgueil: "oculis vestris viditis quantae abominationi traditum sint" (RHC Oc., vol. 4, p. 15); Ezekiel 5:11: "sanctum meum violasti . . . in cunctis abominationibus tuis"; Ezekiel 43:8: "polluerunt nomen sanctam meum in abominationibus quas fecerunt." "Abominationis" also appears far more often in Ezekiel than in other books of the Bible.
20. The phrases are from letters 510 and 363 (Bernard, *Opera*, vol 8, pp. 468 and 311. For similar themes, see letters 457 and 458 (Bernard, *Opera*, vol 8, pp. 432-33, 434-37), and the passage cited in: Rousset, *Origines*, pp. 156-57.
21. See: Otto of Freising, *Gesta* 2, p. 212.
22. The Index of Christian Art lists only three other examples of the siege of Jerusalem.
23. Baldric of Bourgueil: "Sed quid Templum Salomonis, immo Domini praetermisimus, in quo simulacra sua barbarae nationes contra jus et fac modo collocata venerunter?" (RHC Oc., vol. 4, p. 14; tr. in: Krey, *First Crusade*, p. 33. Robert the Monk: "altaria suis foeditibus inquinata" (RHC Oc., vol. 3, p. 727; tr. in Krey, *First Crusade*, p. 30). Despite the inaccuracy of the charge, crusaders frequently described their Muslim opponents as idol-worshippers, as several scholars have noted (Munro, "Western", pp. 331-32; Southern, *Islam*; Bray; Camille, pp. 129-50.
24. For extant examples, see the works cited in note 8.
25. Verdier. Though Verdier does not associate the theme with the crusades, it is interesting that it appears especially in the twelfth century. Verdier (p. 40), quotes Peter Damian (sermon 48: "Homilia de exaltatione sanctae

crucis", in: PL, vol. 144, col. 775) as drawing a connection between the Tau and the carrying of the cross: "The wicked who refused to carry their cross and follow their redeemer will be dealt with as announced in Ezekiel." The carrying of the cross was closely associated with the preaching of the crusades. According to the *Gesta Francorum* (p. 1), Urban referred to that passage in exhorting his audience.

26. For instance see: Sigebert de Gembloux: "virtute et signo sanctae crucis signati et armait . . .", in: Rousset, *Origines*, p. 105; Riley-Smith, *First Crusade*, pp. 41, 114. Urban II used a similar phrase: "tanta hominum multitudo cruce signata est" (PL, vol. 151, col. 485; see also: Delaruelle, *Croisade*, p. 55, n. 45).

27. For crosses on the forehead as portents, see: Ekkehard, *Hierosolymita* (RHC Oc., vol. 5, ch. 10, p. 19). For Abbot Baldwin, see: Guibert of Nogent, RHC Oc., vol. 4, pp. 182-83. Both are cited by McGinn (*Iter*, pp. 68-9, n. 110).

28. Bernard, *De laude* (in Bernard, *Opera*, vol. 3, p. 222, lines 14-24): " . . . eodem pro domo Dei fervere milites zelo, quo ipse quondam militum Dux, vehementissime inflammatus . . . introivet in templum, negotiantes expulit, nummulariorum effudit aes et cathedras vendentium columbas evertit, indignissimum iudicans orationis domum huiuscemodi forensibus incestari. Talis proinde sui Regis permotus exemplo devotus exercitus, multo sane indignius longeque intolerabilius arbitrans sancta pollui ab infidelibus quam a mercatoribus infestari, in domo sancta . . . occupantur" (tr. in: Herlihy, p. 296).

29. Bernard, *Opera*, vol. 3, p. 222, biblical citation for line 21.

30. O'Meara, pp. 95-157 (esp. pp. 144-45).

31. In the *Chanson des chétifs*, see: Hatem, p. 382. See also: Rojdestrensky, pp. 39-40. Especially interesting in the context of the crusades are Mâle's comments on the iconographic transformation during the twelfth century of St. Michael to "a knight giving battle" (Mâle, pp. 261-62).

32. See: Schiller, vol. 1, p. 146.

33. Demus, p. 605. Verbeek (p. xlvii) proposed that they represent four old empires that will give way to the kingdom of Christ, an idea derived from Rupert of Deutz. But given the prominence of the kings — they are considerably larger than the other figures in the chapel — it seems unlikely that they were intended to be read this way.

34. For instance see: Constable, "Second Crusade", pp. 229-30, 239; Rousset, *Origines*, pp. 75-6, 131. Theodosius also appears occasionally (see: Erdmann, *Origin*, p. 239).

35. Seidel ("Holy Warriors", pp. 36-7) stresses the Reconquista, and Norman (pp. 47, 56, 98, 147-48) has extended her arguments to the crusades.

36. Crusading continued to be important to members of the Wied family well into the thirteenth century. Röhricht (*Beiträge*, vol. 2) lists several Wieds: Count Dietrich on the Third Crusade (p. 351); Count George, his brother Archbishop Dietrich, and a Gerard of Wied on the Fifth Crusade (p. 377). I am grateful to Jonathan Riley-Smith for his help with this point.

15

Donations to the Hospitallers in England in the Wake of the Second Crusade

Michael Gervers

The evidence upon which this chapter is based derives largely from English private charters of the twelfth century. Since such charters, not to mention a fair percentage of royal and episcopal ones as well, are not regularly dated until a good century and a half after the end of the Second Crusade, some of the conclusions presented here must remain tentative.

There is no doubt that the Order of the Hospital of St. John of Jerusalem grew out of the First Crusade, and that its official foundation can be attached to a papal charter issued in 1113.[1] It was not, however, until probably 1128 that the Order first appeared in England. There is no indication that before that time the Hospitallers held any property in the country whatsoever. Within the decade, though, and on at least one occasion before the death of King Henry I in 1135, a few grants were made. The first recorded donor was Letitia, of the Ferrières family, who granted a mill at Passenham, Northamptonshire *in tempore primi Henrici regis*.[2] Probably at about the same time, Richard son of William Sorrell granted eighty acres of arable land in Chrishall, Essex.[3] Before his death in 1142, Robert d'Oilly conveyed land at Gosford in Oxfordshire, which for a short time served as a living for a sister of the Order.[4] Sometime during the 1140s (a date of c. 1145 has been suggested), Jordan son of Ralph of Bricett founded the English priory of the Order of St. John at Clerkenwell, near London.[5] This was a significant act, indeed, as theretofore the English lands of the Hospitallers appear to have been administered by the Order's French priory at St. Gilles.[6] In the absence of a priory to serve as an administrative center, there could be no English Order to speak of. Without such a center, there was no place for the regional administrative unit known as the preceptory. These preceptories were small rural foundations consisting often of a manor house and the possession of the advowson of a nearby church or chapel. There was usually one such center per county, and occasionally two, provided the Order held sufficient property there to warrant it. Not infrequently, there were site changes between the twelfth and thirteenth centuries, and during the transition two preceptories may have been operational simultaneously.

The establishment of preceptories followed closely upon that of the priory at Clerkenwell. While the distinction is not always clear between manors which served as preceptories and manors which did not, a network began to grow with about three in the 1140s, seven in the 1150s, three in the 1160s, two in the 1170s, three in the 1180s and one to five in the 1190s.[7] All of these started as major conveyances described in the deed of grant as land, a manor, a church, or all three.

It was generally the acquisition of the church which determined the location of the preceptory. This is not to say, however, that all Hospitaller churches became the sites of administrative centers. The Order possessed far more churches than preceptories, as is evidenced by the case of Essex where, in the twelfth century, it held seven churches and one preceptory. Of those early grants of churches which led to the establishment of preceptories throughout England, four were made c. 1148 - 54,[8] another four in the 1160s and 1170s,[9] two in the 1180s[10] and four others before 1199.[11]

From the foregoing it is apparent that the Hospitallers received relatively little support in England prior to the fall of Edessa in the last days of December 1144. It is tempting to surmise that the foundation of the priory at Clerkenwell by Jordan Bricett c. 1145 was an immediate and emotional response to the fate of Edessa, and that the major grants of manors and churches in the later 1140s and the 1150s, leading to the foundation of rural preceptories, were prompted at least in part by the spirit of the crusade. In this regard, certainly, the 1150s was for the Hospitallers the most active decade of the century.

Was this, then, the wake of the Second Crusade? Perhaps, but to do justice to the Order's economic and territorial expansion in England, one may extend that wake for the full length of the period between the Second and Third Crusades, that is from c. 1150 to the visit of the Patriarch of Jerusalem, Heraclius, to England seeking support for a crusade in 1185.[12]

Rather than attempt to view the growth of the Hospitallers' estate in the country as a whole, we shall for the moment confine our remarks to a consideration of the county of Essex. The county is significant for this purpose as it is the best documented. The Order appears from surviving sources to have acquired more individual pieces of property there than in any other county in England. It is also the county for which all extant conveyances to the Order have been dated.[13] Twelve hundred of the approximately 3,000 deeds of grant preserved in the British Library in the Order's Great Cartulary concern Essex. Of these, 135, approximately 11 percent, belong to the twelfth century. Two or three may be as early as the 1130s, while six or seven can probably be assigned to the 1140s. There is then a sudden jump to between twenty-seven and thirty-five conveyances, somewhere between 20 percent and 26 percent, for the 1150s; between 11 percent and 15 percent for the 1160s; between 19 percent and 25 percent for the 1170s; between 18 percent and 23 percent for the 1180s; and between 6 percent and 11 percent for the 1190s. As was the case for major donations of churches and manors throughout England as a whole, the 1150s appear to have been the most active decade of the century. Following a brief drop in the 1160s, the 1170s and 1180s provide rather similar percentages.

Ninety-nine (73 percent) of the twelfth-century transactions consisted of arable land. While the quantity in nearly a third of these is unspecified, amounts in another third represent small conveyances of one to three acres. Given the likelihood that most of the unspecified amounts transferred were also small, it is probable that nearly 85 percent of the individual grants of arable were under ten acres in size. While the remainder range up to a maximum of ninety acres, the majority are often so small that their economic value is difficult to determine. The second most common type of conveyance was rent, of which there were fourteen, equalling 10 percent of the total. These range in amount from 1d to £1/0/0, or 240d.

Were these many small grants a reflection of popular piety, or token donations made by wealthy landowners, perhaps to placate members of an energetic young order seeking to build a domain in an already heavily settled county? We have suggested elsewhere that the latter may, in some cases, have been the more likely scenario.[14] Small grants were certainly made by small landholders, but they were also made by lords of considerable means who could obviously have given more had they been so inclined. For example, Simon of Wares, who by eight separate charters gave approximately fifty acres of land to the Augustinian Canons at their Essex priory of Little Dunmow, made grants of but one acre each to the Hospitallers and the Templars. The contrary also occurred. William son of Audelin, the steward of King Henry II, and his wife Juliana, granted to the Hospitallers the entire vill and church of Little Maplestead (the site of the Order's Essex preceptory in the thirteenth century), yet made only a one-acre grant to the same Dunmow canons. Each donor quite obviously had his or her preferred recipient.[15]

It cannot be said that the Hospitallers stood by and waited for prospective donors to come their way, or that the development of their estate was carried out by happenstance. It is quite likely, for example, that the Order solicited a certain Alfred de Bendaville for a church at a place in Essex called Chaureth, which he granted it in 1151. Chaureth became their first Essex preceptory and remained so until the second quarter of the thirteenth century when it was replaced by the more accessible site at Little Maplestead. Both lay in northern Essex, however, and it was in the north that the Order's economic activity in the county would be concentrated for the duration of its existence in England. In this context, an extremely interesting phenomenon occurs in the third quarter of the twelfth century. From c. 1150 to c. 1165, never before and probably not much thereafter, the Order can be clearly documented acquiring in perpetuity, or leasing at term, significant properties in exchange for annual rent or gersum, rather than settling for whatever might come by way of free alms. Seven conveyances, fully 15 percent of all surviving transactions issued to the Hospitallers in Essex in the 1150s and 1160s, are of this nature.[16] Thus, probably very shortly after the acquisition of Chaureth church in 1151, we find the Order paying £1/3/4 (280d) for a serf, his issue and chattels. The year after, in 1152, apparently in the same parish as the church, it undertook to pay 10s (120d) annually on a five-year lease of half a hide (approximately sixty acres) of land, in addition to a silver mark (160d) to a third party for the first two years of that lease. Also in that year, it agreed to pay 4s (48d) annually for three virgates (approximately ninety acres) of land with pannage for fifty pigs in the neighboring parish. At about the same time, it acquired a peasant holding in Chaureth for 12d annually and 12d down. Transactions such as these suggest that once the site for a preceptory had been determined, the Order was prepared to acquire with its own resources what was not forthcoming in free alms. Once it was clear that the Order was a feature on the landscape, donations seem to have come more easily of their own accord.

In view of the foregoing, can it be said that the Hospitallers' establishment and early growth in England were due to circumstances surrounding the Second Crusade? In an indirect way, it seems that they can. To confirm this supposition, one must compare the growth of the Hospitallers with that of the Templars and even of the Cistercians. All three orders appear to have been introduced to England in the same year, that is, in 1128.[17] In marked contrast to the Hospitallers, however, the initial growth of the Cistercians and Templars was phenomenal. While there is no evidence for the foundation of a Hospitaller priory or preceptory before c. 1145, the Cistercians had received a full 31 percent of their twelfth-century monastic foundations, and the Templars 26 percent of their administrative sites, before 1140. By the end of the 1150s, at which time the Hospitallers had acquired approximately 33 percent of their twelfth-century foundations, the Cistercians had received 77 percent and the Templars 62 percent. Thereafter, the contrast is reversed, particularly vis-à-vis the Cistercians. From 1160 to 1199 the number of their foundations increased by only 23 percent, compared with 38 percent for the Templars and 67 percent for the Hospitallers. For the latter, 54 percent was acquired in the last two decades of the century, compared with 23 percent for the Templars and 8 percent for the Cistercians. Perhaps most significant of all is that during the 1180s, sites for the Hospitallers' administrative network increased by 31 percent, for the Templars 17 percent and for the Cistercians only 5 percent.[18] During the second half of that decade the patriarch of Jerusalem visited England, Jerusalem fell to Saladin, the Saladin tithe was imposed in England and France, and the Third Crusade began.

One may suggest by way of conclusion a preliminary interpretation of the foregoing figures. The Cistercians and the Templars grew together during the first three decades of their existence in England, often with royal support and patronage. Cistercian growth dropped off markedly after 1153. This situation may be connected to the lack of success of the Second Crusade and the dissatisfaction expressed in some quarters with the involvement of Bernard of Clairvaux, or even to his death in that year. It may equally have had to do with the re-establishment of peace in England, after the nineteen-year anarchy under King Stephen, with the crowning of King Henry II in 1154. What then, can be said for the military orders, both of which flourished in the 1150s, especially the Templars? One may propose that the military orders received patronage in England precisely because they were military orders, and that that patronage was encouraged by popular support for the protection of the Holy Land. Why else, one might ask, would both the Templars and the Hospitallers choose to embellish their priories in London with round churches reminiscent of the Church of the Holy Sepulchre, if it were not to impress visually upon English society their direct connection with the Jerusalem mission?[19] It may also be argued that the sharp increase in the 1180s of grants to the military orders leading to the establishment of preceptories belongs in the context of the events leading up to the Third Crusade. Finally, and most importantly, if the Hospitallers in England received very little material support before c. 1145, it may well have been because before that time they were not, in fact, a military order. We know that St. Bernard encouraged the Hospitallers to participate in the Second Crusade in 1146.[20] There is no previous conclusive evidence that direct involvement in warfare was part of their professional mandate.[21] Their acceptance in 1146 may have been due not so much to the personal prestige of St. Bernard as to the realization that a military image was a better magnet for patronage than was service to pilgrims and the sick. Despite the unsuccessful conclusion of the Second Crusade, that expedition provided the springboard for a new departure from which the Hospitallers never looked back. They responded to what the number and chronology of English conveyances suggest was a marked preference on the part of donors to support military involvement in the defense of the Holy Land.

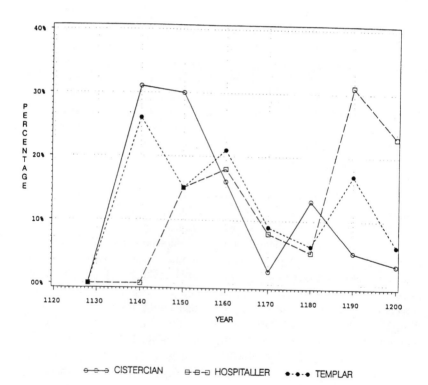

Fig. 5. Graph showing percentage growth of Cistercian, Templar and Hospitaller administrative centers in England from 1128 to 1200.

NOTES

1. *Cart. gén.*, vol. 1, no. 30.
2. *Cart. gén.*, vol. 1, no. 337.
3. *Cart. St. John II*, no. 215, pp. 134-35.
4. Knowles & Hadcock, pp. 300, 304.
5. Round, pp. 226, 228; see also: Taylor, p. 17.
6. BM, *Index to Charters*, p. 650a (Harl. 83 C.41); Riley-Smith, *Knights*, pp. 353, 357; Round, p. 226.
7. These numbers are based on information provided by Knowles & Hadcock, pp. 300-309. Four of the five preceptories included under the total for the 1190s are only known to have been granted before 1199, when they were confirmed by King John. Two others, not accounted for among those listed, were founded sometime before c. 1180, and one before 1189.
8. Mount St. John (Yorks. N), c. 1148; Chaureth (Essex), 1151; Ossington (Notts.) and Standon (Herts.), before 1154.
9. Slebech (Pembroke), c. 1161-76; Melchbourne (Beds.), before 1176; Harefield (Middlesex), c. 1176; Carbrooke (Norfolk), before 1180.
10. Buckland (Somerset), c. 1180; Little Maplestead (Essex), 1186.
11. Barrow (Derby); Trebeigh (Cornwall), Swinford (Leics.), Winkburn (Notts.). Barrow was founded during the reign of Henry II, and the three others sometime during the second half of the twelfth century.
12. On Heraclius' visit to England, see: Tyerman (1988), pp. 50-53.
13. *Cart. St. John I* and *Cart. St. John II*.
14. *Cart. St. John II*, pp. xxxix - xl.
15. *Cart. St. John II*, p. xxxix.
16. *Cart. St. John II*, nos. 334, 340, 355, 361, 372, 414, 416. No. 388 may also fall within this category (cf. no. 52).
17. *Records of Templars*, pp. xxxviii-xxxix; Donkin, pp. 15, 28-9; Hill, p. 27; Knowles and Hadcock, pp. 112-15.
18. The lists of foundations upon which these calculations are based derive largely from Knowles & Hadcock, pp. 112-15, 292-3, 300-301.
19. Gervers, pp. 363-65.
20. Riley-Smith, *Knights*, pp. 55 and n. 1, 58 and n. 7.
21. The acquisition by the Hospitallers of Bethgibelin castle in southern Palestine has been cited as the first evidence of the Order's involvement in military activity. Such evidence is not conclusive, however, as the context for their tenancy may have been colonial rather than defensive. The Order's military role is otherwise not attested until the following decade (Riley-Smith, *Knights*, pp. 52-3, 57-8, 435-37; see also: the chapter by Martin Hoch in this volume).

the events of the crusade would appear to have been lost in the hiatus between these works.[2] It also came as something of a disappointment to discover that neither of those two late twelfth-century gossips, Walter Map and Gerald Wales, has any comments on the crusade. Gerald, it is true, does have what I take to be an oblique reference: recalling his own preaching of the Third Crusade at Haverfordwest in 1188, he compared his success at moving an audience made up of Welshmen while speaking in a language they did not understand to Bernard's earlier success in preaching in French to the Germans.[3]

Gerald's memory of St. Bernard's role as a crusade preacher, though mentioned by Robert of Torigni, found few other echoes among the English writers of my period. Of the historians I have seen, only Ralph of Diceto made any significant allusion to his role. Ralph described Louis VII's conflict with the Church over the archbishopric of Bourges. The affair was resolved thanks to Bernard's mediation, and the king agreed to back down and go to Jerusalem to atone for the sacrilegious oath he had sworn during the quarrel. He thereupon took the cross and prepared for his crusade. The idea that Louis was concerned principally with a pilgrimage for the expiation of his sins rather than with undoing the damage wrought by the Muslim capture of Edessa has been discussed elsewhere by Aryeh Graboïs; Ralph of Diceto is the only one of these English writers to suggest that the motivation for the crusade was anything other than the needs of the Holy Land.[4]

Henry of Huntingdon and Robert of Torigni had followed the papal bull *Quantum Predecessores* in linking the crusade to the Muslim capture of Edessa, but it was William of Newburgh, writing in the late 1190s, who gave this theme its most full and most sophisticated treatment.[5] William was in no doubt that the crusade had come about as a direct response to the fall of Edessa, and he described the circumstances at length: Edessa had long been a bastion of Christendom; the faith of the people had stood firm at the time of Valens — here William has a historical tradition deriving ultimately from the *Historia Tripartita* — and the city had never at any time fallen to the Muslims — a misconception which may originate in the reference in *Quantum Predecessores* to the idea that Edessa had escaped Turkish occupation during the period of Byzantine collapse in the decades before the First Crusade. The fall of Edessa was blamed on its ruler, Joscelin, who had seduced the daughter of a certain Armenian; the father had then taken revenge by letting the Turks into the city. Where this story came from is not known — the idea that Edessa fell as the result of the treachery of one of its inhabitants is at variance with our other information — but William's account may not be entirely without foundation: William of Tyre similarly had heard reports of Joscelin's unsavory sexual behavior.[6]

No English author made any reference to the crusade on the eastern marches of Germany, but several followed Henry of Huntingdon or Robert of Torigni in mentioning the successes at Lisbon and in Spain. Henry had contrasted the absence of God's grace at the siege of Damascus with the divine aid that had attended the more lowly crusaders in Spain and Portugal and quoted the first epistle of St. Peter (5 v.5): "For God resisteth the proud, but giveth grace to the humble." He took evident pride in noting that the greater part of these men had come from England. But despite this English involvement, no one could add anything; Gervase of Canterbury, for example, was content simply to record the victories at Lisbon and Almeria, stripping away all Henry's theology.[7] It was the expeditions of Louis VII and Conrad III that continued to hold the center of attention.

So what went wrong? For Henry of Huntingdon, God had spurned the efforts of the crusaders: their fornication, adultery and other wickedness had earned His displeasure, and so it was that the armies were betrayed by the emperor of Constantinople and harried by the sword of the enemy; Louis' hope of restoring his reputation at Damascus had come to nothing as he lacked God's grace. Robert of Torigni was scarcely less theological in his explanation. He preferred not to dwell on the hardships, pestilence and enemy attacks suffered during the passage through the Byzantine empire, ascribing them to the oppression of the poor and the spoliation of churches that had attended the start of the expedition.[8] But of the later writers, only William of Newburgh, his near contemporary Gervase of Canterbury, and the early thirteenth-century Cistercian, Ralph of Coggeshall, attempted an answer that was not totally derivative.

Gervase and Ralph are notable for their secular tone. Gervase mentioned the foolhardiness of the crusaders and the efforts of the Saracens before going on to recount the story of how the Damascus expedition was frustrated by the treacherous dealings of the Templars, who accepted a huge bribe from the citizens to raise the siege only to discover too late that what they had thought were gold coins were in fact copper. Ralph of Coggeshall also reported that the siege was raised when the Templars accepted a bribe, although in his case he believed that it had been paid by Nūr al-Dīn.[9] The idea that Templar venality was to blame was not new — earlier writers including John of Salisbury and the Wurzburg Annalist had already repeated the allegation[10] — while other authors, notably William of Tyre and Michael the Syrian, alluded to a bribe which turned out to be in counterfeit money.[11] So far as I am aware, Gervase is the earliest writer to link the counterfeit bribe with the Templars, although the tale may have had a wide circulation; there is another version in the early thirteenth-century *Chronique d'Ernoul*.[12] But despite their popularity among later writers, it is most unlikely that these stories have any factual basis. The accusations against the Templars are clearly a further symptom of the mounting antipathy towards the Order which elsewhere in the later twelfth century found expression in the writings of, among others, William of Tyre and Walter Map,[13] while the story of the valueless bribe probably appealed to clerical writers because of its moral dimension, showing that avarice and treachery do not prosper. Both Gervase and William of Tyre spoke of the frustrated expectations of the recipients as nothing short of miraculous, although in Gervase's case there is more than a hint of sardonic irony.

William of Newburgh is very different. In his account we find theological and mundane explanations for the failure of the crusade juxtaposed at almost every turn.

> After entering Asia Minor . . . [the crusaders] experienced the treachery of the Greek emperor. Our forces, however, had indulged in certain excesses and had incurred his displeasure, and by their arrogant and uncontrolled behavior, they had fired the anger of Almighty God as well against them.[14]

There is here an extraordinary evenhandedness: Greek perfidy, understandable ill-will, divine retribution. All go together. William proceeds to discuss God's disfavor: alluding to the story in Joshua, ch. 7, of the sin of Achan and the Israelite's failure before Ai, he explains how the secret crime of just one man could turn God against His people. In the case of the crusade it was licentiousness in the camp that lay at the root of divine displeasure. Secondly, the crusaders were trusting in their own strength rather than relying on God, and William quotes the same verse from I Peter that Henry of Huntingdon had employed: "God resisteth the proud, but giveth grace to the humble." He then returns to mundane explanations: the crusaders plundered the Greeks; the emperor became hostile and withdrew food supplies; the army wasted away through hunger; it was prey to Muslim ambushes; the weather aggravated the crusaders' plight. Essentially what we have is a reworking of the material to be found in Henry of Huntingdon's account. But, unlike Henry, William was unable to see these events wholly in theological terms. As Professor Partner has remarked, "It is not that his stated critical and theological assumptions are very different from Henry's, but he feels greater trepidation about applying them."[15]

Having brought the remnants of the French and German armies to Jerusalem, William ended his account of the crusade abruptly: "They then returned ingloriously, having achieved nothing of note."[16] There is no reference at all to the Damascus campaign. Instead he described the death of Prince Raymond of Antioch in battle — this was in 1149 — and King Baldwin III of Jerusalem's rescue mission to northern Syria, and he then mentioned the capture of Gaza (c.1150) and Ascalon (1153). Once again God, who resisteth the proud, had given grace to the humble. Interestingly, William has nothing but praise for the Latins settled in the East.

So what conclusions, if any, can we draw? Clearly these late twelfth-century writers had only a limited fund of information at their disposal. New elements, such as Joscelin of Edessa's seduction of the Armenian woman, or the Templars' bribe that turned out to be of copper and not gold, are the sort of tales that could conceivably have found their way back to England with the crusaders returning from the Third Crusade, but it would be unwise to insist on this point.[17] John of Salisbury, the ablest and best-informed English commentator on the Second Crusade, was not writing in England and left no mark on later authors. So, for example, Richard of Devizes is alone in alluding to the allegation, which John had featured prominently, that Eleanor of Aquitaine had an adulterous and incestuous relationship with Raymond of Antioch. Other writers of his generation, Walter Map and Gerald of Wales, preferred to comment on Eleanor's supposed adultery with Henry II's father, Count Geoffrey of Anjou, while William of Newburgh decried her presence in the host during the crusade on the grounds that many other women had followed her lead in joining the expedition, with the result that the chastity which should have prevailed in the camp was compromised.[18]

There was also a distinct lack of curiosity. None of the English historians who described the Second Crusade, nor, so far as I am aware anyone else, addressed the question of why, if the fall of Edessa had been the occasion of the crusade, there had been no attempt at its recovery. More significantly, it is difficult to detect any impact on their accounts of the Second Crusade from the events of 1187-92. Thus no one suggested that the sinfully obstructive behavior of the Latins in the East in the late 1140s prefigured the wickedness which led to the loss of Jerusalem, and no one seems to have drawn any parallels or contrasts between the fortunes of Louis or Conrad and those of Richard, Philip Augustus and Frederick Barbarossa. William of Newburgh, with his multiplicity of human and theological reasons for the failure of the expedition, and his appreciation that successes in the East in the years after 1148 did much to efface the disasters, is by far the most interesting, but even he is circumscribed by his limited information and by an inability to see these events in a broader historical perspective. Substantial numbers of Englishmen and Normans had joined the expedition, but echoes of their recollections are conspicuous only by their absence. It was not that later twelfth-century writers were unaware of the events of the Second Crusade: Ralph Niger, writing at the time of the Third Crusade, reminded his readers that the Muslims habitually curtailed the crusaders' sources of supply and obstructed their routes, and he cited the experiences of Louis and Conrad as proof; elsewhere he lampooned Bishop Otto of Freising for his part in persuading Conrad to participate in the expedition.[19] Interestingly, St. Bernard escaped his stricture. Nor are accounts of the Third Crusade completely devoid of references to the Second: Roger of Howden, for example, had the crusaders tell the Muslims in 1191 that they intended restoring the Christian possessions to the frontiers as at the time of Louis' sojourn in the East.[20] But the English writers were either locked in a historiographical tradition that precluded any original investigation of events before their own lifetime, or presumably took the view that the crusade had been too painful a failure for them to want to explore it any further.

NOTES

1. Constable, "Second Crusade". I wish to thank David Bates and Jonathan Riley-Smith for their comments on an earlier draft of this chapter.
2. Henry of Huntingdon, pp. 279-81; Robert of Torigni, *Chronicles*, pp. 152, 154-55; Roger of Howden, vol. 1, pp. 209-10; *Ann. Waverleia*, pp. 231-33; Ralph of Diceto, vol. 1, pp. 256-58 (cf. p. 291). For Roger of Howden's singular account of the First Crusade, see: Gillingham "Howden", p. 60.
3. Gerald of Wales, vol. 1, p. 76 (cf. vol. 2, p. 152).
4. Ralph of Diceto, vol. 1, pp. 256-57; Graboïs, "Crusade".
5. Wm. of Newburgh, vol. 1, pp. 84-87.
6. Wm. of Tyre, *Chronicon*, p. 635.
7. Henry of Huntingdon, p. 281; Gervase of Canterbury, vol. 1, p. 138.
8. Henry of Huntingdon, pp. 280-81; Robert of Torigni, *Chronicles*, p. 154.
9. Gervase of Canterbury, vol. 1, pp. 137-38; Ralph of Coggeshall, p. 12.
10. John of Salisbury, p. 57; *Ann. Herbipolenses*, p. 7.
11. Wm. of Tyre, *Chronicon*, p. 769; Michael the Syrian, vol. 3, p. 276. Cf. Tritton & Gibb, p. 299; Bar Hebraeus, p. 274. I am indebted to Martin Hoch for these references.
12. *Chron. d'Ernoul*, p. 12.
13. For William, see: Edbury & Rowe, pp. 125-26; Walter Map, pp. 62-7, 72-3.

14. Wm. of Newburgh, vol. 1, pp. 92-5, at p. 92.

15. Partner, p. 59.

16. Wm. of Newburgh, vol. 1, pp. 94-7, at p. 94.

17. Both Roger of Howden and Ernoul record another story of this type: Louis visited Roger of Sicily on his way home from the crusade, and Roger allegedly induced him to place a crown on his head, thereby validating his kingship (*Gesta Regis Henrici II*, vol. 2, p. 202; *Chron. d'Ernoul*, p. 13).

18. John of Salisbury, pp. 11-12, 52-9, esp. pp. 52-3; Richard of Devizes, pp. 25-6; Walter Map, pp. 474-77; Gerald of Wales, vol. 8, p. 300; Wm. of Newburgh, vol. 1, pp. 128-29.

19. Ralph Niger, pp. 80 (cf. p. 70), 224.

20. *Gesta Regis Henrici II*, vol. 2, p. 174.

from where did they come? To consider these questions, let us focus on Jerusalem, where illuminated manuscripts are one familiar and important source of evidence. The Church of the Holy Sepulchre is another, and for our purposes here, the more important source, both in terms of architecture and sculpture.

Two published manuscripts introduce the period with which we are concerned. The first is a Missal in the Bibliothèque Nationale in Paris, ms. lat. 12056.[2] Buchthal has analyzed this codex with great sensitivity, and he is surely correct to see a close connection to the famous Melisende Psalter in its style. Some of its medallions of saints depend on full-length portraits in the Psalter. Buchthal commented, "The illuminator of the Missal . . . is . . . versatile and adaptable . . . but his acquaintance with Byzantine style is very much second hand; his figures betray themselves at first glance as western copies. His decorative work, on the other hand, stands in a class by itself . . . ."[3] In fact, he describes the essential character of much of this ornament as derived from Italian sources: "whatever remains of northern [English] elements is now almost submerged in [the] wealth of south Italian geometrical interlace, and the exuberant taste for brilliant and contrasting color."[4] Buchthal hypothesized an Anglo-Italian artist working with a scribe who was bilingual in Latin and Armenian. The calendar is indisputably characteristic of other Jerusalem service and prayer books. In date, the Missal must come shortly after the Psalter because of its dependence on the work. I propose to date it c. 1140, for reasons argued elsewhere.[5] It is noteworthy for us to see this codex as an example of crusader painting in the scriptorium of the Holy Sepulchre shortly before the advent of the Second Crusade.

In comparison to this codex, we also have a manuscript of the Gospel of St. John, Paris, Bibliothèque Nationale, ms. lat. 9396.[6] Sumptuously produced, it has a full page illustration of the Evangelist, is written in golden letters, and overall has a pronounced aristocratic character, comparable to the Melisende Psalter. Buchthal saw a number of specific features in its decoration which he also recognized as parallels with the Psalter: the imitation of Byzantine models in a non-Byzantine manner by a Latin master for the figure of John and for the insertion of the Hand of God. The decorative border of the miniature is reminiscent of the work of Basil in the Melisende Psalter, and as with the Missal, the artist seems much more confident in doing the ornament in contrast to the figural work. The finest expression of this ornamental inclination is found in the opening initial "I", and here again Italian sources are evident: the interlace as in Monte Cassino work, the Italian taste for white outlines on the foliate designs at top and bottom. Buchthal related it to the manuscripts in the circle of the Melisende Psalter; he thought it might even have been written for a member of the crusader royal family. I propose to date it in the early 1140s, as a second generation work — the latest of the Psalter-related codices from the Jerusalem scriptorium in this period.

Whatever their exact dates, these two codices demonstrate important characteristics of crusader art just before the Second Crusade. It was an art which was carried out mostly by westerners, only occasionally by easterners, for aristocratic and ecclesiastical patrons of the Latin Kingdom. In form, the art imitated Byzantine figural and Italian ornamental models with some reference to Northern European aspects of the latter. But essentially it was a Mediterranean art in source and spirit, and its western component was strongly rooted in Italian sources.

How do these works differ from slightly later crusader manuscripts? Without going into this matter in any detail, I shall refer to two examples from a Gospel Book in Paris (Bibliothèque Nationale, ms. lat. 276).[7] These paintings will demonstrate that in the period immediately following the Second Crusade, 1150-75, there was a loss of contact with the tradition of the Melisende Psalter, an intensification of the study of Byzantine figural models, and a continuation of the use of Italian ornamental sources. Certainly, however, there was no sudden infusion of new western artistic ideas from France or Germany, that is, those regions which supplied the bulk of the manpower for the Second Crusade.

With these examples in mind, we can turn our attention to the most important crusader monument in progress before, during and after the Second Crusade, namely, the Church of the Holy Sepulchre (figs. 6 and 7). The history of this church is a large issue, the full discussion of which we cannot enter into here. I shall only propose the following chronology, argued elsewhere, within which one may consider some specific problems.[8]

1. In the years following the First Crusade up to c. 1120, the focus of crusader attention at the Church of the Holy Sepulchre had been the complete renovation and redecoration of the aedicule of the Holy Sepulchre, and the erection of the cloister of the canons to the east of the Byzantine *triporticus*.

2. The crystallization of a crusader plan to rebuild and enlarge the Byzantine church on the site occurred in the period after 1131, and work began under the supervision of Patriarch William when manpower and resources were available.

3. The main construction and decoration of the Church of the Holy Sepulchre occurred during the 1140s, with a major change of plan

occasioned when the building was struck by lightning in January 1146.

4. The church was dedicated on July 15, 1149, by the then reigning patriarch, Fulcher, despite the fact that certain aspects of the building were unfinished, in particular, the south transept facade, the bell tower and some parts of the mosaic decoration for the church. Within the framework of this chronological outline, we can comment on a few important aspects of this ambitious project.

First, the plan of the Church of the Holy Sepulchre obviously predated the Second Crusade and must have been worked out in detail by the early 1140s.[9] In contrast to other early crusader churches, or Byzantine churches in Syria-Palestine, it reflects a carefully selected part of a standard pilgrimage-road type seen in Romanesque churches of France and Spain.[10] The idea of the crossing, choir and ambulatory with radiating chapels is clearly based on western Romanesque sources. What is striking about the plan is the ingenious way the essential coherence of the basic components serves to unify the interior of the church, making possible the integration of a complex of holy sites — the Sepulchre, Calvary, the Prison of Christ, and other commemorative chapels; crusader monuments — the tombs of the crusader kings; and certain Byzantine architectural elements — the rotunda, north wall and gallery, and Calvary chapel within one harmonious space. The fact that no particular church provides an exact parallel to the parts of the plan used in Jerusalem indicates that the western model was adapted according to the special needs of the specific and very complicated site of the Church of the Holy Sepulchre.

Second, one of the most striking features of the new church was the use of broad, gracefully pointed arches throughout the interior and on the exterior of the building.[11] The decision to use these pointed arches must also have occurred early in the planning and construction of the church, so we must suppose that this decision was made by the early 1140s. It has been tempting in the past to suppose that, like the plan, the origin of these arches should be sought in the West, in Burgundy, where pointed arches are found at Cluny III from c. 1100, in the 1130s in St. Lazare at Autun, or in the Ile de France, where the new Gothic pointed arches debuted at Sens, and St. Denis in the 1140s.[12] But unlike the needs of the plan, there was no necessity for the crusader architects to look far afield for these arches. Indeed, the character of the round arched pilgrimage-road church, dating from the late eleventh century on, which provided the core idea for the plan, would not have suggested pointed arches at all. On the contrary, significant examples of pointed arches were available in the immediate vicinity of the Holy Sepulchre: nearby in Ramla, in the Bir al-Annezieh, the great cistern of St. Helena so-called, put up in 789 A.D., with huge pointed arches of the same impressively graceful shape, in the Aqsa Mosque, the largest and most significant church-like building in Jerusalem at this time, and in the Church of St. Anne, which was probably under construction in the 1130s providing a trial example for some of the ideas employed at the Holy Sepulchre.[13] The fact is that we need to consider the local context for the new architecture these architects were erecting. It is important to entertain motivations other than eclectic dependence on western models here when the evidence demonstrates that local buildings and ideas were significant stimuli and sources of inspiration.

These features, among others, of the crusader Church of the Holy Sepulchre were no doubt decided on and mostly built before the Second Crusade arrived in Jerusalem. The situation is different for other aspects of the church to which we now turn.

Third, the dome over the nave-crossing was probably, I suggest (based on Alan Borg's observations), the result of a change in plan.[14] We note that the only time William of Tyre mentions the Church of the Holy Sepulchre specifically in the text of his history pertaining to the period 1140-49, he describes a calamitous event:

> About the time of the feast of Epiphany [January 1146], a thunderbolt sent from on high struck the church of the Sepulchre of the Lord on Mt. Sion [sic] and exposed it to great danger. The omen terrified the entire city and was, as we believe, a portent of disaster. A comet also was visible for many days, and certain other unusual signs, prophetic of future events, appeared.[15]

Whatever the omen was interpreted to be, it is probable that the lightning struck the church at its highest point. At the time, that point may have been some kind of tower under construction over the four sturdy piers of the crossing. In the wake of the damage to this hypothetical tower which the church apparently sustained, the steep dome over a high drum may have been chosen for the crossing. This choice would explain the slightly irregular rectangular plan of the piers: not exactly erected on a square, the alterations to the fabric of the crossing observable in the supporting arches, and the sculptural decoration of the interior drum and exterior dome corbels by wholly new ateliers in contrast to those working on the lower levels.[16] It has also been recently argued that the motivation for choosing the dome would have been based in large measure on the context of the church in a city of domed buildings.[17] Besides the rotunda of the Holy Sepulchre itself, the most conspicuous examples were found over the Dome of the Rock and on the Aqsa of the Templars. It is timely to recall, moreover, that in the early 1140s, a papal legate had come to Jerusalem to dedicate the Dome of the Rock as the *Templum Domini* in 1142. Thus, there was recent impetus to contemplate the significance of domed Christian buildings in crusader Jerusalem quite apart from Byzantine or Romanesque sources farther afield.

Finally, we come to the sculptural decoration of the south transept facade of the Church of the Holy Sepulchre (fig. 7).[18] Here we can witness the evidence of local sources which provided the impetus to crusader architects, sculptors, and mosaicists to provide the Holy Sepulchre with the most sumptuous architectural setting and entrance in keeping with its Levantine context. Into the two-storey double portal configuration, significant nonfigural architectural sculpture was inserted, based on local sources:

a. the godroons (from the Bab al-Futuh in Cairo, the Church of St. Anne in Jerusalem, et al.)

b. the classical Roman moldings (partly spolia, partly copied, to articulate the first and second storeys)

c. the lace-like hood molding (partly derived from Early Christian sources as, for example, the Tomb buildings at Bara in the Syrian mountains near Qalaat Seman)

d. the wind-swept capitals (capitals that remind us of Byzantine inspired examples from San Marco, apparently based here on local Byzantine models), among other aspects

e. along with the sculptural decoration, there was also the decision to decorate the facade, including the tympanum over the left (west) door with mosaics, certainly a Mediterranean idea found in widespread Byzantine and Italian examples.

Some of these examples, it could be argued, were decorations decided on before the Second Crusade ever reached Jerusalem in 1147. But even if the date of their initiation cannot be determined precisely, the most famous extant figural decorations from this facade, the lintels over the doors — a figural lintel over the left door, a vine-scroll lintel over the right door — can be dated after the Second Crusade. The likelihood is that neither lintel was finished by the dedication of the Church on July 15, 1149, and both may only have been begun at that time. Thus, in terms of a test case of the impact of the Second Crusade on the project to rebuild the Church of the Holy Sepulchre, we have here perhaps our most telling example in the figural arts.[19]

Not surprisingly, the initial evaluation of these two sculptural ensembles found them to be related to one part of France or another in style and iconography. More significantly, however, recent critical studies of these works have proposed that they have much more to do with Italy — with Tuscany in the case of the configuration, style and iconography of the figural lintel, and the Abruzzi in the case of the vine-scroll lintel — than with France.[20] Once again, it was not the northern European areas of France or Germany which apparently provided the artistic background for the sculptors of these lintels.

Finally, there is the case of the bell tower. Everyone agrees that this was the last major architectural element to be done on the church, and at the earliest it could have been finished only in the 1150s.[21] In its original configuration, the campanile was probably a five-storey structure, with the first two storeys bonded to the western end of the south facade, and the upper three storeys freestanding with arched fenestration on all four sides as indicated in a woodcut of 1486 (fig. 6). The idea of an independent or quasi-independent bell tower associated with the main entrance facade of a church is, of course, widespread in Italy in the eleventh and twelfth centuries.[22] In the Holy Land, the characteristically rectangular Syrian minarets would have provided the immediate context and direct visual models, especially the famous minaret of the great mosque in Aleppo of 1089-94.[23] Taken together, these sources were adapted to produce the final result on the facade of the Holy Sepulchre, which was distinctive from either in its heavier proportions, the use of buttresses, and the relative decorative austerity.

The significance of these observations can be assessed only in a preliminary way at this point. However, what is striking is that in a circumstance in which the main source of manpower for the Second Crusade was derived from France and Germany, the notable characteristics of certain works of art, insofar as they have relations with western sources through their artists, form and content, are Italian — in painting, in sculpture, and in architecture. This suggests a variety of points, of which I mention the following:

1. The nature of crusader art as seen in Jerusalem in the 1140s seems to have attained a stable character which depended on its own creative resources. Crusader artists and architects used sources from East and West to meet the needs of their resident patrons. The results in architecture and the figural arts were varied, but were characterized by a unique blend of western sensibilities, some quite orientalized, combined with eastern ideas drawn from the Levantine context.

2. No art as yet identified as crusader during the years of the mid- and late 1140s seems to have anything to do with patrons, or artists, who were participants in the Second Crusade itself.

3. Whatever impact the Second Crusade may have had on the art of the crusaders in the Holy Land by mid-1149, it was relatively insignificant in terms of any direct influence from those areas of the West whence the bulk of the crusaders came.

4. By the 1140s, the art of the crusaders demonstrably had much to do with those "crusaders" who formed the most direct linkage with the West, namely, the Italians from the various maritime cities whose importance in the Crusader States has been the subject of two major recent studies.[24]

5. As Marie Luise Bulst-Thiele correctly observed, we should call "Crusader Art" the art of the Frankish, that is, western European colonists of the Latin Kingdom of Jerusalem.[25] While that correct title is no doubt too cumbersome for general use, what we typically refer to as crusader art, or art of the crusaders in the Holy Land, should be understood mainly as being sponsored by these settlers, whoever the artists may have been. Thus, although the First Crusade provided the point of departure for what we call today "Crusader Art", by the time of the Second Crusade, indeed well before the 1140s, the art was substantially in the hands of the settlers in the Latin Kingdom.

In sum, the art of the crusaders in the Holy Land seems to have differed very little in 1149/50 from what it looked like in the 1140s immediately prior to 1147 in terms of any direct influence generated as a result of the Second Crusade expedition. On reflection, this directs our attention to the importance of the resident "crusaders", that is, the Frankish settlers and their offspring as the real instigators of this art as patrons and sponsors. This suggests that in order to understand the art of the crusaders in the Holy Land we must endeavor to understand not only who the artists and architects were, but also the historical context, visual environment and motivations of these settlers, not simply as transient colonists, but as Europeans who came to Syria-Palestine and made it their home, some families over several generations.

Fig. 6. Church of the Holy Sepulchre, Jerusalem, south facade entrance (woodcut after a
sketch by Erhard Reuwich of Utrecht, 1486)

Fig. 7. Church of the Holy Sepulchre, Jerusalem, south facade entrance (view in the early
twentieth century with figural and vine-scroll lintels in place)

NOTES

1. The history of the Latin Kingdom in the 1140s is addressed by a variety of historians, of which the most recent important accounts are: Mayer, *Crusades*, pp. 87-110; Richard, *Latin Kingdom*, vol. A, pp. 34-41; and Prawer, *Histoire*, vol. 1 (1975), pp. 328-402.
2. Buchthal, pp. 14-23, 141-42, pls. 20-32.
3. Buchthal, p. 20.
4. Buchthal, p. 19.
5. In a study tentatively entitled "The Art of the Crusaders in the Holy Land" (vol. 1: The Twelfth Century), currently in preparation, I have argued for dating this codex somewhat earlier than that proposed by Buchthal.
6. Buchthal, pp. 23-24, 142, pl. 33.
7. Buchthal, pp. 24-33, 142-43, pls. 39a (for the Byzantinizing Christ), 35b (for the Italianate decorative motif).
8. The bibliography on the crusader church of the Holy Sepulchre is enormous. The most important art historical studies remain the following: Boase, pp. 69-84; Enlart, *Monuments*, vol. 2 (1928), pp. 136-80; Schmaltz, pp. 167-241; Vincent & Abel, vol. 2, pts. 1-2 (1914), pp. 260-91; Vogüé, *Eglises*, pp. 173-226. A monograph on the crusader church of the Holy Sepulchre remains a major desideratum. Alan Borg has begun work on such a study, and presented some preliminary findings in lectures delivered in the 1970s, none of which has as yet been published. The following chronology is based on my study referred to in n. 5.
9. For the plan of the crusader church, see: Enlart, *Monuments* (Atlas, album 1: 1926), pl. 2-3; Corbo, pt. 2 (1981) pls. 6, 7.
10. For major examples of plans of the Romanesque pilgrimage churches in western Europe, see: Conant, p. 94; fig. 28.
11. For views of the pointed arches that characterize the church of the Holy Sepulchre, see: Enlart, *Monuments* (Atlas, album 1: 1926), pls. 91-94.
12. On the use of the pointed arches in Romanesque and Gothic churches, see: Bony, pp. 15-21, 45 ff.
13. For the cistern at Ramla, see: Creswell, vol. 2, pp. 161-64, fig. 152, pl 33. For the Aqsa Mosque, see: Hoag, pp.21-22. For the church of St. Anne, see: Enlart, *Monuments*, vol. 2 (1928), pp. 189-97. My dating of the church of St. Anne is based on the study mentioned in n. 5.
14. Borg expressed his opinions in a lecture given at the Courtauld Institute in 1977. I am indebted to him for a typescript of that presentation.
15. Wm. of Tyre, *History*, vol. 2 (1976), p. 162. See also: Wm. of Tyre, *Chronicon*, vol. 2 (1986), bk. 16, ch. 17, p. 738: "Eodem tempore, circa Epiphaniorum dies [January 1146], fulmen divinitus immissum ecclesiam Dominici Sepulchri et Montis Syon [sic] ictu perculit periculoso, omen, ut credimus, portendens infaustum et universam deterrens civitatem. Visus est

et cometa per dies multos et alia quedam preter morem apparuerunt signa, futurorum disignativa."

16. For the measured plan, see: Vincent & Abel, vol. 2, pts. 1 & 2 (1914), p. 118, fig. 67. I am also relying here on observations made by Borg and Kenaan-Kedar.

17. See: Kenaan-Kedar.

18. The most recent studies on the south transept facade include Rosen-Ayalon and Buschhausen. See also: Boase, pp. 80-83; Kenaan.

19. For detailed photos of the lintels, see: Boase, pls. II, III, pp. 290-91.

20. For the figural lintel, see: Borg. For the vine-scroll lintel, see: Kühnel.

21. For the bell tower, see: Enlart, *Monuments*, vol. 2 (1928), pp. 151-55.

22. For important examples of the campanile on eleventh- and twelfth-century churches in Italy, see: Ricci, pls. 1, 69, 151.

23. For the minaret of the great mosque in Aleppo, see: Hoag, p. 213, fig. 265.

24. Favreau-Lilie, "Kirchen"; Favreau-Lilie, *Italiener*, passim.

25. Bulst-Thiele, "Mosaiken", pp. 442-43.

18

Cistercian Houses in the Kingdom of Jerusalem

Denys Pringle

In the later twelfth and thirteenth centuries, a network of Cistercian daughter-houses was established throughout the Latin East, both on the Syrian mainland and also in Cyprus and in Frankish Greece.[1] In contrast to other religious orders, however, and despite the great interest that St. Bernard is known to have shown in the affairs of the kingdom, there seems to have been an initial reluctance on the part of the Cistercians to establish themselves in the Kingdom of Jerusalem itself.

Sometime between 1118 and 1131, King Baldwin II actually gave to the abbot of Clairvaux the site of the ruined Byzantine church that enclosed the tomb of the Prophet Samuel on Mount Joy, overlooking Jerusalem, together with an endowment of 1000 *aurei* with which to found a monastery,[2] but it was the Order of Prémontré who were eventually to build there.[3] The reasons for St. Bernard's declining this offer are given by his biographer, Geoffrey of Clairvaux:

> Finally, like a flourishing vine, he extended his shoots in all directions, except that in the land of Jerusalem, although a site had been prepared for him by the King, he would not agree to send his brothers, because of the attacks of the pagans and the intemperateness of the climate.[4]

One may suspect that a site next to one of the main roads to Jerusalem would not have been altogether suitable anyway.

This story finds echoes, however, in Gerard of Nazareth's *Life* of Elias, abbot of the Benedictine monastery of Palmarea, located somewhere on the northwestern shore of the Sea of Galilee. In the 1130s, at about the time when Baldwin II was in correspondence with Bernard of Clairvaux, Abbot Elias sent one of his monks to France to fetch a brother who might instruct his community in Cistercian ways. The outcome of the mission is unrecorded. Elias did, however, try to make his brothers wear the Cistercian habit, but the oppressive summer heat and humidity of the area beside the lake proved too much for them, and they simply refused, to Elias' intense disgust.[5]

Despite these and other false starts, in 1157 a Cistercian house was founded by monks from Morimond (on the borders of Champagne and Lorraine) at Belmont, south of Tripoli,[6] and in 1169 a daughter-house of Belmont, called St. John in the Woods (*in nemore*), was established near Jerusalem.[7] Meanwhile, in 1161, Morimond had established another house in the East, called *Salvatio*.[8] In 1222, a house of Cistercian nuns, St. Mary Magdalen's, also existed in Acre, and from 1239 this was dependent directly on Cîteaux.[9]

The convent in Acre was located somewhere near the church of St. Giles, in the walled suburb known as Montmusard, to the north of the city.[10] All remaining traces of this suburb were probably systematically destroyed when the Turkish artillery defenses were erected around Acre in the second half of the eighteenth century.[11] It is therefore unlikely that any archaeological evidence for St. Mary Magdalen's will ever come to light. But what of the other two houses: St. John's and *Salvatio*? Various suggestions have been made, including locations in the County of Tripoli, Cyprus and the Kingdom of Jerusalem.[12]

The Kingdom of Jerusalem seems the likeliest location for *Salvatio*, since it was to its abbot, Richer, that King Amalric (1163-74) recounted his experience on campaign in Egypt, when St. Bernard had appeared to him in a vision.[13] Bernard Hamilton has also noted that, in 1186, two Cistercian abbots acted as intermediaries between the rebel barons in Nablus and King Guy in Jerusalem. If, as seems likely, these were the abbots of St. John's and *Salvatio*, it would follow that both houses probably lay not only in the Kingdom of Jerusalem, but close to the city of Jerusalem itself; this would also explain why nothing more is heard of them after 1187, when the hill country of Judaea was lost to Saladin.[14]

A place called *Sainz Iehanz du Bois* is indeed referred to near Jerusalem in the Rothelin version of the Continuation of William of Tyre's Chronicle (c. 1261), and it appears as *Saint Iohan de Boys* in the *Pelrinages et Pardouns de Acre* of c. 1280.[15] This is the place which the German pilgrim Theodoric referred to around 1175 as "St. John, or . . . the place which is called 'In the Wood', where his father Zechariah and his mother Elizabeth lived, and where St. John himself was born; where also St. Mary . . . came and saluted St. Elizabeth."[16] This place may be identified as the village known today as ᶜAin Kārim, some eight kilometers (or five miles) southwest of Jerusalem.

In fact, two churches are known to have existed in ᶜAin Kārim in the twelfth century. The larger of these (Palestine Grid ref. 1655.1307) had been built in the fifth or sixth century over the rock-cut cave in which John the Baptist was supposed to have been born.[17] The striking similarity of the present building to the nearby Church of the Holy Cross, however, suggests that it had been almost entirely rebuilt by the Byzantines in the mid-eleventh century;[18] it may therefore possibly still have been in Orthodox hands at the time of the crusader conquest. In April 1166, however, the "House of the Blessed John . . . in the Mountains" (*domum beati Johannis . . . in montanis*) was included among the possessions of the canons of the Templum Domini.[19] It therefore seems unlikely that this, the principal church in ᶜAin Kārim, could have been the one occupied by the Cistercians from 1169.

The second church in ᶜAin Kārim stands across the valley, some 500 meters southwest of the larger one (Palestine Grid ref. 1651.1302).[20] Today it is associated with the Visitation of St. Elizabeth by the Virgin Mary, but in Byzantine and crusader times it was associated with Elizabeth's concealment of the infant John from Herod's soldiers. According to the mid-second-century Proto-Gospel of James, Elizabeth went to the Mountain to hide her child; the Mountain parted, and received the baby and its mother until the danger had passed.[21] By the sixth or seventh century, the cave had become a place of pilgrimage.[22] Its location was known to the Russian Abbot Daniel, who in 1106/7 distinguishes it from the church of John's birth:

> And this place may be recognized in the rock even to the present day. And above this place there is now built a little church, and beneath the little church is a little cave and another little church built on to the cave in front of it. From this cave flows very good water, and Elizabeth and John drank this water while they were living in the cave in the mountain guarded by an angel until the death of Herod. And this mountain is very great and has much forest on it, and around it there are many forested valleys.[23]

The cleft rock, though no church, is mentioned by the Greek John Phocas in 1185.[24] It is not until the fourteenth century, however, that Western pilgrims begin to mention this church. In 1330, for example, Antony of Cremona writes, "Not far from the house of Zechariah (i.e. the larger church) is a church, towards the mountain in a wooded place, where St. Elizabeth hid the Blessed John the Baptist."[25] Five years later, James of Verona records that it was occupied by Armenians,[26] and other sources indicate an Armenian presence from the 1240s until at least 1469.[27]

Probably because of the difficulty experienced by pilgrims in getting access to the larger church of St. John, the smaller church had, by the end of the fourteenth century, come instead to be associated with the Visitation and with the Circumcision of John.[28] By 1422, however, the upper church was in ruins,[29] and by the 1480s the Armenian monks had left. Brother Felix Faber (1480-83) and later writers also mention the existence of paintings of saints in the ruined upper church.[30]

In 1679, the site was acquired by the Franciscan Custody of the Holy Land, and the lower vaulted church was restored once more as a chapel.[31] An engraving by Cornelius van Bruyn, made in October 1681, shows the south wall of the upper church still standing up to the springing of the vaulting, and also some remains of the apse. In 1861, the lower church was partly reconstructed, and a bell-tower was added in 1891.[32]

Between 1938 and 1946, both the upper and lower church were rebuilt to the designs of the Italian architect Antonio Barluzzi. During the demolition of the nineteenth-century elements, the medieval and earlier remains of both churches and of the surrounding structures were recorded by Fr. Bellarmino Bagatti. Bagatti was unaware of the possible Cistercian associations of the site, but it is from his patient efforts that much of our present knowledge of it is derived.[33]

The medieval church faces southeast and was built against the hill slope, on two levels (see Figs. 8-9). The lower level, entered from the courtyard, was in effect a crypt, giving access to the spring and to the Rock of Concealment, while the upper level comprised the main church, which extended further to the southeast, and probably communicated with an upper level of conventual buildings to the south and east.

The walls of the twelfth-century church and conventual buildings are constructed with facings of coursed roughly dressed stone blocks. Fine diagonally tooled ashlars of characteristic twelfth-century type are used for the quoins, the door and window surrounds, and for the apse. Masonry marks on these blocks include the Greek or Latin letters A, B, Δ, Θ, K, L, N, O, Π, and possibly Ω and W.[34] Barluzzi's church (1946) incorporated most of the medieval elements which came to light when the 1861 chapel was demolished, including the crypt (apart from the vault, and much of the north and west walls), much of the south wall of the upper church, four courses of the apse, and part of the north wall near the northeast corner.

The crypt was about 7 m. square, and seems originally to have been groin-vaulted. Its east wall represents a facing-up in masonry of an almost vertical scarp in the natural rock. Set into it was a semicircular apse, and to the right of this, a barrel-vaulted passage runs back into the rock to end in another semicircular apse. Despite this passage's slightly pointed profile, it seems to predate the twelfth-century church, for it encloses a well-head from which a terracotta pipe of late Roman or Byzantine type ran out under the west wall. The main door seems to have been on the west, and there was a secondary door in the north wall. In the south wall, a pointed-arched niche encloses a shapeless lump of stone, identified as the Rock of Concealment. In the southwest corner, a staircase leads up inside the south wall to the upper church.[35]

The western part of the upper church was built directly over the crypt, and the eastern part on a level terrace cut in the rock. It was a single-celled building, with a semicircular apse on the east, contained by a straight external wall, set at an angle. Internally, the church measured about 8 m. by 20 m. (including the apse).[36]

The apse, built of finely dressed ashlars, was approached up two steps from the nave. The position of the altar, on the chord of the hemicycle, is indicated by a monolithic base slab (1.95 m. x 1.35 m.), with a step cut in its front corresponding to the uppermost chancel step. In the south wall of the apse, there was a large walk-in cupboard, or more likely a sacristy, some 2 m. square; and there was a small aumbry, 80 cm. square, in a corresponding position on the north side of the apse.[37]

Only the eastern part of the upper church's north wall survived, and this only to a height of 2.5 m. (it has since been demolished). The south wall, however, survived, 4 m. high. Towards the east, it was partly rock-cut, and had no openings. The stair from the crypt emerged roughly one-third of the way along it from the west, and at the far west end, another door opened on to the roof of the building adjoining it to the south.[38]

The vaulting system of the upper church is indicated by two hollow-chamfered springers for transverse arches, set in the south wall. Van Bruyn's drawing (1691) shows clearly that these related to groin-vaults. But while it is possible to reconstruct the two central bays, as he shows them, of roughly equal size and each with a rounded-arched window, the eastern- and westernmost bays must have been much narrower.[39]

The floors of the nave and sanctuary seem to have been of plaster, and traces of a low rock-cut or stone bench were also found against the north and south walls. No evidence was found for any division of the nave, but it has to be remembered that only the eastern part of the pavement survived.[40]

The paintings of saints seen on the walls by medieval pilgrims and the traces still visible on the apse wall most probably date from the period of Armenian occupation, but there is some evidence that the twelfth-century church was also painted.[41]

The church stood within an irregular enclosure, extending some 50 m. x 42 m., with a gate on the northeast leading into a courtyard before the church. A number of vaulted buildings existed at this level, notably, to the south of the church, a large groin-vaulted room (see Fig. 8, no. 2). In the south corner of the enclosure, a fragment of walling and vaulting, now incorporated into the Franciscan convent buildings, indicated the existence of other buildings in this area, at the same level as the church (no. 4).[42]

There can be little doubt that this double church and associated buildings belonged to a monastic establishment of the twelfth century.[43] But when exactly was it built? Abbot Daniel records an upper and a lower church already existing here by 1106. However, there is also archaeological evidence for earlier ecclesiastical buildings on the site, dating from the fifth or sixth centuries.[44] Unless the crusader builders were exceptionally quick off the mark, it is therefore perhaps more likely that what Daniel saw were structures of an earlier period, possibly restored like the larger church in ᶜAin Kārim during the eleventh century.

The twelfth-century buildings described above were therefore probably built after Daniel's visit, and unless the monks who arrived from Belmont in 1169 simply moved into an existing complex, conveniently vacated by another community, the likelihood is that it was they who built — or rebuilt — it. Some support for this interpretation is provided by the coin sequence from the site, which, after a gap from the eighth century onwards, starts up again in the mid-twelfth century and continues through to the fourteenth.[45] We may also consider the general similarity between the main church at ᶜAin Kārim and that at Belmont itself (see Fig. 10).[46] Both are simple structures, with no aisles or transepts. At Belmont the nave is in fact narrower, but some 10 m. longer, and instead of groin-vaults, it has a continuous barrel-vault. Like ᶜAin Kārim, it terminates in a semicircular apse, contained by a straight external wall and flanked by large walk-in cupboards, or sacristies, inside the walls. Although the internal nave division that one would expect in a Cistercian church such as Belmont is no longer apparent, the separate doors in the south wall for the choir monks and lay brothers can still be seen. At ᶜAin Kārim, the two doors in the south wall could also conceivably have served this purpose, though in so small a church it is uncertain just how marked the nave division would have been.[47]

While the identification of the twelfth-century church of St. John in the Woods with the present church of the Visitation in ⁽Ain Kārim is thus reasonably well established, *Salvatio*, the other twelfth-century Cistercian house in the Kingdom of Jerusalem, is more difficult to pinpoint. Topographical sources provide no clues, for although the name could suggest a site associated with the life of the Saviour, all of the churches and monasteries attested at such places in the twelfth century are known to have been held by other orders.[48] Most of them lie, in any case, in or very close to Jerusalem itself — an unlikely location for a Cistercian house of this date. We are therefore left looking for an unidentified twelfth-century monastic site, somewhere near, but not too close to, Jerusalem.

It so happens that just such a site exists, in a secluded location in the bottom of a valley, at ⁽Allar as-Sufla (Horvat Tannur), some 19 km. southwest of Jerusalem and 15 km. southwest of ⁽Ain Kārim (Palestine Grid ref. 1548.1247). These ruins were seen in the 1870s by Ch. Clermont-Ganneau, who identified them as belonging to a small crusader convent;[49] the church was also described by the officers of the Survey of Western Palestine in 1881.[50] More recently the buildings have been discussed by Dr. Meron Benvenisti, who interprets them instead as a crusader farmstead, associated with a domestic hall.[51] Survey of the entire complex by Peter E. Leach and myself in 1981, however, suggests that the nineteenth-century interpretations were, after all, correct.

The church lies on the east side of a complex of vaulted buildings, to which it appears to be secondary (Fig. 11-12). Internally, it measures about 19 m. (E-W) by 8.5 m., and the nave is divided into three groin-vaulted bays by transverse arches, which spring from a continuous cavetto-moulding with plain ovolo corbels beneath. The semicircular apse can no longer be seen above the level of the collapsed rubble, but may be inferred both from the spacing of the nave bays, and by the presence in the east wall of a small lancet window at just the right level.

No trace of any door could be found in the west wall. Subsidence of the masonry in the central bay of the south wall, however, indicates the existence of a door here, below the present ground level. Only the north wall stands to any height above the cornice level, and the two surviving windows in its central and eastern bays are plain splayed openings with pointed heads and plastered sides.

The masonry of the building is similar to that at ⁽Ain Kārim, with thick walls of roughly shaped blocks and a weak mortared rubble core, and with more finely dressed stone reserved for quoins and details. The inside was coated with a hard, fine, white lime plaster.

Remains of five other vaulted structures exist west of the church. The earliest seem to have been nos. 2 and 3 (see Fig. 12), which, with the northward continuation of the church's east wall, would have formed three sides of a courtyard some 26 m. from east to west. Vault no. 2 would have opened directly on to the court through two or possibly three arches. Evidently it had an upper storey, for the remains of a staircase carried on an arch survive in the southwest corner of the courtyard. In a secondary period, vault no. 1 was built in the angle between vault no. 2 and the church. And another pair of vaults (nos. 4 and 5), possibly a grange or storehouse of some kind, lie a short way to the northwest.

Clearly the ruins at ʿAllar as-Sufla are those of a monastic establishment. While there are obvious dangers, in the absence of positive proof, in seeking to identify them with *Salvatio*, the possibility that they are indeed the remains of that house nevertheless seems high. The isolated position, in the bottom of a valley, beside a running stream, could hardly be more characteristic for a Cistercian house. A stronger argument, however, lies in its general architectural similarity to St. John in the Woods. The churches of both houses are remarkably alike in size, plan and vaulting. Some similarities between the two sets of associated buildings may also be detected, despite the lack of a regular plan in both cases. Our understanding of them is of course hindered by the fact that neither survives in its entirety; in particular, the upper storeys have gone. Nor is it clear how the two complexes might have evolved if the communities that they housed had continued in existence for more than eighteen and twenty-six years respectively. The buildings at Belmont, for instance, were evidently laid out in such a way as to leave room for a transept and enlarged sanctuary to be added to the church at a later date, though that was never done. Too little remains of ʿAllar as-Sufla and ʿAin Kārim for us to tell whether what we see was not intended likewise to be capable of eventual expansion. Even so, in both cases, a general similarity is discernible in the placing of the church to the east, and the principal conventual buildings to the south and southeast of an enclosed courtyard.

The characteristic feature of both houses, and also of Belmont, is their modest scale. It is therefore perhaps ironic that in order to find what by Western standards would seem a more typical example of "Cistercian" planning in the Holy Land, we must look not to them, but to the church that the Premonstratensians built for themselves at Mount Joy, on the site, and with the money, that had been given by Baldwin II to Bernard of Clairvaux in the second or third decade of the twelfth century.[52]

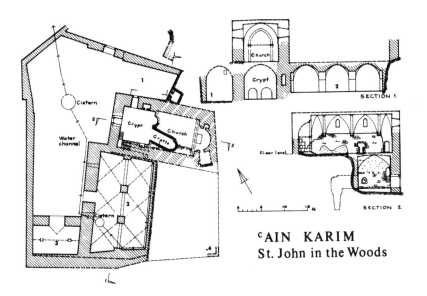

AIN KARIM
St. John in the Woods

Fig. 8. ^cAin Karim, St. John in the Woods: plan of the monastic complex (Drawn by
Peter E. Leach, after Bagatti *Santuario* and BSAJ Survey 1981).

ᶜAIN KARIM
St. John in the Woods

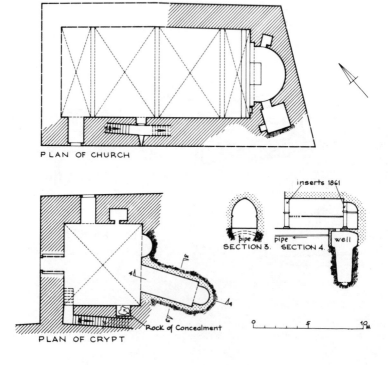

PLAN OF CHURCH

PLAN OF CRYPT

inserts 1861

SECTION 3.   SECTION 4.

pipe

pipe

well

Rock of Concealment

0   5   10ₘ

Fig. 9. ᶜAin Kārim, St. John in the Woods: plan of the church (Drawn by Peter E. Leach, after Bagatti *Santuario* and BSAJ Survey 1981).

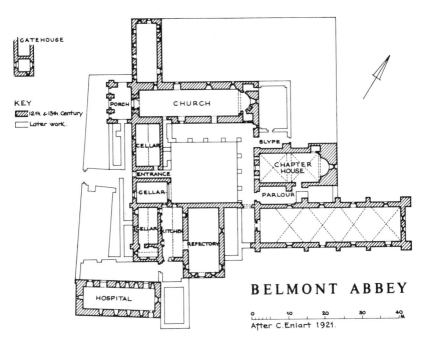

KEY
12th. c13th. Century
Later work.

GATEHOUSE

PORCH

CHURCH

CELLAR

ENTRANCE

CELLAR

CELLAR KITCHEN

REFECTORY

SLYPE

CHAPTER HOUSE

PARLOUR

HOSPITAL

BELMONT ABBEY

0   10   20   30   40 M

After C. Enlart 1921.

Fig. 10. Belmont Abbey (Dair Balamand), Lebanon: plan of the monastic complex
(Drawn by Peter E. Leach, after Enlart, "Belmont").

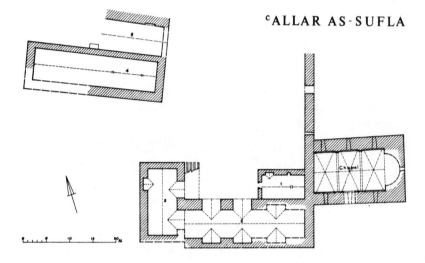

Fig. 11. ᶜAllar as-Sufla (Horvat Tannur): plan of a twelfth-century monastic complex, possibly that of *Salvatio* (Drawn by Peter E. Leach, from BSAJ Survey 1981).

^cALLAR AS-SUFLA

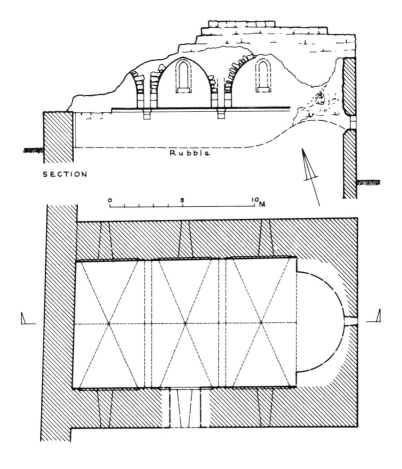

SECTION

Fig. 12. ^cAllar as-Sufla (Horvat Tannur): plan of the church (Drawn by Peter E. Leach, from BSAJ Survey 1981).

NOTES

This chapter is dedicated with gratitude and affection to the memory of the late Fr. Bellarmino Bagatti, O.F.M. (1905-1990), in recognition of the help and advice that he gave me over a number of years in documenting and recording the medieval churches of the Crusader Kingdom of Jerusalem. I am also grateful for helpful criticism of the preliminary draft from Professor Bernard Hamilton. The research project of which this represents but a small part has been sponsored since 1979 by the British School of Archaeology in Jerusalem.

1. See chapter 19 by Jean Richard in this volume. See also: Hamilton, "Cistercians"; Panagopoulos.
2. Bernard, *Opera*, letter 253, vol. 8, pp. 149-55.
3. Savignac & Abel; Mayer, "Sankt Samuel".
4. "Postremo quasi uitis abundantissima suos undique palmites propagauit, excepto quod in terram Jerosolymitanam, quamuis locus esset a Rege paratus, ob incursus Paganorum et aeris intemperiem, non acquieuit mittere fratres suos" (Bernard, *Opera* (PL), vol.185 (1), col. 316.
5. Kedar, "Gerard of Nazareth", pp. 68, 75; Kedar, "Palmarée", p. 263.
6. Janauschek, vol. 1 (1877), p. 139, no. 354; Hamilton, "Cistercians", p. 405, Hamilton, *Latin Church*, p. 102; Enlart, "Belmont"; Enlart, *Monuments*, vol. 2 (1928), pp. 45-63; Breycha-Vauthier.
7. Janauschek, vol. 1 (1877), p. 158, no. 405; Hamilton, "Cistercians", p. 407; Hamilton, *Latin Church*, p. 102.
8. Janauschek, vol. 1, p. 144, no. 365; Hamilton, "Cistercians", p. 405; Hamilton, *Latin Church*, p. 102. The foundation took place during the reign of Baldwin III and the lifetime of Queen Melisende.
9. Hamilton, "Cistercians", pp. 410-12; Hamilton, *Latin Church*, pp. 300, 304.
10. *Cart. gén*, vol. 2 (1896), no. 1828, pp. 344-45; Michelant & Raynaud, p. 235. Dichter (pp. 101-103) confuses the Cistercian nuns of St. Mary Magdalen's with the Convertites, or Reformed Magdalens, who were also established in the Monmusard quarter (cf. Michelant & Raynaud, p. 236), and their church with another church of St. Mary Magdalen, documented in 1187, which was evidently situated in the Genoese quarter of the city (cf. Favreau-Lilie, "Kirchen", p. 19).
11. Jacoby, p. 215.
12. Richard, *Comté de Tripoli*, p. 61; Hamilton, "Cistercians", pp. 406-407.
13. Bernard, *Opera* (PL), vol. 185(1), col. 368.
14. *Cont. Guillaume de Tyr*, p. 31; *Chron. d'Ernoul*, pp. 131-32; Hamilton, *Latin Church*, p. 102, n. 5; cf. Hamilton, "Cistercians", pp. 405-407.

15. Michelant & Raynaud, pp. 170-71, 233.

16. " . . . ad sanctum Iohannem siue ad locum, qui appellatur Siluestris . . . ubi pater eius Zacharias et mater Elysabeth manserunt, et ubi ipse sanctus Iohannes natus est, ubi etiam sancta Maria . . . ipsam sanctam Elysabeth salutauit" (Bulst [-Thiele] + Bulst, *Theodericus*, ch. 38, p. 42; tr.: Theoderich, p. 57).

17. Cangioli, *S. Giovanni*; Saller; Bagatti & Alliata.

18. Pringle, "Church-building", pp. 12-13, 26; figs. 12-13.

19. Chalandon, p. 313; Röhricht, *Additamentum*, no. 422a, pp. 25-6.

20. Bagatti, *Santuario*; Cangioli, *Visitazione*.

21. Amann, p. 262; *NT Apocrypha*, vol. 1 (1963), p. 387.

22. Bagatti, *Santuario*, pp. 21-23, pl. 12.25; Vikan, p. 17, fig. 12.

23. Tr. by W.F. Ryan in: Wilkinson, Hill & Ryan, p. 151.

24. Johannes Phocas (PG, vol. 133, col. 956); cf. Wilkinson, Hill & Ryan, p. 332.

25. "Non multum longe ab ista domo Zachariae est una ecclesia uersus montes, in loco siluestri, ubi Sancta Helysabeth abscondit ipsum beatum Johannem Baptistam" (Röhricht, "Itinerarium", pp. 173-74; Baldi, p. 51, no. 60.3).

26. Röhricht, "Pèlerinage", pp. 222-23; Baldi, pp. 51-2, no. 63.1.

27. Bagatti, *Santuario*, pp. 100-102.

28. It was here that pilgrims sang the *Magnificat* and *Benedictus*: Baldi, no. 65, p. 54; no. 70, p. 57; no. 73, pp. 59-60.

29. Baldi, no. 71.1, p. 58; Bagatti, *Santuario*, p. 28.

30. *Book of Felix Fabri*, vol. 2, pp. 637-38; Baldi, no. 74.2-3, pp. 61-2; no. 82.4, p. 69; no. 83.3, p. 71; no. 84.2, p. 73; no. 86.2, p. 76.

31. Bagatti, *Santuario*, pp. 32-3, 105-106.

32. Bagatti, *Santuario*, pp. 39-44.

33. Bagatti, *Santuario*, pp. 45-97.

34. Bagatti, *Santuario*, pp. 56, 57, 64-5, 68; figs. 21, 23-4, 27, 30; pl. 19.41.

35. Bagatti, *Santuario*, pp. 44-5.

36. On the upper church, see: Bagatti, *Santuario*, pp. 56-62.

37. Bagatti, *Santuario*, pp. 56-9, 62.

38. Bagatti, *Santuario*, pp. 59-61.

39. Bagatti, *Santuario*, p. 62.

40. Bagatti, *Santuario*, pp. 61-62.

41. Bagatti, *Santuario*, pp. 40, 41-2, 49, 56, 58; pls. 10.20-22.

42. Bagatti, *Santuario*, pp. 63-72.

43. Bagatti, *Santuario*, pp. 93-4.

44. Bagatti, *Santuario*, pp. 94-5.

45. Cf. Bagatti, *Santuario*, pp. 84-8.

46. See note 6 above.

47. On the comparative planning of Cistercian monasteries in France, see, for example: Dimier & Porcher, pp. 39-41. The existence of an upper and lower church at ᶜAin Kārim was due no doubt to the fact that the building served both as a monastic church and as a place of pilgrimage. Other twelfth-century examples of double churches serving this dual function existed in the Valley of Jehoshaphat, at Bethany and Abu Ghosh, and on Mount Tabor (see: Pringle, "Planning", pp. 350-58).

48. For a provisional list of archaeologically attested church sites, see: Pringle, "Edifices".

49. Clermont-Ganneau, vol. 2 (1896), pp. 455, 458-59.

50. Conder & Kitchener, vol. 3 (1883), pp. 62-3.

51. Benvenisti, *Crusaders*, pp. 235-36; Benvenisti, "*Bovaria*", p. 152.

52. See note 3 above. For the plan, see: Savignac & Abel, p. 273, fig. 1.

19

The Cistercians in Cyprus

Jean Richard

The Cistercian establishment in Cyprus was an outgrowth of monasteries of the Order of Cîteaux which had been set up in the Latin States of the Holy Land.[1] These monasteries were founded in the second half of the twelfth century as dependencies of Morimond (*Salvatio* in 1157, Belmont in 1161). Dependencies of La Ferté first appeared in the thirteenth century with the incorporation of Jubin. This monastery had been established early in the previous century in the Black Mountain region near Antioch; it followed an eremitical rule to which attention has recently been drawn.[2] Thereafter came the foundation of St. Sergius near Gibelet.[3] It is uncertain whether institutions for Cistercian nuns existed in the twelfth century. The first appearance of one of these, the abbey of St. Mary Magdalene of Acre, occurs in 1222. It apparently acknowledged the abbot of Belmont as father superior.[4]

In his role as the new sovereign of Cyprus, Guy of Lusignan acted as a generous benefactor to the religious establishments of the Holy Land, which had been impoverished by Saladin's conquest. During the course of that conquest, both *Salvatio* and St. John's *in nemore*, a daughter-house of Belmont, had disappeared. It is known that Guy donated an annuity of 200 bezants from the *commerc* of Nicosia to Jubin before that institution came under the control of the Cistercians. It had received another annuity based on the casal of *Sonia* before 1215.[5]

At some undetermined point, the Abbey of St. Mary Magdalene of Acre acquired a house in Nicosia. It appears that it was at the instigation of the archbishop of Nicosia, Eustorge of Montaigu, that the abbess and convent undertook to set up a new abbey there in 1229, and, while retaining authority over it, to elect an abbess to administer the fledgling house. Thereafter, the abbess of St. Mary Magdalene of Nicosia would be elected by her own convent, but in the presence of the abbess or prioress of Acre. The archbishop laid down certain conditions, which were accepted.[6] Among these, the abbot of Belmont was to be acknowledged as the superior of both houses, as well as of another daughter-house of Acre founded in Tripoli and similarly dedicated to St. Mary Magdalene. The General Chapter of 1239 rejected this claim, however, and placed all three houses directly under the authority of Cîteaux.[7]

The foundation on Cyprus of a Cistercian monastery for monks was clearly being considered at approximately the same date, for the abbot of Belmont had acquired land at Pyrgos before 1224 with the intention of installing an abbey there. His plans were, however, opposed by William of Rivet who held Pyrgos in fief. Despite papal intervention, the acquisition could not be finalized until William, one of the appointed regents of Emperor Frederick II, died in Armenia on a diplomatic mission in 1230. In 1237, the abbot of Belmont received the go-ahead from the General Chapter, and the abbot of Jubin was instructed to supervise the setting up of the new monastery. From 1238 he shared this charge with the abbot of St. Sergius.[8]

The original site proved to be unsuitable. In 1243, the General Chapter decided that the two abbots should visit "the place to which the abbot of Belmont wished the abbey of Cyprus to be transferred." The legate, Odo of Châteauroux, gave his assent to this transfer, which appears to have been effected as early as 1249.[9] In the early days of that year, Count John of Montfort, who had joined Saint Louis on the island, died and was buried in the church of the new abbey of Beaulieu near Nicosia.[10] John is known to have been worshipped as a saint; Makhairas evoked the miraculous healings which occurred following his intercession, and pilgrims described his relics which were preserved and displayed in the same church.[11]

The new site had been bought from the Franciscans, who had established their first settlement there. In accordance with their customary procedure, they settled in a hermitage on the outskirts of the town until King Henry I built them a new convent within the town walls. The archbishop of Nicosia hampered the new installation, which the General Chapter of 1253 had confirmed, for it had been built without his consultation.[12] He claimed that in accordance with Franciscan practice, that Order should have turned over the site it had left behind to him, as bishop of the diocese, rather than to have given it to another order of monks. In 1254, Pope Innocent IV directed the archdeacon of Acre and the bishop of Tripoli to investigate the matter, and Alexander IV confirmed the acquisition in 1256.

There is no indication that the settlement in Pyrgos resulted in any permanent construction on the site. Golubovich and Jeffery have dismissed Camille Enlart's hypothesis proposing Stasouza, in the village of Kalokhorio, as the site finally occupied by the new convent and called Beaulieu.[13] It must, in fact, have been situated on the outskirts of Nicosia, for it is referred to as *Bellilocum juxta Nicosiam, Bellilocum extra muros Nicosienses*,[14] and by Stephen of Lusignan as "Notre Dame des Champs".[15] According to an episode which took place during the war against the Genoese in 1374, a Cypriot messenger succeeded in outwitting the Genoese surveillance by slipping out of the town across the aqueduct which brought water to Nicosia from the fountain of Trakhonas under the walls of the city, "at Beaulieu".[16]

These first two Cistercian foundations on Cyprus undoubtedly resulted from the need of a population following the Latin rite to benefit from the presence of religious communities representing the major orientations of thirteenth-century religious life. This population was limited in number and, since those available locally for a monastic calling must have been few, it was necessary to bring monks from the West.[17]

A third settlement responding to another type of demand was also created. In 1237, the pope requested the General Chapter to accept the monastery which had recently been built by the "Countess of Cyprus" as a daughterhouse directly dependent upon Cîteaux. Chapter consented and entrusted the abbot of Jubin with the inspection of the site in question and with bringing in nuns from various convents.[18] The matter dragged on for some time. Not until 1242 did the abbot of Cîteaux write to the archbishop and Chapter of Nicosia confirming his acceptance of the conditions set down by the prelate for this foundation. It is apparent from his letter that the site chosen lay between those occupied by the Dominicans and the Franciscans, the latter being the very building which would be transferred to the Cistercians and become the Abbey of Beaulieu.[19] It is, however, a passage from the *Lignages d'Outre-mer* which explains the motivation behind the new foundation. The house was established by Alix of Montbéliard, widow of Philip of Ibelin, formerly regent of Cyprus, to receive their daughter, Mary of Ibelin, who was about to take the veil and was no doubt destined to become its abbess.[20] The fact that it was a princely foundation explains why the petition of the Countess Alix went by way of the pope.

For whatever reason, the new abbey was dedicated to St. Theodore. The letter of 1243 provides no indication that it occupied the site of a former

Greek church. Nonetheless, it may be remembered that St. Theodore, the martyr of Amasea, was worshipped as a holy knight. The monastery's gardens were greatly admired by Nicholas of Martoni.[21]

The abbot of Belmont requested the General Chapter of 1238 to accept the incorporation of the Cypriot abbey of Episcopia (i.e. Bellapais). Founded by Guy of Lusignan, this monastery originally followed the Augustinian rule. This was replaced by the Premonstratensian rule under Archbishop Thierry (1206-1211), although Episcopia would not be affiliated to the Order of Prémontré until Pope Gregory IX decided to make the transfer after 1228. In 1232, at the request of Archbishop Eustorge, he nevertheless retained it under that bishop's authority. It is probably due to dissatisfaction with their new status that the monks of Episcopia made contact with the abbot of Cîteaux in order to explore the possibility of being incorporated into the Order. The General Chapter assented, and an inquiry was to have been conducted by the abbots of Jubin and St. Sergius, but in the end the affair came to nothing.[22]

The campaigns of Sultan Baîbars in Syria initiated a new period in the history of the Cistercians in Cyprus. Already in 1260/61 the abbots of Beaulieu and Belmont excused themselves from attending the General Chapter, probably because of the fear caused by the arrival of the Mongols in Syria.[23] But in 1269, the excuse given by the abbot of Beaulieu for his absence was that his monastery had had to receive the monks from Jubin and Belmont who were fleeing the devastation of their houses by the Saracens.[24] Belmont's monks were soon able to return to their monastery, where their presence was testified to in 1283.[25] They do not appear to have taken refuge anew in Cyprus when Tripoli fell in 1289. In compliance with the wish expressed by the General Chapter in 1290, the abbey may have survived, but at the cost of being transferred abroad, perhaps to Sicily.[26]

The monks from Jubin, on the other hand, lost their monastery definitively in 1268. In 1271, they appealed to the General Chapter to be allowed to live in one of their granges until provided with another monastery.[27] They settled in a building which until then had been an appendage of their house and which is known as the Priory of St. Blaise of Nicosia. The income which the monks had at their disposal in Cyprus and Crete was retained when the abbey was transferred to Genoa between 1291 and 1297. It is likely that a few monks were left in Nicosia to oversee their estate on Cyprus, for several fourteenth-century documents testify to the presence of a prior of St. Blaise.[28]

A collector's account issuing from the Apostolic Chamber provides evidence for the material situation of the Cistercian establishments in Cyprus in 1357. The collector recorded the total amount received from the tithe levied in the kingdom:

> *ab abbate Belliloci, bisantios 325*
> *pro abbacia Magdalene, bisancios 15*
> *pro abbacia sancti Theodori, bisantios 50*
> *a priore sancti Blaxii, bisantios 19.*[29]

It thus appears that Beaulieu was particularly well endowed, a point confirmed by entries in the Order's tax book.[30] The income of St. Theodore's abbey, though more modest, remained comfortable, while that of St. Mary Magdalene was poor.

In 1306, the abbot of Beaulieu (apparently called Biauleuc in Cypriot French)[31] was Henry Chappe, a member of an old aristocratic family. He had joined the great barons against King Henry II, was a signatory of the manifesto inviting Henry to hand over the kingdom to his brother, and died in 1309 on a diplomatic mission in Armenia. The following year, Constable Aimery sought refuge in the convent after the king's restoration. During the fourteenth and fifteenth centuries, the abbots are frequently mentioned in papal bulls as executors.[32] It is clear that they acted as superiors to the monastery of St. Theodore, for in 1337, Abbess Elizabeth Antiaume complained to the pope that the tutelage had become intolerable, that several abbesses had been forced to resign as a result of it, and that the number of sisters had fallen to nine. Benedict XII consequently withdrew the abbot's authority,[33] but it was later restored: a rental, confirmed by Pope John XXIII in 1415, was issued with the consent of the abbot of Beaulieu, who was described as the "Father Abbot" of the nuns of St. Theodore's.[34] Further, on February 24, 1469, "*a l'abaie de Bialeuq, a la chanbre de l'abé*", Prioress Martha of Chérines and two of her nuns asked Brother Jerome, abbot of Beaulieu, "as their superior", to give his consent to another rental.[35]

Jerome was the last regular abbot of Beaulieu. Before 1451, the pope had transferred the governance of the abbey to the Chaldean archbishop, titular of Tarsus. He was the head of the Chaldean community in Cyprus and had adhered to the Florentine decree of union. It soon became apparent, however, that the Chaldean prelate knew nothing of the Latin rite. The pope then revoked his nomination and appointed Jerome to the abbacy, granting him on May 25, 1451 a dispensation *defectu natalium*.[36] But, on February 25, 1469 (the day after Jerome agreed from Nicosia to the above-mentioned rental), Anthony of Chanas, bishop of Limassol, solicited and obtained from Pope Paul II the lifetime reunion of the monastery of Beaulieu, "St. John of Montfort as it is called", with his own bishopric. The argument favoring this reunion was based on the fact that the monastery was poor and that the majority of Beaulieu's income came from the Limassol diocese.[37]

These documents, which were discovered by M. de Collenberg, confirm Stephen of Lusignan's report that the Bernardines left Cyprus during the reign of King James II (1462 - 1473). Their abbey had been given over *in commendam*, while the monastery was assigned to the *Zoccolanti*, that is to the Franciscans of the Strict Observance. The latter would reside in the building, then known only as St. John of Montfort, until it was demolished by Venetian engineers in 1567.[38] Their convent should not be confused with the monastery of St. Francis which remained in the hands of the Conventual Friars.

The demolition of St. Theodore's must have occurred at the same time. More information is available concerning the temporals of this monastery during the fourteenth and fifteenth centuries. In 1338, the nuns were granted permission by Pope Benedict XII to lease its land at Sterviga due to the difficulty they had had in finding serfs ("parèques") to exploit it. Theretofore, their property had been divided into a number of tenures and a "reserve" exploited by the tenant farmers according to a system of corvées.[39] Another property, the *presterie* of Malandes (perhaps Malounda) in the diocese of Nicosia, was leased in perpetuity for 170 bezants a year to John Soulouan, a Nicosian commoner. In 1415, the grant was confirmed by the Abbess Françoise to John's son, James Soulouan. The vineyard at Klirou called "tou Farmaca" was leased out in 1469 for 45 bezants a year.[40] These transactions reflect the gradual decline of the abbey's resources. The nuns seem, however, to have continued to live according to their rule. On the other hand, the brief list of names appearing in the lease of 1469 (two, in addition to their prioress, which does not exclude the possibility that others could not be present at Beaulieu on this occasion) suggests that their number had already been reduced; nine nuns were accounted for in 1337. St. Mary Magdalene's is last referred to in 1357.

The buildings of Beaulieu and St. Theodore's disappeared when the Venetians destroyed that part of the town in 1567.[41] The archeological excavations carried out by Enlart in 1901 in the area located north of the old Armenian cemetery, near the Wolseley Barracks, unearthed a monastic complex.[42] The stone slab covering the tomb of the Friars (*Sepulcrum Fratrum*) and dated 1516 identifies it as the convent granted to the Franciscans of the Observance, that is, to Beaulieu.[43] Although nothing remained of the walls which had been razed and whose freestones had been salvaged for the building of new walls, Enlart was fortunate to discover the paving still in place and nearly intact. His description (fig. 13) shows a quadrangular cloister bordered by a gallery leading northwards to a church with a square apse and a raised chancel (the disposition of the stalls is still recognizable); westwards to an extensive chapter room; and southwards to a large double navel refectory. The classical Cistercian groundplan is thus clearly identifiable, the *Zoccolanti* having introduced only minor modifications.

The identification of the remains of Beaulieu nevertheless raises a question. Since the monastery was located outside the walls that Henry II of Lusignan constructed around Nicosia, the attempted reconstruction of these walls by historians must be altered.[44]

St. Theodore's was erected between the "place" (*locus*) of the Dominicans and the house of the Franciscans. At the time, the latter occupied the same location as the Cistercians had between 1244 and 1249. The emplacement of St. Dominic, partially occupied today by the Paphos Gate, suggests that the Cistercian nunnery, with its vast garden, was located outside the sixteenth-century walls, somewhere between the Paphos Gate and the site of Beaulieu.

It was probably the Cistercian nunnery alone that carried the Order's observance on Cyprus into the sixteenth century. As a community of Cistercian monks, Beaulieu disappeared first, having fallen victim to the importance of its temporals and the envy which they had aroused. The weakness of the Order's recruitment on the island was likely responsible in part for its disappearance. Nevertheless, thanks to the sepulchre of John of Montfort, Beaulieu had become enviably famous as a place of worship. The thirteenth-century foundations proved to be secure since they maintained the Cistercian tradition on the island long after the departure of the Franks from the Holy Land.

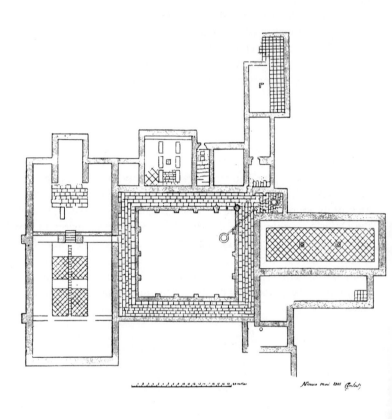

Fig. 13. Ground plan of Beaulieu Abbey, Nicosia, Cyprus (from Enlart "Nicosie")

NOTES

I am grateful to Mrs. Nicole Corregan for translating this work into English.

1. Hamilton, "Cistercians".
2. Kedar, "Gerard of Nazareth", pp. 66-67, 71. It is uncertain whether Jubin was dedicated to St. George or to St. Mary before it was incorporated into the Order (see: Richard, "Jubin").
3. Petit. For the identification of places mentioned in the charters, see: Richard, "Questions", p. 59. The location of the casal *Effdar superius*, which belonged to Saint Sergius, must be reconsidered. It is Fdar-al-Fawqa, situated in the interior, and not the coastal settlement of al-Fidar.
4. He occurs sealing the charter of 1222, mentioned below.
5. Richard, "Jubin". On the disappearance of *Salvatio*, see: Hamilton, "Cistercians", p. 407.
6. Mas-Latrie, "Chypre", pp. 343-44.
7. *Statuta Cisterciensis*, vol. 2 (1934), pp. 196, 214.
8. Hamilton, "Cistercians", pp. 413-14.
9. The decision of Odo of Châteauroux, to which the pope refers in his bull of 1254, would have been made during his stay as legate in Cyprus with the king of France in 1248-1249, rather than in 1251 as is generally believed.
10. John of Montfort has often been mistaken for the son of Philip of Montfort, lord of Tyre, who died in 1283. Cypriot authors have made him out to be a count of Rohais (Edessa) and a constable, or marshall, of Cyprus, which is also wrong. John was the son of Amaury, count of Montfort and constable of France, who had conceded his rights to the Languedoc to the king of France.
11. Felix Faber (p. 235) alone identifies the site of the chapel of St. John of Montfort in the Augustinian convent, now the Omerieh mosque. All other pilgrims place it in Beaulieu.
12. *Statuta Cisterciensis*, vol. 2 (1934), p. 397. Camille Enlart was mistaken in believing that the Cistercians had exchanged their house in Nicosia with the Franciscans and gone to live in a rural site (Enlart, "Nicosie"); cf. Golubovich, vol. 2 (1913), pp. 375-78.
13. For descriptions of the ruins of a church at Stasouza-Kalokhorio, see: Enlart, *Chypre*, vol. 2, p. 420; Enlart, *Cyprus*, pp. 321-25. See also: Jeffery, p. 189.
14. This designation occurs in Archivio segreto Vaticano, Registrum Avenionense 72, f° 277 (1342).
15. Lusignan, *Chypre*, pp. 63, 89, 90v.
16. Makhairas, vol. 1, p. 508.

17. So writes the bishop of Gibelet when he asks the abbot of La Ferté to send monks for St. Sergius (Hamilton, "Cistercians", p. 415). This is confirmed by a study based on the *Lignages d'Outre-mer* (Vandevoorde, p. 183). Vocations for women seem to have been more numerous.

18. *Statuta Cisterciensis*, vol. 2 (1934), p. 171.

19. Mas-Latrie, *Histoire*, vol. 3 (1861), pp. 644-45.

20. "Phelippe, l'autre fis de Balian de Ybelin et de la royne Marie, fu baill de Chipre et esposa Aalis de Monbeliart qui fu feme de conte Bertot d'Alemaigne, et orent un fis et une fille, Johan et Marie qui fu nonain et fu pour lui estorée l'abeie de Saint Theodore à Nicossie" (*Lignages d'Outre-mer*, Vatican Library ms. lat. 4789, according to p. 79 of the typescript edition provided by Marie-Adelaïde Vandevoorde). Cf. Collenberg, "Ibelin", p. 204.

21. Nicolas de Martoni, p. 635. These gardens, planted with vegetables and fruit trees, *intra menia dicte civitatis*, covered an area of approximately 20 *modia*.

22. *Statuta Cisterciensis*, vol. 2 (1934), p. 193; Mas-Latrie, *Histoire*, vol. 3 (1861), pp. 632-33; Hackett, p. 64.

23. *Statuta Cisterciensis*, vol. 2 (1934), p. 481.

24. *Statuta Cisterciensis*, vol. 3 (1935), p. 76.

25. This date, often given as 1282, should be corrected to conform with the Cypriot year which began on March 1 (Richard, "Tripoli", pp. 223-24). Belmont would, therefore, have survived Baïbars' campaign against Tripoli (Enlart, "Belmont").

26. *Bellus mons* is mentioned in the middle of the fourteenth century, with contributions ranging from £6 to £16 (*Tax-book*, pp. 80-1). The abbeys in the Holy Land which were abandoned (St. Sergius, St. John of the Wood, *Salvatio*) also occur, but with no indication of taxes. Such is the case of *Sancta Trinitas de Refech*, an abbey identified with Refesio, near Sciacca, in Sicily (White, *Sicily*, pp. 171-77). Refesio is believed to have been granted to Belmont by the bishop of Agrigento, when the monks were obliged to abandon their convent under threat by Saladin (ibid., p. 176). In a bull granted to Refesio in 1198, Innocent III confirms that it belonged to the Cistercians, but makes no reference to Belmont. On the other hand, a *vidimus* of this bull, dated 1271, was issued at the request of "frater Gualterius, cantor monasterii Bellimontis in Syria, Tripolitani diocesis, Cisterciensis ordinis, et preceptor monasterii Sancte Trinitatis de Refesio, filie Bellimontis" (pp. 290-93). It is tempting to relate the drawing up of that document to the temporary evacuation of Belmont by the monks in 1269; they would have adopted Refesio as the new seat of their convent by transferring the name to it when Belmont was definitively abandoned in 1289. Cf. *Statuta Cisterciensis*, vol. 3 (1935), p. 248.

27. *Statuta Cisterciensis*, vol. 3 (1935), p. 102.

28. Richard, "Jubin". George de Carmandino, prior of St. Blaise in 1353, was appointed abbot of Beaulieu in 1357.

29. Richard, "Collecteur", p. 28. In the *Liber taxarum*, Beaulieu renders 12 florins, and in the *Liber censualis of 1471-1474* 312 florins (Mas-Latrie, "Chypre", p. 355, with reference for the *Liber taxarum* to Archivio segreto Vaticano, Armarium XXXIII, no. 7, f° 119; the *Liber censualis* was held by Firmin Didot).

30. According to the *Tax-book* (pp. 82-3), *Bellus locus in Cypro* was taxed £20 for the *contributio moderata* and £56 13s. 4d. for the *excessiva*.

31. The Greek transliteration is *Pialeki* (Makhairas, vol. 1, pp. 32, 496).

32. Janauschek, p. 238; Collenberg, "Choix", p. 397; Collenberg, "Schisme", pp. 681, 682, 688, 692; Collenberg, "Chypre", pp. 153, 173, 177. A monk, Conrad *d'Alemania*, appears in 1347. The abbot, John, is replaced by George *de Carmandino* in 1357; and George by Aubert, formerly prior of the monastery, in 1361.

33. Benedict XII, *Lettres*, vol. 1 (1903), no. 510, p. 59; vol. 1, no. 4771, p. 422. The abbess and three of her nuns were granted an indult at the same time (Collenberg, "Grâces", p. 224).

34. "Dilecti filii abbatis Belliloci...patris abbatis prefati monasterii sancti Theodori consilio et assensu" (Archivio segreto Vaticano, Registrum Lateramense 182, f°ˢ 10v - 12, printed in: *Acta pseudopontificum*, p. 210.

35. Richard, *Livre*, pp. 130-31.

36. Collenberg, "Chypre", p. 161. Jerome was the son of an Armenian priest and a Benedictine nun.

37. Collenberg, "Chypre", p. 176.

38. Lusignan, *Cipro*, p. 33.

39. Benedict XII, *Lettres*, vol. 2 (1910), no. 6196, p. 90 (31 August 1338).

40. See notes 33 and 35 above.

41. Lusignan, *Chypre*, p. 90; Lusignan, *Cipro*, p. 15v. In compensation, the strict Franciscans had been given "the church of St. James lying next to [the house of] the count of Tripoli and adjacent to the residence of the House of Lusignan." No such compensation is known to have been received by the nuns of St. Theodore, and it is uncertain whether they were then still resident at the convent.

42. Keshishian, p. 158.

43. Enlart, "Nicosie". The map on p. 218 is dated May 1901.

44. The location of St. Dominic's Gate is identified by Keshishian (*Nicosia*, p. 69). According to him, St. Theodore was situated between this gate, which was part of the late thirteenth-century wall, and the Paphos Gate, built in 1567 as part of the new wall. See also his map on pp. 80-81.

Bibliography

Compiled by David I. Harvie

Ackerman	Ackerman, Robert W. "The Knighting Ceremonies in the Middle English Romances." *Speculum*, vol. 19 (1944), pp. 285-313.
Acta pseudopontificum	*Acta pseudopontificum Clementis VII, Benedicti XIII, Joannis XXIII.* Ed. Aloysies L. Tautu. Pontificia commissio ad redigendum codicem juris canonici orientalis, *Fontes*, vol. 13, pt. 2. Rome, 1971.
Adso, *De ortu*	Adso, abbot of Montier-en-Der. *Adso Dervensis de Ortu et Tempore Antichristi necnon et Tractatus qui ab eo dependunt.* Ed. D. Verhelst. Corpus Christianorum, Continuatio Mediaevalis, vol. 45. Turnhout, 1976.
Albert of Aachen	Albert of Aachen. *Alberti Aquensis Historia Hierosolimitana.* In: RHC Oc., vol. 4 (1879), pp. 265-713.
Alcuin	Alcuin, [Pseudo-]. *Vita Antichristi ad Carolum Magnum.* In: Adso, *De ortu*, pp. 105-37.
Alphandéry	Alphandéry, Paul. *La chrétienté et l'idée de croisade.* 2 vols. Paris, 1954-1959.
Amann	Amann, Emile, ed. *Le Protoévangile de Jacques et ses remaniements latins.* Paris, 1910.
Ambroise	Ambroise, Georges. *Les moines du moyen âge: leur influence intellectuelle et politique en France.* 2nd ed. Paris, 1946.
Ann. Herbipolenses	*Annales Herbipolenses.* In: MGHS, vol. 16 (1859), pp. 1-12.
Ann. Reicherspergenses	*Annales Reicherspergenses.* In: MGHS, vol. 17 (1861, rpt. 1990), pp. 443-76.

Ann. Waverleia   *Annales monasterii de Waverleia.* Ed. Henry Richard Luard. In: *Annales monastici*, vol. 2 of 5 vols. RS, vol. 36. London, 1864-69, pp. 129-411.

Annales   *Annales: Economies. Sociétés. Civilisations.* vol. 1-. Paris, 1929-

Anselm, *Opera*   Anselm of Canterbury. *Opera omnia.* 6 vols. Ed. Franciscus Salesius Schmitt. Edinburgh, 1946-61.

Arbois de Jubainville   Arbois de Jubainville, Henry d'. *Histoire des ducs et des comtes de Champagne.* 6 vols. in 7 bks. Paris, 1859-1869.

Archives Maine   *Archives historiques du Maine.* Le Mans, 1900-.

Arquillière   Arquillière, H. X. "Origines de la théorie des deux glaives." *Studi Gregoriani*, vol. 1 (1947), pp. 501-21.

Atlas Anjou   *Atlas historique français. Anjou.* Vol. 1: text, Vol. 2: atlas. Monumenta historiae Galliarum. Paris, 1973.

Auberger   Auberger, Jean-Baptiste. *L'Unanimité cistercienne primitive: mythe ou réalité?* Cîteaux: Studia et documenta, vol. 3. Achel, 1986.

Bagatti, *Santuario*   Bagatti, Bellarmino. *Il Santuario della Visitazione ad ᶜAin Karim (Montana Judaeae): Esplorazione archeologica e ripristino.* Studium Biblicum Franciscanum. Collectio maior, no. 5. Jerusalem, 1948.

Bagatti & Alliata   Bagatti, Bellarmino & Eugenio Alliata. "Nuovi elementi per la storia della chiesa di S. Giovanni ad ᶜAin Karem." *Liber Annuus Studii Biblici Franciscani*, vol. 36 (1986), pp. 277-96, pls. 9-28.

Baldi   Baldi, Donatus, ed. *Enchiridion Locorum Sanctorum.* 2nd ed. Jerusalem, 1955.

Baldric of Bourgueil   Baldric of Bourgueil, archbishop of Dol. *Historia Jerosolimitana.* In: RHC Oc., vol. 4 (1879), pp. 1-111.

Baldwin, "Critics"   Baldwin, John W. "Critics of the Legal Profession: Peter the Chanter and His Circle." In: *Proceedings of the Second International Congress of Medieval Canon Law.* Eds. Stephen Kuttner & J. Joseph Ryan. Monumenta iuris canonici, Subsidia, vol. 1. Vatican City, 1965, pp. 249-59.

Baldwin, "Papacy"   Baldwin, Marshall W. "The Papacy and the Levant during the Twelfth Century." *Bulletin* (Polish Institute of Arts and Sciences in America), vol. 3 (1945), pp. 277-87.

Bar Hebraeus   Bar Hebraeus [Gregory Abû'l-Faraj]. *The Chronography of Gregory Abû'l-Faraj, commonly known as Bar Hebraeus.* Ed. & tr. Ernest A. Wallis Budge. 2 vols. Oxford, 1932.

Barber, *Knight*   Barber, Richard. *The Knight and Chivalry.* London, 1970.

Barber, "Origins" — Barber, Malcolm. "The Origins of the Order of the Temple." *Studia Monastica*, vol. 12 (1970), pp. 219-40.

Barteau — Barteau, Françoise. "Mais à quoi songeaient donc les Croisés?" *Revue des langues romanes*, vol. 88 (1984), pp. 23-38.

Barthélemy — Barthélemy, Edouard de, comte. *Diocèse ancien de Châlons-sur-Marne, histoire et monuments suivi des cartulaires inédits de la commanderie de la Neuville-au-Temple, des abbayes de Toussaints, de Monstiers et du prieuré de Vinetz.* 2 vols. Paris, 1861.

Bartolf of Nangis, *Gesta* — [Bartolf of Nangis], *Gesta Francorum Iherusalem expugnantium.* In: RHC Oc., vol. 3 (1866), pp. 487-543.

Batany — Batany, Jean. "Du *bellator* au chevalier dans le schéma des trois ordres (étude semantique)." In: *Actes du 101ᵉ Congrès national des sociétés savantes: section philologique et historique. Lille, 1976.* Paris, 1978, pp. 23-34.

Bec — Bec, Pierre. "'Amour de loin' et 'dame jamais vue.' Pour une lecture plurielle de la chanson VI de Jaufré Rudel." In: *Miscellanea di studi in onore di Aurelio Roncaglia.* Modena, 1989, pp. 101-18.

Bédier & Aubry — Bédier, Joseph & Pierre Aubry. *Les chansons de croisade.* Paris, 1909.

Benedict of Nursia, *Regula* — Benedict of Nursia, saint. *Benedicti Regula.* Ed. Rudolphus Hanslik. Corpus scriptorum ecclesiasticorum latinorum, vol. 75. Vienna, 1960.

Benedict XII, *Lettres* — Benedict XII, pope. *Benoît XII (1334-1342). Lettres communes: Analysées d'après les registres dits d'Avignon et du Vatican.* 3 vols. Ed. J.M. Vidal. Lettres Communes des Papes D'Avignon. Bibliothèque des Ecoles Françaises d'Athènes et de Rome. 3rd ser. Paris, 1903-1911.

Benencasa — Benencasa. *Casus* to the *Decretum Gratiani.* In: *Corpus iuris canonici* (1605), vol. 1.

Benson, "Chodorow" — Benson, Robert L. Review of: Stanley Chodorow, *Christian Political Theory and Church Politics in the Mid-Twelfth Century.* In: *Speculum*, vol. 50 (1975), pp. 97-106.

Benson, "Plenitudo" — Benson, Robert L. "Plenitudo Potestatis: Evolution of a Formula from Gregory IV to Gratian." *Studia Gratiana*, vol. 14 (1967), pp.196-217.

Benton, *Guibert of Nogent* — Benton, John F., ed. *Self and Society in Medieval France. The Memoirs of Abbot Guibert of Nogent.* New York, 1970.

Benton, "Suger"   Benton, John F. "Suger's Life and Personality." In: *Abbot Suger and Saint-Denis*. Ed. Paula Lieber Gerson. New York, 1986, pp. 3-15.

Benvenisti, "*Bovaria*"   Benvenisti, Meron. "*Bovaria-babriyya*: A Frankish Residue on the Map of Palestine." In: *Outremer*, pp. 130-52.

Benvenisti, *Crusaders*   Benvenisti, Meron. *The Crusaders in the Holy Land*. Tr. Pamela Fitton. Jerusalem, 1970.

Berges   Berges, Wilhelm von. "Reform und Ostmission im 12. Jahrhundert." In: Beumann, pp. 317-36.

Bernard, *De considthe ratione*   Bernard of Clairvaux. *De consideratione ad Eugenium papam*. In: Bernard, *Opera*, vol. 3 (1963), pp. 392-493 (Eng. ed.: Bernard, *On Consideration*).

Bernard, *De laude*   Bernard of Clairvaux. *De laude novae militiae ad milites Templi*. In: Bernard, *Opera*, vol. 3 (1963), pp. 213-40.

Bernard, *Epistolae*   Bernard of Clairvaux. *Epistolae St. Bernardi*. In: Bernard, *Opera*, vols. 7-8 (1974, 1977).

Bernard, *Letters*   Bernard of Clairvaux. *The Letters of St. Bernard of Clairvaux*. Ed. & tr. Bruno Scott James. London-Chicago, 1953.

Bernard, *On Consideration*   Bernard of Clairvaux. *Five Books on Consideration: Advice to a Pope* [*De consideratione ad Eugenium papam tertiam libri quinque*]. Tr. John D. Anderson & Elizabeth T. Kennan. The Works of Bernard of Clairvaux, vol. 13. Cistercian Fathers Series, no. 37. Kalamazoo, 1976.

Bernard, *Opera*   Bernard of Clairvaux. *Sancti Bernardi Opera*. 8 vols.: vol. 1 (1957): *Sermones Super Cantica Canticorum 1-35*; vol. 2 (1959): *Sermones Super Cantica Canticorum 36-38*; vol. 3 (1963): *Tractatus et Opuscula*; vol. 4 (1966): *Sermones I*; vol. 5 (1968): *Sermones II*; vol. 6 (1970): *Sermones III*; vol. 7 (1974): *Epistolae 1-180*; vol. 8 (1977): *Epistolae 181-547*. Vols. 1-2, eds. Jean Leclercq, Henri M. Rochais & C.H. Talbots. Vols. 3-8, eds. J. Leclercq & H.M. Rochais. Rome, 1957-1977.

Bernard, *Opera* (PL)   Bernard of Clairvaux. *Opera*. In: PL, vols. 182-85.

Bernard, *Tractatus*   Bernard of Clairvaux. *Tractatus de Baptismo Aliisque* .... In: PL, vol. 182. Paris, 1879, cols. 1031-1046.

Bernard of Parma   Bernard of Parma. *Glossa ordinaria* to the *Liber Extra*. In: *Corpus iuris canonici* (1605), vol. 2.

Berry   Berry, Virginia Gingerick. "The Second Crusade." In: Setton, vol. 1 (1969), pp. 463-512.

Beumann	Beumann, Helmut, ed. *Heidenmission und Kreuzzugsgedanke in der deutschen Ostpolitik des Mittelalters.* 2nd ed. Wege der Forschung, vol. 7. Darmstadt, 1973.
BHVB	*Bericht des historischen Vereins für die Pflege der Geschichte des ehemaligen Fürstbistums Bamberg.* Bamberg, vol. 1– (1834-).
Bischof Otto	*Bischof Otto I. von Bamberg. Reformer, Apostel der Pommern, Heiliger (1139 gestorben, 1189 heiliggesprochen). Gedenkschrift zum Otto-Jubiläum 1989.* Eds. Lotham Bauer, Franz Bittner, Lothar Braun & Franz Machilek. *BHVB*, vol. 125 (1989), pp. 9-576.
Boase	Boase, T.S.R. "Ecclesiastical Art in the Crusader States in Palestine and Syria." In: Setton, vol. 4 (1977), pp. 69-139, pls. I-XLIX (pp. 289-337).
BM, *Index to Charters*	*Index to the Charters and Rolls in the Department of Manuscripts, British Museum*, vol. 1: *Index Locorum.* Ed. H.J. Ellis & F.B. Bickley. London, 1900.
Bonnaud-Delamare	Bonnaud-Delamare, R. "Le fondement des institutions de la paix au XIe siècle." In: *Mélanges d'histoire du moyen âge dédiés à la mémoire de Louis Halphen.* Paris, 1951, pp. 19-26.
Bony	Bony, Jean. *French Gothic Architecture of the 12th and 13th Centuries.* Berkeley-Los Angeles-London, 1983.
Book of Felix Fabri	*The Book of the Wanderings of Brother Felix Fabri.* 4 vols. Tr. A. Stewart. Library of the Palestine Pilgrims' Text Society, vols. 7-10. London, 1893-1896.
Borg	Borg, Alan. "Observations on the Historiated Lintel of the Holy Sepulchre, Jerusalem." *Journal of the Warburg and Courtauld Institutes*, vol. 32 (1969), pp. 25-40.
Bouchard	Bouchard, Constance Brittain. *Sword, Mitre and Cloister.* London-Ithaca, 1987.
Bray	Bray, Jennifer. "The Mohammetan and Idolatry." *Studies in Church History*, vol. 21 (1984), pp. 89-98.
Bredero	Bredero, A.H. "Jerusalem dans l'Occident médiéval." In: *Mélanges Crozet*, vol. 1, pp. 259-71.
Breycha-Vauthier	Breycha-Vauthier, A.C. "Deir Balamand: Témoin de Cîteaux en Terre libanaise." *Bulletin du Musée de Beyrouth*, vol. 20, pp. 7-20.
Brial	Brial, M. "Mémoire sur la véritable époque d'une assemblée tenu à Chartres, relatif à la croisade de Louis le Jeune." *Mémoires*

de l'Academie des inscriptions et belle-lettres, vol. 4(2) (Paris, 1818), pp. 508-29.

Brown, "Eleanor"   Brown, Elizabeth A.R. "Eleanor of Aquitaine: Parent, Queen, and Duchess." In: *Eleanor of Aquitaine: Patron and Politician*. Ed. William W. Kibler. Austin, 1976, pp. 9-34.

Brown, *Normans*   Brown, Reginald Allen. *The Normans and the Norman Conquest*. London, 1969.

Brundage, *Canon Law*   Brundage, James A. *Medieval Canon Law and the Crusader*. Madison-London, 1969.

Brundage, "Cruce signari"   Brundage, James A. "'Cruce signari': The Rite for Taking the Cross in England." *Traditio*, vol. 22 (1966), pp. 289-310.

Brundage, *Documentary*   Brundage, James A. *The Crusades. A Documentary Survey*. Milwaukee, 1962.

Brundage, "Holy War"   Brundage, James A. "Holy War and the Medieval Lawyers." In: Murphy, *The Holy War*, pp. 99-140.

Brundage, "St. Anselm"   Brundage, James A. "St. Anselm, Ivo of Chartres, and the Ideology of the First Crusade." In: *Les mutations socio-culturelles au tournant des XIe-XIIe siècles* (Abbaye Notre-Dame du Bec. Le Bec-Hellouin, 11-16 Juillet 1982). Ed. Raymonde Foreville. Paris, 1984, pp. 175-87.

Brundage, "Transformed Angel"   Brundage, James A. "The Transformed Angel (X 3.31.18): The Problem of the Crusading Monk." In: *Studies in Medieval Cistercian History Presented to Jeremiah F. O'Sullivan*, vol. 1. Cistercian Studies Series, no. 13. Spencer, Mass., 1971, pp. 55-62.

Buchthal   Buchthal, Hugo. *Miniature Painting in the Latin Kingdom of Jerusalem*. Oxford, 1957 (rpt. London, 1986).

Bulst-Thiele, *Magistri*   Bulst-Thiele, Marie Luise. *Sacrae Domus militiae Templi Hierosolymitani Magistri*. Abhandlungen der Akademie der Wissenschaften in Göttingen, Philologisch-Historische Klasse. 3rd ser., no. 86. Göttingen, 1974.

Bulst-Thiele, "Mosaiken"   Bulst-Thiele, Marie Luise. "Die Mosaiken der 'Auferstehungskirche' in Jerusalem und die Bauten der 'Franken' im 12. Jahrhundert." *Frühmittelalterlichen Studien*, vol. 13 (1979), pp. 442-71.

Bulst [-Thiele] + Bulst, *Theodericus*   Bulst [-Thiele], Marie Luise & W. Bulst. eds. *Theodericus Libellus de Locis Sanctis*. Editiones Heidelbergenses, vol. 18. Heidelberg, 1976.

Bur   Bur, Michel. *La formation du comté de Champagne, v.950-v.1150*. Mémoires des annales de l'Est, no. 54. Nancy, 1977.

Burchard of Worms   Burchard, bishop of Worms. *Decretum [Burchardi Wormacien-sis Ecclesiae Episcopi]*. In: PL, vol. 140 (1880), cols. 537-1058.

Buschhausen   Buschhausen, Hugo. "Die Fassade der Grabeskirche zu Jerusalem." In: Folda, *Crusader Art*, pp. 71-96.

Calixtus II, *Epistolae*   Calixtus II, pope. *Epistolae et privilegia*. In: PL, vol. 163 (1893), cols. 1093-1338.

Camille   Camille, Michael. *The Gothic Idol: Ideology and image making in medieval art*. Cambridge, 1989.

Cangioli, *S. Giovanni*   Cangioli, F. *Il Santuario e il Convento di S. Giovanni in ᶜAin Karim*. Jerusalem, 1947.

Cangioli, *Visitazione*   Cangioli, F. *Il Santuario della Visitazione*. Jerusalem, 1945.

Cardini   Cardini, Franco. *Alle radici della cavalleria medioevale*. Florence, 1981.

Cart. d'Azé   *Cartulaire d'Azé et du Genéteil, prieurés de l'abbaye Saint-Nicholas d'Angers*. Ed. E. du Brossay. Archives historiques du Maine, vol. 3, 1903.

Cart. de Vendôme   *Cartulaire de l'abbaye cardinale de la Trinité de Vendôme*. 5 vols. Ed. C.H. Métais. Paris, 1893-1904.

Cart. gén.   *Cartulaire général de l'Ordre des Hospitalliers de Saint-Jean de Jérusalem (1100-1310)*. Ed. Joseph Marie Delaville le Roux. 4 vols. Paris, 1894-1906.

Cart. Mâcon   *Cartulaire de Saint-Vincent de Mâcon, connu sous le nom de Livre enchaîné*. Ed. M.Camille Ragut. Mâcon, 1864.

Cart. Marmoutier   *Cartulaire Manceau de Marmoutier*. 2 vols. Ed. E. Laurain. Laval, 1911-1945.

Cart. Saint-Aubin   *Cartulaire de l'abbaye de Saint-Aubin d'Angers*. 3 vols. Ed. Arthur Bertrand de Broussillon. Paris, 1903.

Cart. St. John I   *The Cartulary of the Knights of St. John of Jerusalem in England, Prima Camera, Essex*. Ed. Michael Gervers. In preparation.

Cart. St. John II   *The Cartulary of the Knights of St. John of Jerusalem in England, Secunda Camera, Essex*. Ed. Michael Gervers. British Academy: Records of Social and Economic History, n.s., vol. 6. London, 1982.

Cart. Temple   *Cartulaire général de l'Ordre du Temple 1119?-1150*. Ed. Marquis d'Albon. 2 vols. Paris, 1913-1922.

Caspar, "Eugens III"   Caspar, Erich. "Die Kreuzzugsbullen Eugens III." with an appendix containing the text of *Quantum praedecessores nostri*, ed. Peter Rassow. In: *Neues Archiv der Gesellschaft für ältere deutsche Geschichtskunde*, vol. 45 (1924), pp. 285-305.

Cate

Cate, J.L. "The Crusade of 1101." In: Setton, *History*, vol. 1, pp. 343-67.

Chalandon

Chalandon, F., ed. "Un diplome inédit d'Amaury I, roi de Jérusalem, en faveur de l'Abbaye du Temple Notre Seigneur (Acre, 6-11 avril 1166)." *Revue de l'Orient latin*, vol. 8 (1900-1901), pp. 311-17.

Chanson d'Antioche

Chanson d'Antioche, La. 2 vols. Ed. Suzanne Duparc-Quioc. Paris, 1977-78.

Chartes Bourbonnais

Chartes du Bourbonnais 918-1522. Eds. Jacques Monicat & Bernard de Fournoux. Moulins, 1952.

Chaurant

Chaurant, Jacques. *Thomas de Marle, sire de Coucy, sire de Marle, seigneur de La Fère, Vervins, Boves, Pinon et autres lieux*. Marle, 1963.

Chenu

Chenu, Marie Dominique. "Monks, Canons, and Laymen in Search of Apostolic Life." In: Chenu, Marie Dominique. *Nature, Man and Society in the Twelfth Century*. Tr. Jermone Taylor & Lester K. Little. Chicago-London, 1968, pp. 202-38.

Chodorow

Chodorow, Stanley. *Christian Political Theory and Church Politics in the Mid-Twelfth Century: The Ecclesiology of Gratian's Decretum*. UCLA Center for Medieval and Renaissance Studies, no. 5. Berkeley-Los Angeles, 1972.

Chron. Albrici

Chronica Albrici monachi Trium Fontium a monacho novi monasterii Hoiensis interpolata. In: MGHS, vol. 23 (1874, rpt. 1986), pp. 631-950.

Chron. de Morigny

Chronique de Morigny (1095-1152). Ed. Léon Mirot. Collection de textes pour servir à l'étude et à l'enseignement de l'histoire, no. 41. Paris, 1909. 2nd ed., Paris, 1912.

Chron. de Parcé

La Chronique de Parcé. Ed. Henri de Berranger. Archives départmentales de la Sarthe. Inventaires et Documents. Le Mans, 1953.

Chron. Mauriniacensi

Chronico Mauriniacensi, auctoribus Teulfo et aliis ejusdem loci Monachis. In: RHGF, vol. 12 (1781), pp. 68-88.

Chron. St.-Pierre-le-Vif

Chronique de Saint-Pierre-le-Vif de Sens [Chronicon sancti Petri vivi Senonensis]. Eds. Robert-Henri Bautier & Monique Gilles. Paris, 1979.

Chron. Turonensis

Chronica Turonensis. In: RHGF, vol. 12 (1781), pp. 461-78.

Chron. d'Ernoul

Chronique d'Ernoul et de Bernard le Trésorier. Ed. Louis, comte de Mas-Latrie. Paris, 1871.

Classen, "Eschatologische 1"

Classen, Peter."Eschatologische Ideen und Armutsbewegungen im 11. und 12. Jahrhundert." In: *Povertà e ricchezza nella spiritualità dei secoli XI e XII. Convegni del Centro di Studi sulla spiritualità medievale, VIII.* L'accademia Tudertina, Todi, 1969, pp. 127-62.

Classen,
"Eschatologische 2"

Classen, Peter. "Eschatologische Ideen und Armutsbewegungen im 11. und 12. Jahrhundert." In: *Ausgewählte Aufsätze von Peter Classen.* Ed. Josef Fleckenstein. Vorträge und Forschungen, vol. 28. Sigmaringen, 1983, pp. 307-46.

Classiques de l'histoire

Classiques de l'histoire de France au Moyen Age. Eds. Louis Halphen, et al. L'Association Guillaume Budé. Paris, 1923-.

Clermont-Ganneau

Clermont-Ganneau, Charles Simon. *Archaeological Researches in Palestine During the Years 1873-1874.* 2 vols: vol. 1 (1899); vol. 2 (1896). London, 1896-1899.

Cokayne, *Complete Peerage*

Cokayne, George Edward, Vicary Gibbs, et al., eds. *The Complete Peerage of England, Scotland, Ireland, Great Britain and the United Kingdom, extent, extinct or dormant.* Rev. ed. 13 vols. London, 1910-59.

Collection de documents

Collection de documents inédits sur l'histoire de France. Paris, 1835-.

Collection de textes

Collection de textes pour servir à l'étude et à l'enseignement de l'histoire. 51 vols. Paris, 1886-1929.

Collenberg, "Choix"

Collenberg, Wipertus-Hugo Rudt de. "Le choix des exécuteurs dans les bulles de provision au XIVe siècle." *MEFR(MA)*, vol. 92 (1980), pp. 393-440.

Collenberg, "Chypre"

Collenberg, Wipertus-Hugo Rudt de. "Le royaume et l'Eglise latine de Chypre et la papauté, de 1417 à 1471." *Epeteris* (Center of Scientific Research, Nicosia), vols. 13-16 (1984-1987), pp. 63-193.

Collenberg, "Grâces"

Collenberg, Wipertus-Hugo Rudt de. "Les grâces papales autres que les dispenses matrimoniales accordées à Chypre de 1305 à 1378." *Epeteris*, vol. 8 (1975-77), pp. 187-252.

Collenberg, "Ibelin"

Collenberg, Wipertus-Hugo Rudt de. "Les Ibelin aux XIIIe et XIVe siècles." *Epeteris*, vol. 9 (1977-79), pp. 117-265 (rpt. in his *Familles de l'Orient latin, XIIe-XIVe siècles.* London: Variorum, 1983, ch. 4).

Collenberg, "Schisme"

Collenberg, Wipertus-Hugo Rudt de. "Le royaume et l'Eglise de chypre face au Grand Schisme." *MEFR(MA)*, vol. 94 (1982), pp. 621-701.

Collet

Collet, Giancarlo. *Das Missionsverständnis der Kirche in der gegenwärtigen Diskussion.* Tübinger Theologische Studien, vol. 24. Mainz, 1984.

Colloquio, *Livonia*   Atti del colloquio internazionale di storia ecclesiastica in occasione dell'VIII centenario della chiesa in Livonia (1186-1986), Rome, 24-25 June, 1986. *Gli inizi del Cristianesimo in Livonia-Lettonia.* Vatican City, 1989.

Conant   Conant, Kenneth John. *Carolingian and Romanesque Architecture, 800-1200.* 2nd ed. Baltimore, 1966.

Conder & Kitchener   Conder, Claude Reignier & Herbert Horatio Kitchener. *The Survey of Western Palestine: Memoirs of the topography, orography, hydrography and archaeology.* 3 vols. London, 1881-1883.

Congar   Congar, Yves. "L'écclésiologie de S. Bernard." In: *Analecta sacri ordinis Cisterciensis* (Saint Bernard théologien: actes du congrès de Dijon, 15-19 septembre 1953), vol. 9, pts. 3-4 (1953), pp. 136-90.

Constable, "Lost Sermon"   Constable, Giles. "A Report of a Lost Sermon by St. Bernard on the Failure of the Second Crusade." In: *Studies in Medieval Cistercian History*, vol. 1. Cistercian Fathers' Series, no. 13. Spencer, Mass., 1971, pp. 49-54.

Constable, "Second Crusade"   Constable, Giles. "The Second Crusade as Seen by Contemporaries." *Traditio*, vol. 9 (1953), pp. 213-79.

Constable, "Study"   Constable, Giles. "The Study of Monastic History Today." In: *Essays on the Reconstruction of Medieval History.* Eds. Vaclav Mudroch & G.S. Couse. Montreal-London, 1974, pp. 21-51.

Constable, "Suger"   Constable, Giles. "Suger's Monastic Administration." In his: *Monks, Hermits and Crusaders in Medieval Europe.* London: Variorum, 1988, pp. 1-51.

Cont. Guillaume de Tyr   *La Continuation de Guillaume de Tyr 1184-1197.* Ed. Margaret Ruth Morgan. Documents relatifs à l'Histoire des Croisades, vol. 14. Académie des Inscriptions et Belles-Lettres. Paris, 1982.

Cont. Praemon.   *Continuatio Praemonstratensis a. 1113-1155 (Sigeberti Gemblacensis).* Ed. Ludwig C. Bethmann. In: MGHS, vol. 6 (1844, rpt. 1925, 1980), pp. 447-56.

Corbo   Corbo, Virgilio Canio. *Il Santo Sepolcro di Gerusalemme.* 3 parts. Collectio maior, no. 29. Jerusalem, 1981-1982.

Corpus iuris canonici (1605)   *Corpus iuris canonici una cum glossis et additionibus.* 3 vols. in 5 parts. Venice, 1605.

Corpus iuris canonici (1879)   *Corpus iuris canonici. Ed. Lipsiensis II.* Eds. Emil Albert Friedberg & Aemilius Ludwig Richter. 2 vols. Leipzig, 1879-1881 (rpts. Leipzig, 1922; Graz, 1955, 1959).

Corpus Vitrearum	*Corpus Vitrearum Medii Aevi.* Vol. 1: *Les Vitraux de Notre-Dame et de la Sainte-Chapelle de Paris.* Eds. Marcel Aubert, Louis Grodecki, Jean Lafond & Jean Verrier. Comité international d'histoire de l'art. Paris, 1959.
Cowdrey, "Peace & Truce"	Cowdrey, H.E.J. "The Peace and the Truce of God in the Eleventh Century." *Past and Present*, vol. 46 (1970), pp. 42-67.
Cowdrey, "Pope Gregory"	Cowdrey, H.E.J. "Pope Gregory VII's Crusading Plans of 1074." In: *Outremer*, pp. 27-40.
Creswell	Creswell, Keppel Archibald Cameron, Sir. *Early Muslim Architecture.* 2nd ed. 2 vols. Oxford, 1969.
Crist	Crist, Larry. "Dieu ou ma dame: The Polysemic Object of Love in Jaufré Rudel's 'Lanquan li jorn.'" *Marche romane*, vol. 29 (1979), pp. 61-75.
Crocker	Crocker, Richard L. "Early Crusade Songs." In: Murphy, *The Holy War*, pp. 78-98.
Curzon	Curzon, Henri de. *La Règle du Temple.* Paris, 1886.
Dante, *Vita nuova*	Dante Alighieri. *Das neue Leben [Vita nuova].* Ed. Ulrich Leo; tr. Karl Federn. Exempla Classica no. 90. Frankfurt/M-Hamburg, 1964.
De tempore antichristi	*De tempore antichristi.* In: Adso, *De ortu*, pp. 129-37.
Delaruelle, "Bernard"	Delaruelle, Etienne. "L'idée de Croisade chez Saint Bernard." In: *Mélanges St. Bernard.* 24ᵉ Congrès de l'Association bourguignonne des sociétés savantes, 8ᵉ centenaire de la mort de Saint Bernard. Dijon, 1953, pp. 53-67.
Delaruelle, *Croisade*	Delaruelle, Etienne. *L'idée de croisade au moyen âge.* Turin, 1980.
Demm	Demm, Eberhard. *Reformmönchtum und Slawenmission im 12. Jahrhundert.* Historische Studien, vol. 419. Lübeck-Hamburg, 1970.
Demurger	Demurger, Alain. *Vie et mort de l'Ordre du Temple 1118-1314.* Paris, 1985.
Demus	Demus, Otto. *Romanesque Mural Painting.* New York, 1970.
Denny	Denny, Don. "A Romanesque Fresco in Auxerre Cathedral." *Gesta*, vol. 25 (1986), pp. 197-202.
Dichter	Dichter, Bernard. *The Orders and Churches of Crusader Acre.* Acre, 1979.
Dimier & Porcher	Dimier, M.-Anselme & Jean Porcher. *L'Art cistercien.* 3rd. ed. La Nuit des Temps, vol. 16. Editions Zodiaque: La Pierre-Qui-Vire, 1982.

Dion
Dion, Adolphe de. *Le Puiset au XIe et au XIIe siècles, châtellenie et prieuré*. Chartres, 1886.

Donkin
Donkin, R.A. *The Cistercians: Studies in the geography of medieval England and Wales*. Toronto, 1978.

Douglas
Douglas, David Charles. *William the Conqueror: The Norman Impact upon England*. London, 1964 (rpt. 1966).

Duby, *Bouvines*
Duby, Georges. *Le dimanche de Bouvines: 27 juillet 1214*. Paris, 1973.

Duby, *Hommes*
Duby, Georges. *Hommes et structures du moyen âge*. 2 vols. Paris, 1988.

Duby, "Jeunes"
Duby, Georges. "Au XIIe siècle: Les 'Jeunes' dans la société aristocratique." *Annales*, vol. 19 (1964), pp. 835-46.

Duby, *Marriage*
Duby, Georges. *Le chevalier, la femme et le prêtre: le marriage dans la France féodale*. Paris, 1981.

Duby, "Origines"
Duby, Georges. "Les origines de la chevalerie." In: *Ordinamenti militari in Occidente nell'alto medioevo. 30 Marzo - 5 Aprile 1967*. Vol. 2. Settimane di studio del centro italiano di studi sull'alto medioevo, no. 15. Spoleto, 1968, pp. 739-61 (Eng. tr. in his *The Chivalrous Tradition*, London, 1979, pp. 158-70).

Duby, "Sociétés"
Duby, Georges. "Les sociétés médiévales. Une approche d'ensemble." In: Duby, *Hommes*, vol. 2, pp. 361-79.

Duby, *Trois ordres*
Duby, Georges. *Les trois ordres ou l'imaginaire du féodalisme*. Paris, 1978.

Duncalf
Duncalf, Frederick. "The Pope's Plan for the First Crusade." In: *The Crusades and Other Historical Essays Presented to Dana C. Munro by His Former Students*. Ed. Louis John Paetow. New York, 1928, pp. 44-57.

Duparc-Quioc, "Coucy"
Duparc-Quioc, Suzanne. "La famille de Coucy et la composition de *La Chanson de Jérusalem*." *Romania*, vol. 65 (1938), pp. 245-52.

Durparc-Quioc, *Cycle*
Duparc-Quioc, Suzanne. *Le Cycle de la Croisade*. Paris, 1955.

Ebo, *Vita*
Ebo. *Vita S. Ottonis Episcopi Babenbergensis*. Ed. & tr. Jan Wikarjak. In: MPH, n.s., vol. 7(2). Warsaw, 1969.

Edbury, *Crusade*
Edbury, Peter W., ed. *Crusade and Settlement*. Cardiff, 1985.

Edbury & Rowe
Edbury, Peter W. & John Gordon Rowe. *William of Tyre: Historian of the Latin East*. Cambridge, 1988.

Ehrenkreutz, "Naval History"
Ehrenkreutz, Andrew S. "The Place of Saladin in the Naval History of the Mediterranean Sea in the Middle Ages." *Journal of the American Oriental Society*, vol. 75 (1955), pp. 100-116.

Bibliography

223

Ehrenkreutz, *Saladin* — Ehrenkreutz, Andrew S. *Saladin*. Albany, 1972.

Ekkehard, *Chronica* — Ekkehard. *Ekkehardi Chronica*. In: *Frutolfs und Ekkehards Chroniken und die anonyme Kaiserchronik*. Ed. & tr. Franz-Josef Schmale and Irene Schmale-Ott. Ausgewählte Quellen zur deutschen Geschichte des Mittelalters, vol. 15. Darmstadt, 1972, pp. 267-334.

Ekkehard, *Hierosolymita* — Ekkehard. *Hierosolymita: De oppressione, liberatione ac restauratione Jerosolymitanae Ecclesiae*. In: RHC Oc., vol. 5 (1894), pp. 1-40.

Eldridge — Eldridge, Laurence. "Walter of Châtillon and the Decretum of Gratian: An Analysis of 'Propter Sion non tacebo'." *Studies in Medieval Culture*, vol. 3 (Kalamazoo, 1970), pp. 59-69.

Enlart, "Belmont" — Enlart, Camille. "L'abbaye cistercienne de Belmont en Syrie." *Syria*, vol. 4 (1923), pp. 1-22, pls. I-IX.

Enlart, *Chypre* — Enlart, Camille. *L'art gothique et la Renaissance en Chypre*. 2 vols. Paris, 1899 (for English ed., see: Enlart, *Cyprus*).

Enlart, *Cyprus* — Enlart, Camille. *Gothic Art and the Renaissance in Cyprus*. Ed. & tr. Sir David Hunt. London, 1987 (for French ed., see: Enlart, *Chypre*).

Enlart, *Monuments* — Enlart, Camille. *Les Monuments des Croisés dans le Royaume de Jérusalem: Architecture religieuse et civile*. 2 vols & 2 albums. Haut-Commission de la République française en Syrie et au Liban, Service des Antiquités et des Beaux-Arts. Bibliothèque archéologique et historique, vols. 7-8. Paris, 1925 & 1928.

Enlart, "Nicosie" — Enlart, Camille. "L'ancien monastère des Franciscains à Nicosie de Chypre." In: Vogüé, *Florilegium*, pp. 215-19.

Erdmann, "Endkaiserglaube" — Erdmann, Carl. "Endkaiserglaube und Kreuzzugsgedanke im 11. Jahrhundert." In: *Zeitschrift für Kirchengeschichte*, vol. 51, (1932), pp. 384-414.

Erdmann, *Entstehung* — Erdmann, Carl. *Die Entstehung des Kreuzzugsgedankens*. Stuttgart, 1935.

Erdmann, "Heidenkrieg" — Erdmann, Carl. "Der Heidenkrieg in der Liturgie und Kaiserkrönung Ottos I." In: Beumann, pp. 47-64.

Erdmann, *Origin* — Erdmann, Carl. *The Origin of the Idea of Crusade*. Tr. Marshall W. Baldwin & Walter Goffart. Princeton, 1977.

Eugenius III, *Epistolae* — Eugenius III, pope. *Epistolae*. In: RHGF, vol. 15 (1808), pp. 423-83.

Eugenius III, *Epistolae 2* — Eugenius III, pope. *Epistolae et Privilegia*. In: PL, vol. 180 (1902).

Eugenius III, "Quantum"

Eugenius III, pope. "Quantum predecessores." In: Otto of Freising, *Gesta* 1, pp. 55-57 (Eng. ed. in: Otto of Freising, *Deeds*, pp. 71-73; & in: Brundage, *Documentary*, pp. 86-88).

Ex anonymi chronico

Ex anonymi chronico. In: RHGF, vol. 12 (1781), pp. 118-21.

Favreau-Lilie, *Italiener*

Favreau-Lilie, Marie-Luise. *Die Italiener im Heiligen Land, vom ersten Kreuzzug bis zum Tode Heinrichs von Champagne (1008-1197)*. Amsterdam, 1989.

Favreau-Lilie, "Kirchen"

Favreau-Lilie, Marie-Luise. "Die italienischen Kirchen im Heiligen Land (1098-1291)." *Studi veneziani*, n.s., vol. 13 (1987), pp. 15-101.

Fedden & Thomson

Fedden, Robin & John Thomson. *Crusader Castles*. 2nd ed. London, 1957.

Felix Faber

Felix Faber. *Fratris Felicis Fabri Evagatorium in Terrae Sanctae, Arabiae et Egypti peregrinationem*. 3 vols. Ed. C.D. Hassler. Bibliothek des literarischen Vereins in Stuttgart, vol. 2. Stuttgart, 1843.

Ferzoco

Ferzoco, George Piero. *Bernard of Clairvaux and Early Cistercian Thought regarding the Salvific Role of Violence in Twelfth-Century Christian Society*. MA thesis. Peterborough: Trent University, 1985.

Fleckenstein

Fleckenstein, J. & M. Hellmann, eds. *Die geistliche Ritterorden Europas*. Vorträge und Forschungen, vol. 26. Sigmaringen, 1980.

Fliche

Fliche, Augustin. "Urbain II et la Croisade." *Revue d'histoire de l'église de France*, vol. 13 (1927), pp. 289-306.

Fliche & Martin

Fliche, Augustin & Victor Martin, eds. *Histoire de l'église depuis les origines jusqu'à nos jours*. 21 vols. Paris, 1938- 1952 (rpt. 1948-1963).

Flori, "Adoubement"

Flori, Jean. "Les origines de l'adoubement chevaleresque: étude des remises d'armes et du vocabulaire qui les exprime dans les sources historiques latines jusqu'au début du XIIIe siècle." *Traditio*, vol. 35 (1979), pp. 209-72.

Flori, *Chansons*

Flori, Jean. "La notion de chevalerie dans les chansons de geste du XIIe siècle: étude historique du vocabulaire." *Moyen Age*, vol. 81 (1975), pp. 211-44; 407-44.

Flori, "Chevalerie"

Flori, Jean. "Chevalerie et liturgie. Remise des armes et vocabulaire 'chevaleresque' dans les sources liturgiques du IXe au XIVe siècle." *Moyen Age*, vol. 84 (1978), pp. 247-78.

Flori, *Glaive*

Flori, Jean. *L'idéologie du glaive. Préhistoire de la chevalerie*. Geneva, 1984.

Folda, *Crusader Art*   Folda, Jaroslav, ed. *Crusader Art in the Twelfth Century*. British Archaeological Reports. International Series, no. 152. Oxford, 1982.

Folda, "Painting"   Folda, Jaroslav. "Painting and Sculpture in the Latin Kingdom of Jerusalem, 1099-1291." In: Setton, vol. 4 (1977), pp. 251-80.

Fourrier   Fourrier, Anthime. "Retour au *terminus*." In: *Mélanges de langue et de littérature du moyen âge et de la renaissance offerts à Jean Frappier*. Publications romanes et françaises, no. 112. Geneva, 1970, vol. 1 of 2 vols., pp. 299-311.

Fracheboud   Fracheboud, André. "'Je suis la chimère de mon siècle.' Le problème action-contemplation au coeur de saint Bernard." *Collectanea Ordinis Cisterciensium Reformatorum*, vol. 16 (1954), pp. 45-52, 128-36, 183-91.

Frank, "Distant"   Frank, Grace. "The Distant Love of Jaufré Rudel." *Modern Language Notes*, vol. 57 (1942), pp. 528-34.

Frank, "Jaufré"   Frank, Grace. "Jaufré Rudel, Casella and Spitzer." *Modern Language Notes*, vol. 59 (1944), pp. 526-31.

Fried   Fried, Johannes. "Endzeiterwartung um die Jahrtausendwende." *Deutsches Archiv für Erforschung des Mittelalters*, vol. 45 (1989), pp. 381-473.

Frizen   Frizen, Hildegunde. "Die Geschichte des Klosters Schwarzrheindorf von den Anfängen bis zum Beginn der Neuzeit." Ph.D. dissertation. Bonn, 1983.

Frohnes   Frohnes, Heinzgünter, Hans-Werner Gensichen & Georg Kretschmar, series eds. *Kirchengeschichte als Missionsgeschichte*. Vols. 1 & 2, pt. 1, *Die Kirche des früheren Mittelalters*, ed. Knut Schäferdiek. Munich, 1974 & 1978.

Fulcher, *Historia* 1   Fulcher of Chartres. *Historia Hierosolymitana*. In: RHC Oc, vol. 3 (1866), pp. 311-485.

Fulcher, *Historia* 2   Fulcher of Chartres. *Fulcheri Carnotensis Historia Hierosolymitana (1095-1127)*. Ed. Heinrich Hagenmeyer. Heidelberg, 1913.

GC   *Gallia Christiana in provincias ecclesiasticas distributa*. 16 vols. Paris, 1715-1865.

Geoffrey of Auxerre, *Vita 1*   Geoffrey of Auxerre. *Vita prima sancti Bernardi*. In: PL, vol. 185 (1855), cols. 410-16.

Geoffrey of Auxerre, *Vita 3*   Geoffrey of Auxerre. *Fragmenta ex tertia vita sancti Bernardi*. In: PL, vol. 185, pt. 1 (1879), cols. 523D-530.

Gerald of Wales   Gerald of Wales. *Opera*. 8 vols. Ed. J.S. Brewer, et al. RS, vol. 21. London, 1861-1891.

Gervase of Canterbury	Gervase of Canterbury. *Historical Works*. 2 vols. Ed. Wm. Stubbs. RS, vol. 73. London, 1879-80.
Gervers	Gervers, Michael. "Rotundae Anglicanae." In: *Actes du 22ᵉ Congrès international d'histoire de l'art, Budapest, 1969*. Budapest, 1972. Text: vol. 1, pp. 359-76; pls., vol. 3, pp. 109-114.
Gesta Francorum	*Gesta Francorum et aliorum Hierosolimitanorum [The Deeds of the Franks and the other Pilgrims to Jerusalem]*. Ed. Rosalind Hill. London, 1962.
Gesta Guillelmi	Guillaume de Poitiers [Guillelmus Pictavensis]. *Histoire de Guillaume le Conquérant [Gesta Guillelmi II ducis Normannorum, et Regis Anglorum]*. Ed. & tr. Raymond Foreville. Les Classiques de l'histoire de France au moyen âge, vol. 23. Paris, 1952.
Gesta Regis Henrici II	*Gesta Regis Henrici Secundi* (attr. to Benedict of Peterborough). 2 vols. Ed. William Stubbs. RS, vol. 49 (1867).
Gesta Stephani	*Gesta Stephani*. Ed. & tr. K.R. Potter. Edinburgh, 1955.
Gilchrist, "Canon Law"	Gilchrist, John T. "Canon Law Aspects of the Eleventh Century Gregorian Reform Program." *Journal of Ecclesiastical History*, vol 13 (1962), pp. 21-38.
Gilchrist, "Erdmann Thesis"	Gilchrist, John T. "The Erdmann Thesis and the Canon Law 1083-1141." In: Edbury, *Crusade*, pp. 37-45.
Gillingham, "Howden"	Gillingham, John B. "Roger of Howden on Crusade." In: *Medieval Historical Writing in the Christian and Islamic Worlds*. Ed. D.O. Morgan. London, 1982, pp. 60-75.
Gillingham, "Richard I"	Gillingham, John [B.]. "Richard I and the Science of War in the Middle Ages." In: *War and Government in the Middle Ages: Essays in Honour of J.O. Prestwich*. Eds. John Gillingham & J.C. Holt. Woodbridge, 1984, pp. 78-91.
Golubovich	Golubovich, Girolamo P. *Biblioteca biobibliografica della Terra Santa e dell'Oriente francescano*. 9 vols. Florence, 1906-1927.
Graboïs, *Civilisation*	Graboïs, Aryeh. *Civilisation et société dans l'Occident médiéval*. London, 1983.
Graboïs, "Crusade"	Graboïs, Aryeh. "The Crusade of King Louis VII: A Reconsideration." In: Edbury, *Crusade*, pp. 94-104.
Graboïs, "Louis VII"	Graboïs, Aryeh. "Louis VII pélerin." *Revue d'Histoire de l'Eglise de France*, vol. 74 (1988), pp. 5-22.
Graboïs, "Quartier Latin"	Graboïs, Aryeh. "La genèse du Quartier Latin." *Scripta Hierosolymitana*, vol. 23 (1972), pp. 146-64.

Graboïs, "Trêve"	Graboïs, Aryeh. "De la trêve de Dieu à la paix du roi: Etude sur les transformations du mouvement de la paix au XIIe siècle." In: *Mélanges Crozet*. Vol. 1, pp. 585-96.
Gratian, *Decretum* 1	Gratian. *Decretum*. In: PL, vol. 187 (1861).
Gratian, *Decretum* 2	Gratian. *Decretum Gratiani*. In: *Corpus iuris canonici*, vol. 1 (1879).
Gregory I, *Registrum*	Gregory I, pope. *Gregorii I Papae Registrum Epistolarum*. 2 Vols. In: MGH Epist. Vol. 1: Lib. I-VII. Ed. P. Ewald & L.M. Hartmann. Berlin, 1887-1891. Vol. 2: Lib. VIII-XIV. Ed. post P. Ewaldi obitum & L.M. Hartmann. Berlin, 1892-1899 (rpt. 1957, 1978 in 2 vols.).
Gregory VII, *Register*	Gregory VII, pope. *Das Register Gregors VII*. Ed. Erich Caspar. In: MGH Epistolae selectae in usum scholarum IV, vol. 2. Berlin, 1957.
Greschat, *Kirchengeschichte*	*Gestalten der Kirchengeschichte*. 12 vols. Ed. Martin Greschat. Stuttgart-Berlin-Cologne-Mainz, 1981-1985.
Guibert of Nogent, *Gesta*	Guibert of Nogent. *Gesta Dei per Francos*. In: RHC Oc., vol. 4 (1879), pp. 113-263.
Guibert of Nogent, *Vita*	Guibert of Nogent. *Guibert de Nogent: histoire de sa vie (1053-1124)* [*De Vita Sua*]. Ed. Georges Bourgin. Paris, 1907.
Guichenon	Guichenon, Samuel. *Histoire génealogique de la royale maison de Savoie*. 2 pts., 6 vols. Lyon, 1660.
Guth, "Cramers"	Guth, Klaus. "Daniel Cramers Pommerische Chronica von 1602." *BHVB*, vol. 120 (1984), pp. 111-20.
Guth, "Dreifache"	Guth, Klaus. "Der dreifache Schriftsinn. Mittelalterliche Philosophie und Exegese im Gespräch." In: *Actualitas omnium actuum*. Festschrift Heinrich Beck. Ed. E. Schadel. Schriften zur Triadik und Ontodynamik, vol. 3. Frankfurt/M-Bern-New York-Paris, 1989. pp. 219-34.
Guth, *Guibert*	Guth, Klaus. *Guibert von Nogent und die hochmittelalterliche Kritik an der Reliquienverehrung*. Erganzungsbände, vol. 21. Ottobeuren, 1970.
Guth, "Kulturkontakte"	Guth, Klaus. "Kulturkontakte zwischen Deutschen und Slawen nach Thietmar von Merseburg." In: *Historiographia Mediaevalis*. Festschrift für Franz-Josef Schmale zum 65. Geburtstag. Eds. Dieter Berg & Hans-Werner Goetz. Studien zur Geschichtsschreiburg und Quellenkunde des Mittelalters. Darmstadt, 1988. pp. 88-102.
Guttenberg	Guttenberg, Erich Freiherr von & Alfred Wendehorst. *Das Bistum Bamberg*, vol. 1. In: *Auftrage des Max-Planck-Instituts*

für Geschichte bearbeitet. Germania sacra, 2. Abt. Die Bistümer der Kirchenprovinz Mainz. Berlin, 1937.

Hackett   Hackett, John. *A history of the orthodox church of Cyprus.* London, 1901.

Hagenmeyer,   Hagenmeyer, Heinrich, ed. *Die Kreuzzugsbriefe aus den Jahren*
Kreuzzugsbriefe   *1088-1100 [Epistulae et chartae ad historiam primi belli sacri spectantes quae supersunt aero aequales ac Genvinae].* Innsbruck, 1901 (rpt. Hildesheim, 1973).

Halphen   Halphen, Louis. *Le Comté d'Anjou au XIe siècle.* Paris, 1906.

Hamilton, "Cistercians"   Hamilton, Bernard. "The Cistercians in the Crusader States." In: *One Yet Two: Monastic Tradition East and West.* Ed. M. Basil Pennington. Orthodox-Cistercian Symposium, Oxford University, 1973. Cistercian Studies, no. 29. Kalamazoo, 1976, pp. 405-22 (rpt. in his *Monastic Reform, Catharism and the Crusade.* London: Variorum, 1979).

Hamilton, *Latin Church*   Hamilton, Bernard. *The Latin Church in the Crusader States: The Secular Church.* London: Variorum, 1980.

Harnack   Harnack, Adolf. *Militia Christi: The Christian Religion and the Military in the First Three Centuries.* Tr. David McInnes Gracie. Philadelphia, 1981.

Hatem   Hatem, Anouar. *Les poèmes épiques des croisades.* Paris, 1932.

Hauck   Hauck, Albert. *Kirchengeschichte Deutschlands.* 8th ed. 5 vols. in 6 bks. Berlin, 1954.

Hehl   Hehl, Ernst-Dieter. *Kirche und Krieg im 12. Jahrhundert: Studien zum kanonischen Recht und politischer Wirklichkeit.* Monographien zur Geschichte des Mittelalters, vol. 19. Stuttgart, 1980.

Hellmann   Hellmann, Manfred, ed. *Studien über die Anfänge der Mission in Livland.* Sigmaringen, 1989.

Helmholz   Helmholz, Richard H. *Marriage Litigation in Medieval England.* Cambridge, 1974.

Henriquez   Henriquez, Chrysostomos. *Menologium. Regula, constitutiones et privilegia ordinis Cisterciensis.* Antwerp, 1630.

Henry of Breitenau   Henry, abbot of Breitenau. *Passio S. Thiemonis.* In: RHC Oc., vol. 5 (1906), pp. 203-206.

Henry of Huntingdon   Henry, archdeacon of Huntingdon. *Historia Anglorum.* Ed. T. Arnold. RS, vol. 74. London, 1879.

Henry of Livonia   Henry of Livonia. *The Chronicle of Henry of Livonia.* Tr. James A. Brundage. Madison, 1961.

Herbord	Herbord. *Dialogus de Vita S. Ottonis Episcopi Babenbergensis.* Ed. & tr. Jan Wikarjak. In: MPH, n.s., vol. 7(3). Warsaw, 1974.
Herlihy	Herlihy, David, comp. *The History of Feudalism.* New York, 1970.
Hiestand, "Kardinalbischof"	Hiestand, Rudolf. "Kardinalbischof Matthäus von Albano, das Konzil von Troyes und die Entstehung des Templerordens." In: *Zeitschrift für Kirchengeschichte*, vol. 99 (1988), pp. 295-323.
Hiestand, "Konrad"	Hiestand, Rudolf. "'Kaiser' Konrad III, der zweite Kreuzzug und ein verlorenes Diplom für den Berg Thabor." *Deutsches Archiv für Erforschung des Mittelalters*, vol. 35 (1979), pp. 82-126.
Hiestand, *Papsturkunden* 1	Hiestand, Rudolf, ed. *Papsturkunden für Templer und Johanniter.* Vorarbeiten für den Oriens pontificius I. Abhandlungen der Akademie der Wissenschaften in Göttingen, no. 77. Göttingen, 1972.
Hiestand, *Papsturkunden* 2	Hiestand, Rudolf, ed. *Papsturkunden für Templer und Johanniter.* Vorarbeiten zum Oriens pontificius II. N.s. Abhandlungen der Akademie der Wissenschaften in Göttingen, no. 135. Göttingen, 1984.
Hill	Hill, Bennett D. *English Cistercian Monasteries and their Patrons in the Twelfth Century.* Urbana, 1968.
Historia Ludovici VII	*Historia gloriosi regis Ludovici VII, filii Ludovici Grossi.* In: RHGF, vol. 12 (1781), pp. 124-33.
Historia pontificum	*Historia pontificum et comitum Engolismensium.* In: RHGF, vol. 12 (1781), pp. 393-400.
Hoag	Hoag, John D. *Islamic Architecture.* New York, 1977.
Hoffmann	Hoffmann, Hartmut. *Gottesfriede und Treuga Die.* MGH Schriften, vol. 20. Stuttgart, 1964.
Hofmeister	Hofmeister, Philip, OSB. "Mönchtum und Seelsorge bis zum 13. Jahrhundert." *Studien und Mitteilungen zur Geschichte des Benediktiner-Ordens und seiner Zweige*, vol. 65 (1953-54). Munich, 1955, pp. 209-73.
Holtzmann	Holtzmann, Walther. "Studien zur Orientpolitik des Reformpapsttums und zur Entstehung des ersten Kreuzzuges." *Historische Vierteljahrschrift*, vol. 22 (1924-25), pp. 167-99.
Honorius	*Honorius Augustodunensis. Beitrag zur Geschichte geistigen Lebens im 12. Jahrhundert.* Ed. Joseph Anton Endres. Kempten, 1906.
Hölzle	Hölzle, Peter. *Die Kreuzzüge in der okzitanischen und deutschen Lyrik des 12. Jahrhunderts.* 2 vols. Vol. 1: *Untersuchung.* Vol. 2: *Materialen.* Göppinger, 1980.

Hunt

Hunt, Tony. "The Emergence of the Knight in France and England: 1000-1200." In: *Knighthood in Medieval Literature*. Ed. W.H. Jackson. London, 1981, pp. 1-22.

Ibn al-Qalanisi

Ibn al-Qalanisi, Hamza. *The Damascus Chronicle of the Crusades*. Extracted and tr. from the Chronicle of Ibn al-Qalanisi by Hamilton A.R. Gibb. London, 1932.

Idung of Prüfening, "Argument"

Idung of Prüfening. "Argument concerning Four Questions." Tr. Joseph Leahey. In: Idung of Prüfening, *Cistercians*, pp. 143-92.

Idung of Prüfening, "Argumentum"

Idung von Prüfening. "Argumentum super quattuor questionibus: Unus enim et idem homo est et clericus et monachus; monachus in eo, quod fecit professionem monasticam; clericus in eo, quod habet officium clericale." In: Demm, pp. 113-33.

Idung of Prüfening, *Cistercians*

Idung of Prüfening. *Cistercians and Cluniacs: The Case for Cîteaux [Dialogus duorum monachorum & De quatuor quaestionibus]*. Eds. & trs. Jeremiah F. O'Sullivan & Joseph Leahey. Cistercian Fathers Series, no. 33. Kalamazoo, 1977.

Idung of Prüfening, "Dialogue"

Idung of Prüfening. "A Dialogue between Two Monks." Tr. Jeremiah F. O'Sullivan. In: Idung of Prüfening, *Cistercians*, pp. 3-141.

Innocent III, *Opera*

Innocent III, pope. *Opera Omnia*, PL, vol. 214 (1890).

Ivo, "Decretum"

Ivo, bishop of Chartres. "Decretum." In: *Opera Omnia*. PL, vol. 161 (1889), cols. 47-1036.

Ivo, "Panormia"

Ivo, bishop of Chartres. "Panormia." In: *Opera Omnia*. PL, vol. 161 (1889), cols. 1037-1344.

Jacoby

Jacoby, David. "Montmusard, Suburb of Crusader Acre: The First Stage of its Development." In: *Outremer*, pp. 205-217.

Jacqueline, *Episcopat*

Jacqueline, Bernard. *Episcopat et papauté chez Saint Bernard de Clairvaux*. Saint-Marguerite-d'Elle, 1975.

Jacqueline, *Papauté*

Jacqueline, Bernard. *Papauté et épiscopat selon Saint Bernard de Clairvaux*. Paris, 1963.

Jacqueline, "Pape"

Jacqueline, Bernard. "Le pape d'après le livre II du 'De consideratione ad Eugenium papam' de Saint Bernard de Clairvaux." *Studia Gratiana*, vol. 14 (1967), pp. 219-39.

Jacqueline, "Yves de Chartres"

Jacqueline, Bernard. "Yves de Chartres et Saint Bernard." In: *Etudes d'histoire de droit canonique dédiées à Gabriel Le Bras*. Vol. 1 of 2. Paris, 1965, pp. 179-84.

Jacques de Vitry

Jacques de Vitry. *Die Exempla aus den Sermones feriales et communes*. No. 83. Ed. Joseph Greven. Sammlung mittellateinischer Texte, vol. 9. Heidelberg, 1914.

Jaffé-Loewenfeld — *Regesta pontificum romanorum ab condita Ecclesia ad annum post Christum Natum 1198.* Ed. Philipp Jaffé. 2nd ed. 2 vols. Eds. Samuel Loewenfeld, Ferdinand Kaltenbrunner & Paul Ewald. Leipzig, 1885-1888 (rpt. 1965).

Janauschek — Janauschek, Leopold. *Originum cisterciensium tomus primus, in quo praemissis congregationum domiciliis adjectisque tabulis chronologico-genealogicis veterum abbatiarum a monachis habitatarum fundationes ad fidem antiquissimorum fontium primus descripsit.* Vienna, 1877 (rpt. Ridgewood, N.J., 1968).

Jeffery — Jeffery, George. *A description of the historic monuments of Cyprus.* Nicosia, 1918.

Johannes de Legnano — Johannes de Legnano. *Super Clementina "Saepe".* Ed. Ludwig Wahrmund. In: *Quellen zur Geschichte des römisch-kanonischen Prozesses im Mittelalter*, vol. 4, pt. 6. Innsbruck, 1928 (rpt. Aalen, 1962), pp. 1-30.

Johannes Monachus — Johannes Monachus. *Glossa ordinaria* to *Unam sanctam.* In: *Corpus iuris canonici* (1605), vol. 4.

Johannes Phocas — Johannes Phocas. *Descriptio Terrae Sanctae.* PG, vol. 133 (1864), cols. 927-62.

Johannes Teutonicus — Johannes Teutonicus. *Glossa ordinaria* to the *Decretum Gratiani.* In: *Corpus iuris canonici* (1605), vol. 1.

John of Salisbury — John of Salisbury. *Historia Pontificalis: Memoirs of the Papal Court.* Ed. & tr. Marjorie Chibnall. Nelson, 1956 (rpt. with corrections: Oxford Medieval Texts, Oxford, 1986).

Johrendt — Johrendt, J. *Milites und militia im 11. Jahrhundert. Untersuchung zur Frühgeschichte des Rittertums in Frankreich und Deutschland.* (Ph.D. thesis) Erlangen-Nürnberg, 1971.

Kahl, "1147" — Kahl, Hans-Dietrich. "Wie kam es 1147 zum 'Wendenkreuzzug'?" In: *Festschrift H. Ludat. Europa Slavica-Europa Orientalis.* Eds. Klaus-Dietrich Grothusen & Klaus Zernack. Berlin, 1980. pp. 286-96.

Kahl, "Antichristo" — "Der sog. 'Ludus de Antichristo' (De fine saeculorum) als Zeugnis frühstauferzeitlicher Gegenwartskritik." In: *Mediaevistik*, vol. 4 (1991). In press.

Kahl, "Auszujäten" — Kahl, Hans-Dietrich. "'... Auszujäten von der Erde die Feinde des Christennamens.' Der Plan zum 'Wendenkreuzzug' von 1147 als Umsetzung sibyllinischer Eschatologie." In: *Jahrbuch für die Geschichte Mittel- und Ostdeutschlands*, vol. 39 (1990), pp. 133-60.

Kahl, "Bernard 1" — Kahl, Hans-Dietrich. "Die Kreuzzugseschatologie Bernhards von Clairvaux und ihre missionsgeschichtliche Auswirkung."

In: *Bernhard von Clairvaux und der Beginn der Moderne*. Eds. P. Dinzelbacher & D.R. Bauer. In press.

Kahl, "Bernard 2" Kahl, Hans-Dietrich. "Christianisierungsvorstellungen im Kreuzzugsprogramm Bernhards von Clairvaux: Anmerkungen zum geistesgeschichtlichen Kontext des 'Wendenkreuzzugs' von 1147." In: *Przeglad historyczny*, vol. 75 (1984), pp. 453-61.

Kahl, "Bernard 3" Kahl, Hans-Dietrich. "Die Ableitung des Missionskreuzzugs aus sibyllinischer Eschatologie: Zur Bedeutung Bernhards von Clairvaux für die Zwangschristianisierungsprogramme im Ostseeraum." In: *Die Rolle der Ritterorden in der Christianisierung des Ostseegebietes*. Ed. Zenon Herbert Nowak. Ordines Militares, vol. 1. Torún, 1983, pp. 129-39.

Kahl, "Bernard 4" Kahl, Hans-Dietrich. "Bernhard von Fontaines, Abt von Clairvaux." In: *Gestalten der Kirchengeschichte*, vol. 3. Ed. Martin Greschat. Stuttgart - Berlin - Cologne - Mainz, 1983, pp. 173-91.

Kahl, *"Compellere"* Kahl, Hans-Dietrich. *"Compellere intrare*. Die Wendenpolitik Bruns von Querfurt im Lichte hochmittelalterlichen Missions- und Völkerrechts." In: Beumann, pp. 177-274.

Kahl, "Ergebnis" Kahl, Hans-Dietrich. "Zum Ergebnis des Wendenkreuzzuges von 1147." Zugleich ein Beitrag zur Geschichte des Sächsischen Frühchristentums. In: Beumann, pp. 275-316.

Kahl, *"Fides"* Kahl, Hans-Dietrich. *"Fides cum Ydolatria...*: Ein Kreuzfahrerlied als Quelle für die Kreuzzugseschatologie der Jahre 1146/47." In: *Festschrift B. Schwineköper*. Eds. H. Maurer & H. Patze. Sigmaringen, 1982, pp. 291-307.

Kahl, "Geist" Kahl, Hans-Dietrich. "Zum Geist der deutschen Slawenmission des Hochmittelalters." In: Beumann, pp. 156-76.

Kahl, "Kriegsziel" Kahl, Hans-Dietrich. "Die weltweite Bereinigung der 'Heidenfrage'- ein übersehenes Kriegsziel des zweiten Kreuzzugs." In: *Spannungen und Widersprüche. Gedächtnisschrift für František Graus*. Eds. S. Burghards, et al. Basel, 1991. In press.

Kahl, "Mittelalter" Kahl, Hans-Dietrich. "Was bedeutet: 'Mittelalter'?" *Saeculum*, vol. 40 (1989), pp. 15-38.

Kahl, "Slawen" Kahl, Hans-Dietrich. *Slawen und Deutsche in der brandenburgischen Geschichte des 12. Jahrhunderts. Die Letzten Jahrzehnte des Landes Stodor*. In: Mitteldeutsche Forschungen, vol. 30, pts. 1-2. Cologne-Graz, 1964.

Kahl, "Wendenkreuzzug" Kahl, Hans-Dietrich. "Vom Wendenkreuzzug nach Siebenbürgen? Versuch einer Stellungnahme zu überraschenden Hypothesen." In: *Siebenbürgisches Archiv*, 3rd ser., vol. 8 (1971), pp. 142-99.

Kahl, "Zusammenlebens"

Kahl, Hans-Dietrich. "Die Vorprägung des Zusammenlebens von Christen und Juden in Deutschland durch die ältere Kirchengeschichte." In: *Judenklischees und jüdische Wirklichkeit in unserer Gesellschaft*. Ed. J. Albertz. Schriftenreihe der Freien Akademie, vol. 4. Wiesbaden, 1985 (rpt. 1989), pp. 153-88.

Katzenellenbogen

Katzenellenbogen, Adolf. "The Central Tympanum at Vézelay." *Art Bulletin*, vol. 36 (1944), pp. 141-51.

Kedar, *Crusade*

Kedar, Benjamin Z. *Crusade and Mission: European Approaches Towards the Muslims.* Princeton, N.J., 1984.

Kedar, "Gerard of Nazareth"

Kedar, Benjamin Z. "Gerard of Nazareth: A Neglected Twelfth-Century Writer in the Latin East. A Contribution to the Intellectual and Monastic History of the Crusader States." *Dumbarton Oaks Papers*, vol. 37 (1983), pp. 55-77.

Kedar, "Muslim"

Kedar, Benjamin Z. "Muslim Conversion in Canon Law." In: *Proceedings of the Sixth International Congress of Medieval Canon Law. Berkeley, California, 28 July - 2 August 1980.* Eds. Stephan Kuttner & Kenneth Pennington. Vatican, 1985, pp. 321-32.

Kedar, "Palmarée"

Kedar, Benjamin Z. "Palmarée: Abbaye clunisienne du XIIe siècle en Galilée." *Revue bénédictine*, vol. 93 (1983), pp. 260-69.

Keen

Keen, Maurice Hugh. *Chivalry.* New Haven-London, 1984.

Kenaan

Kenaan, Nurith. "Local Christian Art in Twelfth Century Jerusalem." *Israel Exploration Journal*, vol. 23 (1973), pp. 167-75, 221-29.

Kenaan-Kedar

Kenaan-Kedar, Nurith. "Symbolic Meaning in Crusader Architecture: The Twelfth-Century Dome of the Holy Sepulcher Church in Jerusalem." *Cahiers Archéologiques*, vol. 34 (1986), pp. 109-117.

Kennan

Kennan, Elizabeth. *"De consideratione* of Saint Bernard of Clairvaux and the Papacy in the Mid-twelfth Century: A Review of Scholarship." *Traditio*, vol. 23 (1967), pp. 73-115.

Kertelge

Kertelge, Karl, ed. *Mission im Neuen Testament.* Quaestiones disputatae, vol. 93. Freiburg/Br., 1982.

Keshishian

Keshishian, Kevork K. *Nicosia, capital of Cyprus, then and now.* Nicosia, 1978.

Kinnamos

Kinnamos, John. *Deeds of John and Manuel Comnenus.* Tr. Charles M. Brand. New York, 1976.

Kist

Kist, Johannes. *Fürst- und Erzbistum Bamberg.* 3rd ed. Bamberg, 1962.

Knowles & Hadcock

Medieval Religious Houses, England and Wales. New ed. Eds. David Knowles & R. Neville Hadcock. London, 1971.

Königs

Königs, K. *Schwarzrheindorf 1988.* Bonn, 1988.

Konrad

Konrad, R. "Das himmlische und das irdische Jerusalem im mittelterlichen Denken. Mystische Verstellung und geistliche Wirkung." In: *Speculum Historiale. Geschichte im Spiegel von Geschichtsschreibung u. Geschichtsdeutung* (Johannes Spörl aus Anlass seines 60. Gerburtstages, dargebr. von Weggenossen, Freunden u. Schülern). Ed. Clemens Bauer & Lactitia Boehm. Freiburg-Munich, 1965, pp. 523-40.

Krey, *First Crusade*

Krey, August C. *The First Crusade: The Accounts of Eye-Witnesses and Participants.* Gloucester, Mass, 1958.

Krey, "Urban's Crusade"

Krey, August C. "Urban's Crusade, Success or Failure?" *American Historical Review*, vol. 53 (1948), pp. 235-50.

Kristeva

Kristeva, Julia. *Histoires d'amour.* Paris, 1983. [Eng. ed.: *Tales of Love.* Tr. L. Roudiez. New York, 1987].

Krönig

Krönig, Wolfgang von. "Zur Transfiguration der Cappella Palatina in Palermo." *Zeitschrift für Kunstgeschichte*, vol. 19 (1956), pp. 162-79.

Kugler

Kugler, Bernhard. *Studien zur Geschichte des zweiten Kreuzzuges.* Stuttgart, 1866.

Kühnel

Kühnel, Bianca. "Der Rankenfries am Portal der Grabeskirche zu Jerusalem und die romanische Skulptur in den Abbruzzen." *Arte Medievale*, 2nd series, vol. 1 (1987), pp. 87-125.

Kümmel

Kümmel, W. *Die Missionsmethode des Bischofs Otto von Bamberg und seine Vorläufer in Pommern.* Allgemeine Missions-Studien, vol. 4. Gütersloh, 1926.

Kunisch

Kunisch, Johannes. *Konrad III [der Dritte], Arnold von Wied und der Kapellenbau von Schwarzrheindorf.* Düsseldorf, 1966.

La Monte, "Le Puiset"

La Monte, John L. "The Lords of Le Puiset on the Crusades." *Speculum*, vol. 17 (1942), pp. 100-118.

La Monte, "Papauté"

La Monte, John L. "La Papauté et les croisades." *Renaissance*, vols. 4-6 (1946-48), pp. 154-67.

Laarhoven

Laarhoven, J. Van. "'Christianitas' et réforme grégorienne." *Studi Gregoriani*, vol. 6 (1959-61), pp. 1-98.

Labande
Labande, Edmonde-René. "Pour une image véridique d'Aliénor d'Aquitaine." *Bulletin de la Société des antiquaires de l'Ouest.* 4th ser., vol. 2 (1952), pp. 175-234.

Laborde
Laborde, Count Alexandre-Léon Joseph de. *La Bible moralisée.* 4 vols. Paris, 1911-1921.

Ladner
Ladner, Gerhardt B. "The Concepts of 'Ecclesia' and 'Christianitas' and Their Relation to the Idea of Papal 'Plenitudo Potestatis' from Gregory VII to Boniface VIII." *Miscellanea historiae pontificiae*, vol. 18 (1954), pp. 49-77.

Lair
Lair, Jules. "Fragment inédit de la vie de Louis VII préparée par Suger." *Bibliothèque de l'Ecole des Chartes.* Vol. 34 (1873), pp. 583-96.

Laube
Laube, Daniela. *Zehn Kapitel zur Geschichte der Eleonore von Aquitanien.* Geist und Werk der Zeiten, no. 68. Bern-Frankfurt/M-New York, 1984.

Leclercq, "Attitude"
Leclercq, Jean. "L'attitude spirituelle de S. Bernard devant la guerre." *Collectanea Cisterciensis*, vol. 36 (1974), pp. 195-225.

Leclercq, *Bernard*
Leclercq, Jean. *St. Bernard et l'esprit Cistercien.* Editions du Seuil, Maîtres spirituels, vol. 36. Paris, 1966. New ed., Paris, 1975.

Leclercq, *Nouveau visage*
Leclercq, Jean. *Nouveau visage de Bernard de Clairvaux: approches psycho-historiques.* Paris, 1976.

Leclercq, "Prophète"
Leclercq, Jean. "St. Bernard le prophète de la chrétienté." *Etudes*, vol. 277 (1953), pp. 289-303.

Leclercq, "Templiers 1"
Leclercq, Jean. "Un document sur les débuts des Templiers." *Revue d'Histoire Ecclésiastique*, vol. 52 (1957), pp. 81-91.

Leclercq, "Templiers 2"
Leclercq, Jean. "Un document sur les débuts des Templiers." In: *Recueil St. Bernard*, vol. 2 (1969), pp. 87-99.

Lekai
Lekai, Louis J. *The White Monks: A History of the Cistercian Order.* Okauchee, Wisc., 1953.

Lettres Chartreux
Lettres des premiers Chartreux. 2 vols. Vol. 1: Sources chrétiennes, no. 88. Série des textes monastiques d'Occident, no. 10. Paris, 1962. Vol. 2: Sources chrétiennes, no. 274. Série des textes monastiques d'Occident, no. 49. Paris, 1980.

Lewis
Lewis, Andrew W. "Fourteen Charters of Robert I of Dreux (1152-1188)." *Traditio*, vol. 41 (1985), pp. 145-79.

Lotter
Lotter, Friedrich. *Die Konzeption des Wendenkreuzzuges: Ideengeschichtliche, Kirchenrechtliche und Historisch-Politische Voraussetzungen der Missionierung von Elbe-und Ostseeslawen um die Mitte des 12. Jahrhunderts.* Sigmaringen, 1977.

LThK (1935)	*Lexikon für Theologie und Kirche*. Vol. 7. Ed. Michael Buchberger. Freiburg/Br., 1935.
LThK (1962)	*Lexikon für Theologie und Kirche*. Vol. 7. Eds. Josef Höfer & Karl Rahner. Freiburg/Br., 1962.
LThK (1968)	*Lexikon für Theologie und Kirche*. Das 2. Vatikanische Konzil. Suppl. vol. 3, 2nd ed. Eds. Josef Höfer & Karl Rahner. Freiburg/Br., 1968.
Luchaire, *Louis VI*	Luchaire, Achille. *Louis VI le Gros: Annales de sa vie et de son règne (1081-1137)*. Paris, 1889 (rpt. Geneva, 1979).
Luchaire, *Louis VII*	Luchaire, Achille. *Etudes sur les actes de Louis VII*. Paris, 1885.
Lusignan, *Chypre*	Lusignan, Etienne de. *Description de toute l'isle de Cypre*. Paris, 1580.
Lusignan, *Cipro*	Lusignan, Steffano de. *Chorograffia et breve historia universale dell'isola di Cipro*. Bologna, 1573.
Lyxbonensi	*De expugnatione Lyxbonensi*. Ed. & tr. Charles Wendell David. Records of Civilization, vol. 24. New York, 1936.
Maccaronne	Maccaronne, Michele. *Vicarius Christi: storia d'un titulo papale*. Lateranum, n.s. An. 18. Rome, 1952.
MacKinney	MacKinney, Loren C. "The People and Public in the Eleventh Century Peace Movement." *Speculum*, vol. 5 (1930), pp. 181-206.
Makhairas	Makhairas, Leontios. *Recital concerning the sweet land of Cyprus entitled "Chronicle"*, 2 vols. Ed. & tr. R.M. Dawkins. Oxford, 1932.
Mâle	Mâle, Emile. *Religious Art in France: The Twelfth Century*. Princeton, 1978.
Manrique	Manrique, Angel. *Cisterciensium seu ueris ecclesiasticorum annalium a conditio Cistercio*. 3 vols. Vol. 1: *Ad anno 1098 usque ad 1144*. Vol. 2: *Ad anno 1145 usque 1173*. Vol. 3: *Ad anno 1174 usque ad 1212*. Lyon, 1642-1649.
Mas-Latrie, "Chypre"	Mas-Latrie, Louis, comte de, ed. "Documents nouveaux servant de preuves à l'histoire de Chypre." In: *Mélanges historiques*. Collection de documents inédits sur l'histoire de France, vol. 4. Paris, 1882, pp. 339-619.
Mas-Latrie, *Histoire*	Mas-Latrie, Louis de. *Histoire de l'île de Chypre sous le règne des princes de la maison de Lusignan*. 3 vols. Paris, 1852-1861.
Mayer, "Angevins"	Mayer, Hans Eberhard. "Angevins *versus* Normans: The New Men of King Fulk of Jerusalem." *Proceedings of the American Philosophical Society*, vol. 133 (1989), pp. 1-25.

Mayer, "Concordat"	Mayer, Hans Eberhard. "The Concordat of Nablus." *Journal of Ecclesiastical History*, vol. 33 (1982), pp. 531-43.
Mayer, *Crusades*	Mayer, Hans Eberhard. *The Crusades.* Tr. John Gillingham. 2nd ed. Oxford, 1988.
Mayer, "Jérusalem"	Mayer, Hans Eberhard. "Jérusalem et Antioche au temps de Baudouin II." In: *Comptes rendus des séances de l'année 1980, novembre-décembre.* Académie des Inscriptions et Belles-Lettres. Paris, 1981, pp. 717-36.
Mayer, *Kreuzzüge*	Mayer, Hans Eberhard. *Geschichte der Kreuzzüge.* Stuttgart, 1965 (Eng. tr.: Mayer *Crusades*).
Mayer, "Melisende"	Mayer, Hans Eberhard. "Studies in the History of Queen Melisende of Jerusalem." *Dumbarton Oaks Papers*, vol. 26 (1972), pp. 93-182.
Mayer, "Sankt Samuel"	Mayer, Hans Eberhard. "Sankt Samuel auf dem Freudenberge und sein Besitz nach einem unbekannten Diplom König Balduins V." *Quellen und Forschungen aus italienischen Archiven und Bibliotheken*, vol. 44 (1964), pp. 37-71 (rpt. in: *Kreuzzüge und lateinischer Osten*, London: Variorum, 1983, ch. 8).
McGinn, *Iter*	McGinn, Bernard. "*Iter Sancti Sepulchri:* The Piety of the First Crusaders." In: *Essays in Medieval Civilization.* Eds. Bede Karl Lackner & Kenneth R. Philip. Walter Prescott Webb Memorial Lectures, 12. Austin, 1978, pp. 33-71.
McGinn, "St Bernard"	McGinn, Bernard. "Saint Bernard and Eschatology." In: *Bernard of Clairvaux: Studies Presented to Dom Jean Leclercq.* Cistercian Studies Series, vol. 23, Washington, D.C., 1973, pp. 161-95.
McGinn, *Visions*	McGinn, Bernard. *Visions of the End: Apocalyptic Traditions in the Middle Ages.* New York, 1979.
MEFR(MA)	*Mélanges d'archéologie et d'histoire* [from 1971: *Mélanges de l'Ecole française de Rome. Moyen-Age*]. vol. 1- . Rome, 1881
Mélanges Crozet	*Mélanges offerts à René Crozet, à l'occasion de son 70ᵉ anniversaire, par ses amis, ses collègues, ses élèves* .... 2 vols. Eds. Pierre Gallais & Yves-Jean Riou. Poitiers, 1966.
Melville	Melville, Marion. *La vie des Templiers.* Paris, 1974.
Meyer, "Fragment"	Meyer, P., ed. "Fragment d'une Chanson d'Antioche en Provençal." *Archives de l'Orient latin*, vol. 2 (1884), pp. 473-94.
Meyer, *Oberfranken*	Meyer, Otto, Elisabeth Roth & Klaus Guth. *Oberfranken im Hochmittelalter: Politik, Kultur, Gesellschaft.* 2nd ed. Bamberg, 1987.

Meyer & Suntrup	Meyer, Heinz & Rudolf Suntrup, eds. *Lexikon der mittelalterlichen Zahlenbedeutungen*. Münstersche Mittelalter-Schriften, no. 56. Münster, 1987.
MGH Dipl. reg. imp. Germ.	Monumenta Germaniae Historica: Diplomata regum et imperatorum Germaniae. Die Urkurden der deutschen Könige und Kaiser. Vol. 1-. Hanover-Leipzig-Weimar, 1879-.
MGH Epist.	Monumenta Germaniae historica, Epistolae. 8 Vols. Berlin, 1887-1939 (rpt. 1978-1985).
MGH Quell. Geist.	Monumenta Germaniae Historica: Quellen zur Geistesgeschichte des Mittelalters. Weimar, 1955-.
MGH Schriften	Schriften der Monumenta Germaniae Historica. Deutsches Institut für Erforschung des Mittelalters. Stuttgart, 1938-.
MGH Script. rer. Germ.	Monumenta Germaniae Historica: Scriptores rerum Germanicarum in usum scholarum. Hanover-Leipzig-Hahn, 1839-. N.s. vol. 1-. Berlin, 1922-.
MGHS	Monumenta Germaniae Historica, Scriptores. Hanover-Weimar-Berlin-Stuttgart-Cologne, 1826-. (vols 1-30 rpt. Leipzig, 1925; rpt. 1963-64).
Michael the Syrian	Michael I, Jacobite patriarch of Antioch. *Chronique de Michel le Syrien, patriarche jacobite d'Antioche (1166/99)*. Ed. & tr. Jean Baptiste Chabot. 4 vols. Paris, 1899-1924.
Michelant & Raynaud	Michelant, Henri & Gaston Raynaud, eds. *Itinéraires à Jérusalem et descriptions de la Terre Sainte rédigés en français aux XIᵉ, XIIᵉ & XIIIᵉ siècles*. Publications de la Société de l'Orient latin. Série géographique, vol. 3. Geneva, 1882.
Michelet	Michelet, Jules. *Le Procès des Templiers*. 2 vols. Collection de documents inédits sur l'histoire de France. Paris, 1841-1851.
Misch	Misch, Georg. *Geschichte der Autobiographie*. 4 vols. Frankfurt/M, 1949-1969.
Moore	Moore, R.I. "St Bernard's Mission to the Languedoc in 1145." *Bulletin of the Institute of Historical Research*, vol. 47 (1974), pp. 1-10.
Morris, "*Equestris Ordo*"	Morris, Colin. "*Equestris ordo*: Chivalry as a Vocation in the Twelfth Century." In: *Religious motivation: Biographical & sociological problems for the church historian: Papers read at the Sixteenth Summer Meeting and the Seventeenth Winter Meeting of the Ecclesiastical History Society*. Ed. Derek Baker. Studies in Church History Series, vol. 15. Oxford, 1978, pp. 87-96.

Morris, "Propaganda" Morris, Colin. "Propaganda for War: The Dissemination of the Crusading Ideal in the Twelfth Century." In: *The Church and War: Papers Read at the Twenty-first Summer Meeting of the Ecclesiastical History Society*. Oxford, 1982. pp. 79-101.

Morrison Morrison, Karl F. "The Church as Play: Gerhoch of Reichersberg's Call for Reform." In: *Popes, Teachers, and Canon Law in the Middle Ages*. Ed. James Ross Sweeney & Stanley Chodorow. Ithaca, 1989, pp. 114-44.

Moyen Age Le Moyen Age: revue d' histoire et de philologie. Paris, 1888-.

MPH Monumenta Poloniae historica. N.s. 10 vols. Cracow-Warsaw, 1946-1974.

Muldoon, "Boniface VIII" Muldoon, James. "Boniface VIII as Defender of Royal Power: *Unam sanctam* as a Basis for the Spanish Conquest of the Americas." In: *Popes, Teachers and Canon Law in the Middle Ages*. Eds. James Ross Sweeney & Stanley Chodorow. Ithaca, 1989, pp. 62-73.

Muldoon, "Canonists" Muldoon, James. "Extra Ecclesiam non est imperium: The Canonists and the Legitimacy of Secular Power." *Studia Gratiana*, vol. 9 (1966), pp. 551-80.

Munro, "Popes" Munro, Dana C. "The Popes and the Crusades." *American Philosophical Society Proceedings*, 1916, pp. 348-56.

Munro, "Speech" Munro. Dana C. "The Speech of Pope Urban II at Clermont, 1095." *American Historical Review*, vol. 11 (1906), pp. 231-42.

Munro, "Western" Munro, Dana Carleton."The Western Attitude toward Islam during the Period of the Crusades." *Speculum*, vol. 6 (1931), pp. 329-43.

Murphy, *The Holy War* Murphy, Thomas Patrick, ed. *The Holy War*. Fifth Conference on Medieval and Renaissance Studies, Ohio State University, 1974. Columbus, 1976.

Neu Neu, Heinrich von, Franz Josef Helfmeyer & Karl Königs, eds. *825 Jahre Doppelkirche Schwarzrheindorf 1151-1976*. Bonn, 1976.

Neuss, *Bibelillustration* Neuss, Wilhelm. *Die katalanische Bibelillustration*. Bonn, 1922.

Neuss, *Ezechiel* Neuss, Wilhelm. *Das Buch Ezechiel in Theologie und Kunst bis zum Ende des XII. Jahrhunderts*. Beiträge zur Geschichte des alten Mönchtums und des Benediktinerordens. Ed. P. Ildefons Herwegen. Münster, 1912.

Nicolas de Martoni   Nicholas de Martoni. "Le voyage en Terre Sainte de Nicolas de
                         Martoni." Ed. L. Le Grand. *Revue de l'Orient latin*, vol. 3 (1895),
                         pp. 566-669.

Niederkorn   Niederkorn, Jean Paul. "Traditio, a quibus minime cavimus:
                         Ermittelungen gegen König Balduin III von Jerusalem, den
                         Patriarchen Fulcher und den Templerorden wegen Verrats bei
                         des Belagerung von Damaskus 1148." *Mitteilungen des Instituts
                         für Österreichische Geschichtsforschung*, vol. 95 (1987),
                         pp. 53-68.

Niketas Choniates   Niketas Choniates. *O City of Byzantium: Annals of Niketas
                         Choniates*. Tr. Harry J. Magoulias. Detroit, 1984.

Noonan   Noonan, John T. Jr. "Who was Rolandus?" In: *Law, Church, and
                         Society: Essays in Honor of Stephan Kuttner*. Eds. Kenneth
                         Pennington & Robert Somerville. Philadelphia, 1977, pp. 21-48.

Norman   Norman, Joanne S. *Metamorphoses of an Allegory: The Iconog-
                         raphy of the Psychomachia in Medieval Art*. New York, 1988.

NT Apocrypha   *New Testament Apocrypha*, 2 vols. Eds. Edgar Hennecke, Robert
                         McLachlan Wilson & Wilhelm Schneemelcher. London, 1963
                         & 1965.

Nyberg   Nyberg, Tore. "Deutsche, dänische und schwedische
                         Christianisierungsversuche östlich der Ostsee im Geiste des
                         zweiten unde dritten Kreuzzuges." In: *Die Rolle der Ritterorden
                         in der Christianisierung und Kolonisierung des Ostseegebietes*.
                         Ed. Zenon Hubert Novak. Ordines militares, vol. 1, Torun, 1983,
                         pp. 93-114.

O'Meara   O'Meara, Carra Ferguson. *The Iconography of the Facade of
                         Saint-Gilles-du-Gard*. New York, 1977.

Odo of Deuil, *Croisade* Odo of Deuil. *La croisade de Louis VII, roi de France*. Ed. Henri
                         Waquet. Documents relatifs à l'histoire des croisades, vol. 3.
                         Paris, 1949.

Odo of Deuil, *De   Odo of Deuil. *De profectione Ludovici VII in orientem: The
profectione*   Journey of Louis VII to the East*. Ed. and tr. Virginia Gingerick
                         Berry. New York, 1948.

Orderic Vitalis, *History* Orderic Vitalis. *The Ecclesiastical History. [Ordericus Vitalis:
                         Historiae ecclesiasticae]*. 6 vols. Ed. & tr. Marjorie Chibnall.
                         Oxford, 1968-1980.

Orme   Orme, Nicholas. *From Childhood to Chivalry: The Education of
                         English Kings and Aristocracy, 1066-1530*. London-New York,
                         1984.

Othlo, *Liber Visionum* Othlo, monk of St. Emmeram. *Liber Visionum*. Ed. Paul Gerhard
                         Schmidt. In: MGH Quell. Geist., vol. 13. Weimar, 1989.

Otto of Freising, *Chronica*	Otto I, bishop of Freising. *Chronica sive historia de duabus civitatibus.* Ed. Adolfus Hofmeister. In: MGH Script. rer. Germ., vol. 45 (1867, rpt. 1912, 1984), pp. 1-457.
Otto of Freising, *Deeds*	Otto I, bishop of Freising. *The Deeds of Frederick Barbarossa.* Ed. & tr. Charles Christopher Mierow with Richard Emery. New York, 1953.
Otto of Freising, *Gesta* 1	Otto I, bishop of Freising. *Gesta Friderici I Imperatoris.* Eds. George Waitz & Bernhard Simson. In: MGH Script. rer. Germ., vol. 46 (1867, rpt. 1884, 1912, 1978), pp. 1-161.
Otto of Freising, *Gesta* 2	Otto I, bishop of Freising. *Bischof Otto von Freising und Rahewin, die Taten Friedrichs oder richtiger Cronica [Ottonis Episcopi Frisingensis et Rahewini Gesta Frederici seu rectius cronica].* Ed. Franz-Josef Schmale, tr. Adolf Schmidt. Ausgewählte Quellen zur deutschen Geschichte des Mittelalters, n.s., vol. 17. Darmstadt, 1965 (rpt. 1974).
Outremer	Kedar, Benjamin Z., Hans Eberhard Mayer, & R.C. Smail, eds. *Outremer: Studies in the History of the Crusading Kingdom of Jerusalem Presented to Joshua Prawer.* Jerusalem, 1982.
Pacaut, *Elections épiscopales*	Pacaut, Marcel. *Louis VII et les élections épiscopales dans le royaume de France.* Paris, 1957.
Pacaut, *Louis VII*	Pacaut, Marcel. *Louis VII et son royaume.* Paris, 1964.
Painter	Painter, Sidney. *French Chivalry, Chivalric Ideas and Practices in Medieval France.* Baltimore, 1940.
Panagopoulos	Panagopoulos, Beata Kitisiki. *Cistercian and Mendicant Monasteries in Medieval Greece.* Chicago-London, 1979.
Partner	Partner, Nancy F. *Serious Entertainments: the writing of history in twelfth-century England.* Chicago, 1977.
Paterson	Paterson, Linda. "Knights and the Concept of Knighthood in the Twelfth Century Occitan Epic." In: *Knighthood in Medieval Literature.* Ed. William Howland Jackson. Woodbridge, Suffolk, 1981, pp. 23-38.
Paucapalea	Paucapalea. *Die Summa des Paucapalea über das Decretum Gratiani.* Ed. Johann Friedrich von Schulte. Giessen, 1890.
Pennington	Pennington, Kenneth J. "The Rite for Taking the Cross in the Twelfth Century." *Traditio,* vol. 30 (1974), pp. 429-35.
Peter Damian	Peter Damian. *Opera omnia.* PL, vol. 144 (1867).
Peter the Chanter	Peter the Chanter. *Verbum abbreviatum.* In: PL, vol. 205 (1855), cols. 21-370.

Peter the Venerable,
Letters

Peter the Venerable. *The Letters of Peter the Venerable*. 2 vols. Ed. Giles Constable. Cambridge, Mass., 1967.

Peter the Venerable,
Mirac.

Peter the Venerable. *De Miraculis*. In: PL, vol. 189 (1890), cols. 851-954.

Peter the Venerable,
Sel. Ltrs.

Peter the Venerable. *Peter the Venerable: Selected Letters*. Ed. Janet Martin with Giles Constable. Toronto Medieval Latin Texts, vol. 3. Toronto, 1974.

Peter Tudebode

Peter Tudebode. *Historia de Hierosolymitano itinere*. Eds. John Hugh Hill & Laurita L. Hill. Paris, 1977.

Petersohn, "Apostolus"

Petersohn, Jürgen. "Apostolus Pomeranorum. Studien zur Geschichte und Bedeutung des Apostelepithetons Bischof Ottos I. von Bamberg." *Historisches Jahrbuch*, vol. 86 (1966), pp. 257-94.

Petersohn,
"Bemerkungen"

Petersohn, Jürgen. "Bemerkungen zu einer neuen Ausgabe der Viten Ottos von Bamberg. 1. Prüfeninger Vita und Ebo." *Deutsches Archiv für Erforschung des Mittelalters*, vol. 27 (1971), pp. 175-94.

Petersohn, *Ostseeraum*

Petersohn, Jürgen. *Der südliche Ostseeraum im kirchlich-politischen Kräftespiel des Reichs, Polens und Dänemarks vom 10. bis 13. Jahrhundert. Mission, Kirchenorganisation, Kulturpolitik*. Ostmitteleuropa in Vergangenheit und Gegenwart, vol. 17. Cologne, 1979.

Petit

Petit, Ernest. "Chartes de l'abbaye cistercienne de Saint-Serge de Gibelet." *Mémoires de la Société nationale des Antiquaires de France*, vol. 48 (5th ser., vol. 8) (1887), pp. 20-30.

PG

Patrologiae cursus completus. Series Graeca. 167 vols. Ed. Jacques Paul Migne. Paris, 1857-1876.

Philip of Clairvaux

Philip, monk of Clairvaux. Bk. 6, pt. 1 of *S. Bernardi Abbatis Clarevallensis Vita et Res Gestae*. In: PL, vol. 185, pt. 1 (1879), cols. 371-86.

Pissard

Pissard, Hippolyte. *La Guerre sainte en pays chrétien, essai sur l'origine et le développement des théories canoniques*. Bibliothèque d'histoire religieuse, no. 10. Paris, 1912.

PL

Patrologiae cursus completus. Series Latina. 221 vols. Ed. Jacques Paul Migne. Paris, 1841-1905.

Pognon

Pognon, E. "L'échec de la croisade." In: *Saint Bernard: homme de l'église*. Témoinages: Cahiers de la Pierre-qui-Vire, vols. 38-39. Paris, 1953, pp. 47-57.

*Pommersches
Urkundenbuch*

Pommersches Urkundenbuch. 2nd ed. 9 vols. Ed. Klaus Conrad. Cologne-Graz, 1970.

Prawer, *Crusader Institutions* — Prawer, Joshua. *Crusader Institutions*. Oxford, 1980.

Prawer, *Histoire* — Prawer, Joshua. *Histoire du Royaume Latin de Jérusalem*. 2nd ed. 2 vols. Tr. G. Nahon. Paris, 1975.

Prawer, *Kingdom* 1 — Prawer, Joshua. *The Latin Kingdom of Jerusalem: European Colonialism in the Middle Ages*. London, 1972.

Prawer, *Kingdom* 2 — Prawer, Joshua. *The Crusaders' Kingdom: European Colonialism in the Middle Ages*. New York, 1972.

Pringle, "Church-building" — Pringle, [Reginald] Denys. "Church-building in Palestine Before the Crusades." In: Folda, *Crusader Art*, pp. 5-46.

Pringle, "Edifices" — Pringle, [Reginald] Denys. "Les édifices ecclésiastiques du royaume latin de Jérusalem: une liste provisoire." *Revue biblique*, vol. 89 (1982), pp. 92-98.

Pringle, "Planning" — Pringle, [Reginald] Denys. "The Planning of Some Pilgrimage Churches in Crusader Palestine." *World Archaeology*, vol. 18 (1987), pp. 341-62.

Pringle, *Red Tower* — Pringle, [Reginald] Denys. *The Red Tower (al-Burj al-Ahmar). Settlement in the Plain of Sharon at the Time of the Crusaders and Mamluks, A.D. 1099-1516*. British School of Archaeology in Jerusalem, Monograph Series, no. 1. London, 1986.

Pryor — Pryor, John H. *Geography, technology and war. Studies in the maritime history of the Mediterranean, 649-1571*. Cambridge, 1988.

Radcke — Radcke, Fritz. *Die eschatologischen Anschauungen Bernhards von Clairvaux*. (Published Ph.D. dissertation, Greifswald) Langensalza, 1915.

Ralph Niger — Ralph Niger. *De re militari et triplici via peregrinationis Ierosolimitane*. Ed. Ludwig Schmugge. Beiträge zur geschichte und Quellenkunde des Mittelalters, vol. 6. Berlin-New York, 1977.

Ralph of Coggeshall — Ralph of Coggeshall. *Chronicon Anglicanum*. Ed. Joseph Stevenson. RS, vol. 66. London, 1875, pp. 1-208.

Ralph of Diceto — Ralph of Diceto. *Opera historica*. 2 vols. Ed. William Stubbs. RS, vol. 68. London, 1876.

Raoul Glaber — Raoul Glaber. *Les cinq livres des Histoires (900-1044)*. Ed. Maurice Prou. Collection de textes pour servir à l'étude et à l'enseignement de l'histoire, vol. 1. Paris, 1886.

Rassow — Rassow, Peter, ed. "Der Text der Kreuzzugsbulle Eugens III." vom 1. März 1146, Trastevere (J.-L. 8796). *Neues Archiv der*

Gesellschaft für ältere deutsche Geschichtskunde, vol. 45 (1924), pp. 300-305.

Records of Templars

Records of the Templars in England in the Twelfth Century: the Inquest of 1185. Ed. Beatrice A. Lees. Records of the Social & Economic History of England and Wales, vol. 9. London: British Academy, 1935.

Recueil Clairvaux

Recueil des chartes de l'abbaye de Clairvaux. Ed. Jean Waquet. Fasc. 1. Troyes, 1950; Fasc. 2, 1982.

Recueil St. Bernard

Leclercq, Jean, ed. *Recueil des études sur St. Bernard et ses écrits.* 2 vols. Storia e Letteratura, raccolta di studi e testi, vol. 104. Rome, 1962-69.

Renna

Renna, Thomas. "The Idea of Peace in the West, 500-1150." *Journal of Medieval History*, vol. 6 (1980), pp. 143-67

RGG

Die Religion in Geschichte und Gegenwart. 3rd. ed. Ed. Kurt Galling. 6 vols. Tübingen, 1960.

RHC Oc.

Recueil des Historiens des Croisades. Historiens Occidentaux. 5 vols. Académie des Inscriptions et Belles-Lettres. Paris, 1844-1906.

RHGF

Recueil des Historiens des Gaules et de la France. Rerum Gallicarum et Francicarum scriptores. 24 vols. Ed. Martin Bouquet, et al. Paris, 1738-1904. 2nd ed. Vols. 1-19. Ed. Léopold Delisle. Paris, 1869-1880.

Ricci

Ricci, Corrado. *L'Architettura romanica in Italia.* Paris, 1925.

Richard, "Collecteur"

Richard, Jean. "Les comptes du collecteur de la Chambre apostolique dans le royaume de Chypre (1357-1363)." *Epeteris*, vols. 13-16 (1984-87), pp. 1-47.

Richard, *Comté de Tripoli*

Richard, Jean. *Le Comté de Tripoli sous la dynastie toulousaine (1102-1187).* Bibliothèque archéologique et historique, no. 39. Paris, 1945.

Richard, "Jubin"

Richard, Jean. "L'abbaye cistercienne de Jubin et le prieuré Saint-Blaise de Nicosie." *Epeteris*, vol. 3 (1969-70), pp. 63-74 (rpt. in his *Orient et Occident au Moyen-Age. Contacts et relations.* London: Variorum, 1976, ch. 19).

Richard, *Latin Kingdom*

Richard, Jean. *The Latin Kingdom of Jerusalem.* 2 vols. (A/B). Tr. Janet Shirley. Europe in the Middle Ages: Selected Studies, vol. 11A-B. Amsterdam-New York-Oxford, 1979.

Richard, *Livre*

Richard, Jean. *Le livre des remembrances de la Secrète du royaume de Chypre pour l'anneé 1468-1469.* Centre de recherches scientifiques. Sources et études de l'histoire de Chypre, vol. 10. Nicosia, 1983.

Richard, "Papauté"	Richard, Jean. "La Papauté et la direction de la première Croisade." *Journal des Savants* (1960), pp. 49-58.
Richard, "Questions"	Richard, Jean. "Questions de topographie tripolitaine." *Journal Asiatique*, vol. 236 (1948), pp. 53-59 (rpt. in his *Orient et Occident au Moyen-Age. Contacts et relations*. London: Variorum, 1976, ch. 8).
Richard, "Tripoli"	Richard, Jean. "Les comtes de Tripoli de la dynastie antiochénienne et leurs vassaux." In: Edbury, *Crusade*, pp. 213-24.
Richard of Devizes	Richard of Devizes. *Chronicon de tempore Regis Richardi Primi*. Ed. J. T. Appleby. London, 1963.
Richard of Poitiers	Richard of Poitiers, monk of Cluny. *Chronico Richardi Pictaviensis, monachi Cluniacensis*. In: RHGF, vol. 12 (1877), pp. 411-17.
Riché	Riché, Pierre. "Recherches sur l'instruction des laïcs du IXe au XIIe siècle." *Cahiers de Civilisation Médiévale*, vol. 5 (1962), pp. 175-82.
Riley-Smith, *Crusades*	Riley-Smith, Jonathan S.C. *What were the Crusades*. London, 1977.
Riley-Smith, "Crusading"	Riley-Smith, Jonathan [S.C.]. "Crusading as an Act of Love." *History*, vol. 65 (1980), pp. 177-92.
Riley-Smith, *First Crusade*	Riley-Smith, Jonathan, S.C. *The First Crusade and the Idea of Crusading*. London, 1986.
Riley-Smith, *Idea & Reality*	Riley-Smith, Louise & Jonathan S.C. Riley-Smith. *The Crusades. Idea and Reality, 1095-1274*. London, 1981.
Riley-Smith, *Knights*	Riley-Smith, Jonathan S.C. *The Knights of St. John in Jerusalem and Cyprus, c. 1050-1310*. A History of the Order of the Hospital of St. John of Jerusalem, vol. 1. London, 1967.
Riley-Smith, "Persecution"	Riley-Smith, Jonathan S.C. "The First Crusade and the Persecution of the Jews." *Studies in Church History*, vol. 21 (1984), pp. 51-72.
Riley-Smith, "Venetian Crusade"	Riley-Smith, Jonathan S.C. "The Venetian Crusade of 1122-1124." In: *I Comuni Italiani nel regno crociato di Gerusalemme* (Jerusalem, May 24-28th, 1984). Eds. Gabriella Airaldi & Benjamin Z. Kedar. Genoa, 1986, pp. 337-50.
Robert of Torigni, *Appendix*	Robert of Torigni (Robert de Monte), abbot of Mt. St. Michel. *Appendix ad Sigebertum*. In: RHGF, vol. 13, pp. 283-333.
Robert of Torigni, *Chronicles*	Robert of Torigni (Robert de Monte), abbot of Mont St. Michel. "The Chronicle of Robert of Torigni." In: *Chronicles of the*

Reigns of Stephen, Henry II, and Richard I. Vol. 4. Ed. Richard Howlett. In: RS, no. 82. London, 1889.

Robinson, *Authority*

Robinson, I.S. *Authority and Resistance in the Investiture Contest*. Manchester, 1978.

Robinson, "Church & Papacy"

Robinson, I.S. "Church and Papacy." In: *Cambridge History of Medieval Political Thought, c. 350-c. 1450*. Ed. J.H. Burns. Cambridge, 1988, pp. 252-305.

Robinson, "Gregory VII"

Robinson, I.S. "Gregory VII and the Soldiers of Christ." *History*, vol. 58 (1973), pp. 169-92.

Roger of Howden

Roger of Howden. *Chronica*. 4 vols. Ed. William Stubbs. RS, vol. 51 (1868-71).

Röhricht, *Additamentum*

Regesta Regni Hierosolymitani (1097-1291): Additamentum. Ed. Reinhold Röhricht. Innsbruck, 1904.

Röhricht, *Beiträge*

Röhricht, Rheinhold. *Beiträge zur Geschichte der Kreuzzüge*. 2 vols. Berlin, 1878 (rpt. Aalen, 1967).

Röhricht, "Itinerarium"

Röhricht, Reinhold, ed. "Itinerarium ad Sepulcrum Domini (1327-1330)." *Zeitschrift des Deutschen Palästina-Vereins*, vol. 13 (1890), pp. 153-74.

Röhricht, "Pèlerinage"

Röhricht, Reinhold, ed. "Le pèlerinage du moine augustin Jacques de Vérone." *Revue le l'Orient latin*, vol. 3 (1895), pp. 155-302.

Röhricht, *Regesta*

Regesta Regni Hierosolymitani (1097-1291). Ed. Reinhold Röhricht. Innsbruck, 1893.

Rojdestrensky

Rojdestrensky, Olga. *Le culte de Saint Michel et le moyen âge latin*. Paris, 1922.

Rolandus

Rolandus. *Die Summa magistri Rolandi, nachmals Papstes Alexander III*. Ed. Friedrich Thaner. Innsbruck, 1874.

Roscher

Roscher, Helmut. *Papst Innocenz III. und die Kreuzzüge*. Göttingen, 1969.

Rosenstein

Rosenstein, Roy. "New Perspectives on Distant Love: Jaufre Rudel, Uc Bru, and Sarrazina." *Modern Philology*, vol. 87 (1990), pp. 225-38.

Rosen-Ayalon

Rosen-Ayalon, Myriam. "The Facade of the Holy Sepulchre." *Rivista degli Studi Orientali*, vol. 59 (1985), pp. 289-96.

Round

Round, John Horace. "The Foundation of the Priories of St. Mary and of St. John, Clerkenwell." *Archaeologia*, vol. 56 (1899), pp. 223-28.

Rousset, *Origines*

Rousset, Paul. *Les origines et les caractères de la première croisade*. Neuchâtel, 1945.

Rousset, *Réveils*   Rousset, P. *Les réveils missionaires en France du môyen âge à nos jours.* (XIIe-XXe siècles). Paris, 1984.

RS   Rerum Britannicarum medii aevi scriptores [Chronicles and Memorials of Great Britain and Ireland during the Middle Ages]. Published under the direction of the Master of the Rolls [Rolls Series], 99 titles in 251 vols. London, 1858-1896.

Runciman   Runciman, Steven. *A History of the Crusades.* 3 vols. Vol. 1 (1951): *The First Crusade and the Foundation of the Kingdom of Jerusalem.* Vol. 2 (1952): *The Kingdom of Jerusalem and the Frankish East, 1100-1187.* Vol. 3 (1954): *The Kingdom of Acre and the Later Crusades.* Cambridge, 1951-1954.

Rupp   Rupp, Jean. *L'Idée de Chrétienté, dans la pensée pontificale des origines à Innocent III.* Paris, 1939.

Russell   Russell, Frederick H. *The Just War in the Middle Ages.* Cambridge Studies in Medieval Life and Thought. 3rd ser., vol. 8. Cambridge, 1975.

Sackur   Sackur, Ernst. *Sibyllinische Texte und Forschungen: Pseudomethodius, Adso und die tiburtinische Sibylle.* Halle, 1898 (rpt. Turin, 1963).

Saller   Saller, Sylvester John. *Discoveries at St. John's, ^{c}Ein Karim (1941-1942).* Studium Biblicum Franciscanum, Collectio maior, no. 3. Jerusalem, 1946.

Satabin   Satabin, P. "Une lettre inédite de Saint Bernard." In: *Etudes religieuses historiques et littéraires,* vol. 62 (Paris, 1894), pp. 321-27.

Sauvage   Sauvage, René Norbert. *L'abbaye de Saint-Martin de Troarn.* Mémoires de la société des antiquaires de Normandie, 4th ser., vol. 4. Caen, 1911.

Savignac & Abel   Savignac, R. & F.M. Abel. "Chronique: Neby Samouil." *Revue biblique,* vol. 21 (1912), pp. 267-79.

Schiller   Schiller, Gertrud. *Iconography of Christian Art.* 2 vols. Greenwich, Conn., 1971-1972.

Schmaltz   Schmaltz, Karl. *Mater Ecclesiarum: Die Grabeskirche in Jerusalem.* Strassburg, 1918 (rpt. Leipzig, 1982).

Schneider   Schneider, Gerhard. "Der Missionsauftrag Jesu in der Darstellung der Evangelien." In: Kertelge, pp. 71-92.

Schnürer, "Organisation"   Schnürer, Gustav. "Zur ersten Organisation der Templer." *Historisches Jahrbuch,* vol. 32 (1911), pp. 298-316, 511-46.

Schnürer, *Templerregel*   Schnürer, Gustav, ed. *Die ursprüngliche Templerregel*. Studien und Darstellungen aus dem Gebiete der Geschichte, no. 3/1-2. Freiburg/Br., 1903.

Schwinges   Schwinges, Rainer Christoph. *Kreuzzugsideologie und Toleranz: Studien zu Wilhelm von Tyrus*. Monographien zur Geschichte des Mittelalters, vol. 15. Stuttgart, 1977.

Seguin   Seguin, André. "Bernard et la seconde croisade." *Bernard de Clairvaux*. Preface by Jean-de-la-Croix Bouton. Commission d'histoire de l'ordre de Cîteaux. Etudes et Documents, vol. 3. Paris-Aiguebelles, 1953, pp. 379-409.

Seidel, "Holy Warriors"   Seidel, Linda. "Holy Warriors: The Romanesque Rider and the Fight against Islam." In: Murphy, *The Holy War*, pp. 33-54.

Seidel, "Images"   Seidel, Linda. "Images of the Crusades in Western Art: Models as Metaphors." In: *The Meeting of Two Worlds: Cultural Exchange between East and West during the Period of the Crusade*. Eds. Vladimir P. Goss & Christine Verzar Bornstein. Studies in medieval culture, vol. 21. Kalamazoo, 1986, pp. 377-91.

Seidel, *Songs*   Seidel, Linda. *Songs of Glory: The Romanesque Façades of Aquitaine*. Chicago, 1981.

Setton   Setton, Kenneth M., series ed. *A History of the Crusades*. 6 vols.: vol. 1, *The First Hundred Years*, 2nd ed., ed. Marshall L. Baldwin, Madison-London, 1969; vol. 2, *The Later Crusades, 1189-1311*, 2nd ed., eds. Robert Lee Wolff & Harry W. Hazard, Madison-London, 1969; vol. 3, *The Fourteenth and Fifteenth Centuries*, ed. Harry W. Hazard, Madison-London, 1975; vol. 4, *The Art and Architecture of the Crusader States*, ed. Harry W. Hazard, Madison-London, 1977; vol. 5, *The Impact of the Crusades on the Near East*, eds. Norman P. Zacour & Harry W. Hazard, London-Madison, 1985.

Siberry, *Criticism*   Siberry, Elizabeth. *Criticism of Crusading 1095-1274*. Oxford, 1985.

Siberry, "Missionaries"   Siberry, Elizabeth. "Missionaries and Crusaders 1095-1274: Opponents or Allies?" *Studies in Church History*, vol. 20 (1983), pp. 103-10.

Smail   Smail, Raymond Charles. *Crusading Warfare (1097-1193)*. Cambridge Studies in Medieval Life and Thought, n.s., vol. 3. Cambridge, 1956.

Sommerfeldt   Sommerfeldt, John R. "The Social Theories of Bernard of Clairvaux." In: *Studies in Medieval Cistercian History*, vol. 1. Cistercian Studies Series, no. 13. Spencer, Mass., 1971, pp. 35-48.

Southern, *Church*	Southern, Richard William. *Western Society and the Church in the Middle Ages.* Pelican History of the Church, vol. 2. Harmondsworth, 1970.
Southern, *Islam*	Southern, Richard William. *Western Views of Islam in the Middle Ages.* Cambridge, Mass., 1962.
Spitzer	Spitzer, Leo. *L'Amour lointain de Jaufré Rudel et le sens de la poésie des troubadours.* University of North Carolina Studies in the Romance Languages and Literatures, no. 5. Chapel Hill, 1944.
Stammtafeln	*Stammtafeln zur Geschichte der europäischen Staaten.* Comp. Wilhelm Karl Prinz von Isenburg, et. al. Marburg, 1953.
Statuta Cisterciensis	*Statuta capitulorum generalium ordinis cisterciensis ab anno 1116 ad annum 1786.* 8 vols. Eds. Joseph Marie Canivez & Auguste Trilhe. Vol. 1 (1933): *Ab anno 1116 ad annum 1220*; vol. 2 (1934): *Ab anno 1221 ad annum 1261*; vol. 3 (1935): *Ab anno 1262 ad annum 1400*; vol. 4 (1936): *Ab anno 1401 ad annum 1456*; vol. 5 (1937): *Ab anno 1457 ad annum 1490*; vol. 6 (1938): *Ab anno 1451 ad annum 1542*; vol. 7 (1938): *Ab anno 1546 ad annum 1786*; vol. 8 (1941): *Indices.* Bibliothèque de la revue d'histoire ecclésiastique, fasc. 9-14B. Louvain, 1933-1941.
Stevens	Stevens, John. *Words and Music in the Middle Ages.* Cambridge, 1986.
Stickler, "Anselmo da Lucca"	Stickler, Alfonso M. "Il potere coattivo materiale della Chiesa nella riforma gregoriana secondo Anselmo da Lucca." *Studi Gregoriani*, vol. 2 (1947), pp. 235-85.
Stickler, "De ecclesiae"	Stickler, Alfonso M. "De ecclesiae potestate coactive materiali apud magistrum Gratianum." *Salesianum*, vol. 4 (1942), pp. 97-119.
Stickler, "Gladius"	Stickler, Alfonso. "Il Gladius nel registro di Gregorio VII." *Studi Gregoriani*, vol. 3 (1948), pp. 89-103.
Südekum	Südekum, Karl, ed. *Die deutsche Otto - Vita des Konrad Bischof aus dem Jahre 1473.* Neustadt/Aisch, 1983.
Suger, *Epistolae*	Suger, abbot of St. Denis. *Epistolae.* In: RHGF, vol. 15 (1808), pp. 483-532.
Suger, *Vita Ludovici*	Suger, abbot of St. Denis. *Vie de Louis VI le Gros [Vita Ludovici Grossi regis].* Ed. & tr. Henri Waquet. Les classiques de l'histoire de France au moyen âge, vol. 11. Paris, 1929 (rpt. 1964 with corrections & bibliography).
Switten & Chickering	Switten, Margaret & Howell Chickering, eds. *The Medieval Lyric: Anthologies and Cassettes for Teaching.* 5 cassettes; 3

anthologies; commentary volume. Mount Holyoke College: South Hadley, Mass., 1988.

Syria   *Syria*. Revue d'art oriental et d'archéologie. Paris: Haut-Commissaire de la République française en Syrie. Vol. 1-(1920-).

Tax-book   *Tax-book of the Cistercian Order, The*. Ed. Arne Odd Johnsen & Peter King. Norske Videnskaps-Akademi, II. Hist.-Filos. Klasse. *Avhandlinger*, n.s., no. 16. Oslo, 1979.

Taylor   Taylor, Pamela. "Clerkenwell and the Religious Foundations of Jordan de Bricett: a Re-examination." *Historical Research*, vol. 63 (1990), pp. 17-27.

Tellenbach   Tellenbach, Gerd. *Libertas: Kirche und Weltordnung im Zeitalter des Investiturstreits*. Stuttgart, 1936.

Theoderich   Theoderich. *Theoderich's Description of the Holy Places*. Tr. A. Stewart. Library of the Palestine Pilgrims' Text Society, vol. 5. London, 1896.

Theodore et al., *Annales*   Theodore et al., *Annales Palidenses*. In: MGHS, vol. 16 (1859), pp. 48-98.

Tibble   Tibble, Steven. *Monarchy and Lordships in the Latin Kingdom of Jerusalem, 1099-1291*. Oxford, 1989.

Tischler   Tischler, Hans. "Performances of Medieval Songs." *Revue Belge de Musicologie*, vol. 43 (1989), pp. 225-42.

Traditio   *Traditio: Studies in Ancient and Medieval History, Thought and Religion*. Vol. 1-. New York, 1943-.

Treitler   Treitler, Leo. "Music and Language in Medieval Song." In: Switten & Chickering, commentary volume, pp. 12-27.

Tritton & Gibb   Tritton, A.S. and H.A.R. Gibb. "The First and Second Crusades from an Anonymous Syriac Chronicle." *Journal of the Royal Asiatic Society* (1933), pp. 69-101, 273-305.

Trotter   Trotter, D.A. *Medieval French Literature and the Crusades (1100-1300)*. Geneva, 1988.

Tyerman   Tyerman, Christopher. *England and the Crusades, 1095 - 1588*. Chicago-London, 1988.

Ullmann   Ullmann, Walter. "Saint Bernard and the Nascent International Law." *Cîteaux*, vol. 10 (1959), pp. 277-87.

Urkunden Konrads   *Die Urkunden Konrads III und seines Sohnes Heinrich, [Conradi III. et filii eius Heinrici Diplomata]*. Ed. Friedrich Hausmann. In: MGH Dipl. reg. imp. Germ., vol. 9 (1969).

Urkundenbuch Magdeburg	*Urkundenbuch des Erzstiftes Magdeburg.* Eds. Friedrich Israel & Walter Möllenberg. Geschichtsquellen der Provinz Sachsen und des Freistaates Anhalt, n.s. vol. 18. Magdeburg, 1937.
Usamah	Usamah ibn Munqidh. *An Arab-Syrian Gentleman and Warrior in the Period of the Crusades: Memoirs of Usamah Ibn-Munqidh.* Tr. Philip K. Hitti. New York, 1929 (rpt. Princeton, 1987).
Vacandard	Vacandard, [Chanoine Florent-Zéphyr] Elphège. *Vie de Saint Bernard, abbé de Clairvaux.* 2 vols. Paris, 1895 (rpt. 1897, 1902, 1920, 1927).
Valléry-Radot	Valléry-Radot, Irénée. *Le prophète de l'Occident (1130-1153). Bernard de Fontaines abbé de Clairvaux.* Paris, 1969.
Van der Werf, *Chansons*	Van der Werf, Hendrik. *The chansons of the troubadours and the trouvères.* Utrecht, 1972.
Van der Werf, *Melodies*	Van der Werf, Hendrik. *The Extant Troubadour Melodies.* Rochester, 1985.
Van Engen	Van Engen, John H. *Rupert of Deutz.* Berkeley-Los Angeles, 1983.
Van Luyn	Van Luyn, P. "Les *milites* dans la France du XIe siècle." *Moyen Age*, vol. 77, pp. 33-43, 193-200.
Vandevoorde	Vandevoorde, Marie-Adélaïde. "Les lignages d'Outre-mer et la société nobiliaire de l'Orient latin." In: *Positions des thèses des élèves de l'Ecole des Chartes.* Paris, 1990, p. 183.
Verbeek	Verbeek, Albert. *Schwarzrheindorf.* Düsseldorf, 1953.
Verbeke	Verbeke, Werner, Daniel Verhelst and Andries Welkenhuysen, eds. *The Use and Abuse of Eschatology in the Middle Ages.* Mediaevalia Lovaniensia, 1st ser., Studia 15. Louvain, 1988.
Verdier	Verdier, Philippe. "A Mosan Plaque with Ezechiel's Vision of the Sign Thau (Tau)." *Journal of the Walters Art Gallery*, vols. 29-30 (1966-67), pp. 17-47.
Vikan	Vikan, Gary. *Byzantine Pilgrimage Art.* Dumbarton Oaks Byzantine Collection, Publications, no. 5. Washington, DC, 1982.
Villey	Villey, Michel. "L'idée de croisade chez les juristes du Moyen Age." In: *X Congresso internazionale di scienzia storiche* (Roma, 4-11 settembre 1955). Florence, 1955, pp. 365-94.
Vincent & Abel	Vincent, Hugues Le (and F.M. Abel). *Jérusalem: Recherches de topographie, d'archéologie et d'histoire.* 2 vols. Vol. 1 (H. Vincent): *Jérusalem Antique.* Paris, 1912. Vol. 2 in 4 pts. (Vincent & Abel): *Jérusalem nouvelle.* Paris, 1914-1926.

Vita Sugerii — Vita Sugerii abbatis a Willelmo san-Dionysiano ejus discipulo. In: RHGF, vol. 12 (1877), pp. 102-104.

Vogüé, Eglises — Vogüé, [Charles Jean] Melchior [marquis] de. Les églises de la Terre Sainte. Paris, 1860 (rpt. Toronto-Jerusalem, 1973).

Vogüé, Florilegium — Vogüé, [Charles Jean] Melchior [marquis] de. Florilegium Melchior de Vogüé. Paris, 1909.

Walter Map — Walter Map. Courtiers' Trifles [De nugis curialium]. Ed. & tr. M.R. James. 2nd ed. Eds. C.N.L. Brooke and R.A.B. Mynors. Oxford, 1983.

Watt — Watt, John A. "Spiritual and Temporal Powers." In: Cambridge History of Medieval Political Thought. Ed. J.H. Burns. Cambridge, 1988, pp. 367-423.

Weigand — Weigand, Rudolf. "Magister Rolandus und Papst Alexander III." Archiv für katholisches Kirchenrecht. vol. 149 (1980), pp. 3-44.

Weise — Weise, Erich. Die Amtsgewalt von Papst und Kaiser und die Ostmission besonders in der 1. Hälfte des 13. Jahrhunderts. Marburger Ostforschungen, vol. 31. Marburg, 1971.

White, "Gregorian Ideal" — White, Hayden V. "The Gregorian Ideal and St. Bernard of Clairvaux." Journal of the History of Ideas, vol. 21 (1960), pp. 321-48.

White, Sicily — White, Lynn T., jr. Latin monasticism in Norman Sicily. Cambridge (Mass.), 1938.

Wilkinson, Hill & Ryan — Wilkinson, John, J. Hill & W.F. Ryan, eds. & trs. Jerusalem Pilgrimage 1099-1185. Hakluyt Society, 2nd series, vol. 167. London, 1988.

Willems — Willems, E. "Cîteaux et la seconde croisade." Revue d'histoire écclésiastique, vol. 49 (1954), pp. 116-51.

Williams — Williams, Watkin Wynn. Saint Bernard of Clairvaux. Manchester, 1935.

Winter, "Cingulum militiae" — Winter, Johanna Maria van. "Cingulum militiae." Tijdschrift voor Rechtsgeschiedenes, vol. 44 (1976), pp. 1-47.

Winter, Rittertum — Winter, Johanna Maria van. Rittertum. Ideal und Wirklichkeit. Bussum, 1979.

Wm. of Jumièges, Gesta — William of Jumièges. Gesta Normannorum ducum. Ed. J. Marx. Société de l'histoire de Normandie, vol. 43. Rouen, 1914.

Wm. of Malmesbury — William of Malmesbury. De Gestis regum Anglorum. 2 vols. Ed. William Stubbs. RS, vol. 90. London, 1887-89.

Wm. of Nangis	William of Nangis. *Chronique latine de Guillaume de Nangis*. Ed. H. Géraud. 2 vols. Société de l'histoire de France. nos. 33, 35. Paris, 1843.
Wm. of Newburgh	William of Newburgh. *The History of English Affairs*. Ed. in progress. Eds. P.G. Walsh & M.J. Kennedy. Warminster, 1988-.
Wm. of Tyre, *Chronicon*	William, archbishop of Tyre. *Willelmi Tyrensis archiepiscopi chronicon*. 2 vols. Ed. Robert B.C. Huygens. Corpus Christianorum, Continuatio Mediaevalis, vols. 63-63A. Turnholt, 1986.
Wm. of Tyre, *Historia*	William, archbishop of Tyre. *Historia rerum in partibus transmarinis gestarum*. In: RHC Oc., vol. 1 (1844).
Wm. of Tyre, *History*	William, archbishop of Tyre. *A History of Deeds Done beyond the Sea*. 2 vols. Trs. Emily Atwater Babcock & A.C. Krey. New York, 1943 (rpt. 1976).
Wolf & Rosenstein	Wolf, George & Roy Rosenstein, eds. & trs. *The Poetry of Cercamon and Jaufre Rudel*. Garland Library of Medieval Literature, vol. 5, series A. New York-London, 1983.
Wolff, "Eveil"	Wolff, Philippe. *L'éveil intellectuel de l'Europe, IXe-XIIe siècles*. Paris, 1971.
Wollasch	Wollasch, Joachim. "Neue Quellen zur Geschichte der Cisterzienser." *Zeitschrift für Kirchengeschichte*, vol. 84 (1973), pp. 188-232.
Wurm	Wurm, Hermann Joseph. *Gottfried, Bischof von Langres*. Würzburg, 1886.
Zerbi	Zerbi, Piero di. "Riflessione sul simbolo delle due spade in S. Bernardo di Clairvaux." In: *Raccolta di studi in onore di G. Sorranzo*. Contributi dell'Istituto di storia medioevale, vol. 1. Pubblicazioni dell'Università cattolica del Sacro Cuore. Contributi, serie 3: Scienze storiche, 10. Milan, 1967, pp. 1-18.

INDEX

Compiled by Carol Stoppel

DATE DUE

DEC 28 '96			